I0819618

TRENTINO ALTO ADIGE
FRIULI VENEZIA GIULIA
VALLE D'AOSTA
LOMBARDIA
Trieste
Milano
Venezia
PIEMONTE
VENETO
Torino
EMILIA ROMAGNA
LIGURIA
Bologna
Genova
Firenze
Ancona
Perugia
LE MARCHE
TOSCANA
UMBRIA
Pescara
L'Aquila
ABRUZZO
Roma
LAZIO
MOLISE
PUGLIA
CAMPANIA
Bari
Napoli
Potenza
SARDEGNA
Matera
BASILICATA
Lecce
CALABRIA
Cagliari
Catanzaro
Palermo
SICILIA

ITALIAN COOKIES

Sacchetto BISCOTTI
e. 7,00 cad.
Sacchetto CONFETTI
e. 6,00 cad.
ASSICURAZIONE

ITALIAN COOKIES

AUTHENTIC RECIPES AND SWEET STORIES FROM EVERY REGION

DOMENICA MARCHETTI

Photographs by Lauren Volo

Illustrations by Daniela Bracco

First Edition
30 29 28 27 26 5 4 3 2 1

Illustrations credited to Daniela Bracco
Photographs credited to Lauren Volo
Atmosphere and other photographs credited to Domenica Marchetti, found on pages 2, 8, 16, 19, 20, 28, 36, 39, 45, 98, 109, 168, 185, 222, 224, 229, 233

Published by
Gibbs Smith
570 N. Sportsplex Drive
Kaysville, Utah 84037
www.gibbs-smith.com
The authorized representative in the EEA is Simon and Schuster Netherlands BV, Herculesplein 96 3584 AA Utrecht, Netherlands, info@simonandschuster.nl

Designed by Sheryl Dickert and Renee Bond
Printed and bound in China

Library of Congress Control Number: 2025938808
ISBN: 978-1-4236-6846-6
Ebook ISBN: 978-1-4236-6847-3

This product is made of FSC®-certified and other controlled material.

This book is dedicated to my sister, Maria, and our late mother, Gabriella. Our many late-night Christmas cookie baking sessions, accompanied by Fred and Ginger twirling around on TV in the background, will forever be among my most joyful memories.

CONTENTS

ALIMENTARI NOVELLA
ALIMENTARI NOVELLA
CANESTRELLI
CON FARINA
DI
CASTAGNE

INTRODUCTION

It started with a bag of cookies. As I was about to board a van in Genoa to take a small group of tour guests on a day trip, I ducked into a bakery in search of a snack to bring along. Running late, I grabbed the closest thing—a cellophane packet of pretty but plain-looking flower-shaped butter cookies. A lucky choice, as it turns out. Not only were the cookies a big hit with my guests, they were also the best butter cookies I've ever had—impossibly rich and melt-in-your-mouth crumbly, and yet comprising just four ingredients: flour, butter, sugar, and eggs.

I did what any good cookie sleuth would do: I found out where they were made by reading the small print on the back of the package. A few days later, I drove my rented Fiat Panda up into the hills north of Genoa to Torriglia, population 2,300, where the cookies, called *canestrelletti di Torriglia*, have been made for centuries. Much of the small town, once a popular summer getaway for Genoa's city dwellers, is devoted to making and promoting these cookies. Thanks to a clever PR campaign by locals, the *canestrelletti* business has breathed new life into a town that had seen its population and fortunes dwindle during the last half century. There are now at least eight bakeries in Torriglia that turn out canestrelletti and distribute them across the region, and there's an annual sagra (festival) celebrating the cookie that draws thousands.

End of a sweet story? I thought so, too, but it was just the beginning. When I mentioned my excursion to Torriglia to my Genoese friend Emanuela, she said, "Now you have to go to Gavi for the best amaretti." I followed her advice and sure enough Gavi, just over the border in Piedmont, in addition for being known for wine, is also where you will find soft chewy almond cookies known as amaretti di Gavi. In Gavi, I was told to go to nearby Voltaggio for *even better* amaretti. I already knew about crunchy amaretti di Saronno; soon I learned about amaretti di Gallarate. And it wasn't just amaretti. There were Brutti ma Buoni from Borgomanero, Nocciolini di Chivasso, Imperialine di Omegna, Krumiri di Casale Monferrato, and more. Looking at these places on a map, it became clear to me that a swath of northern Italy is populated by cookie towns. Much like Italy's cheeses—Asiago, Gorgonzola, and Taleggio, for example—I discovered that many of Italy's cookies have a place of origin.

I started seeing Italian cookies differently; I realized that they are as regional in character as the country's celebrated regional cuisines. Cookies in the north tend to be butter-based, enriched with eggs and sometimes cornmeal, or finely ground nuts. Or they are whimsical, egg white-whipped concoctions, studded with nuts or chocolate-dipped. Traditional cookies of the south are of a more rustic character. Olive oil or lard takes the place of butter, and honey or *mosto cotto* (grape must syrup) often stands in for sugar. There is wine in the dough, and fewer eggs. In Sicily and Sardinia, Italy's two island regions, almonds are the most important ingredient in sweets, including cookies. Ground almonds, chopped almonds, or almond paste form the base of almost every cookie. The variety of almond cookies is astonishing. But there are exceptions, too, like the wonderfully crumbly *Ciambelline Sarde*, Sardinian ring cookies made with lard.

My own love affair with Italian cookies began many years ago. In the weeks leading up to Christmas, my sister, Maria, and I would sit at the kitchen table cracking open piles of almonds, hazelnuts, and walnuts, which our mother, Gabriella, would toast and skin and grind to make her hazelnut crescents, *calcionelli* (ground nut and honey filled pockets), and other holiday sweets. It was tedious, but when I think back on those evenings spent around the table, anticipating the deliciousness to come, it is with much fondness and nostalgia, and an understanding that the freshness of the nuts was an important detail that Mom did not want to compromise on. Plus, it was less expensive than buying shelled nuts.

Our mom also made pizzelle, those pretty, lacy waffle cookies from her native region of Abruzzo, and rustic wine cookies from Molise, based on a recipe she got from her mother-in-law, my paternal grandmother, Maria. And she baked gingerbread dolls using a waxed paper pattern she made herself, and which Maria (my sister) and I would decorate with icing and sprinkles. It wasn't until decades later, when I found that pattern and others folded up inside Mom's recipe box that I realized that her gingerbread ladies were the re-creation of a traditional cookie found in Abruzzo and Lazio, one that she likely enjoyed herself as a girl. (You'll find a recipe for Pupazze Frascatane on page 112.)

As we grew older, Maria and I started contributing our own cookies to the Christmas plate—pine nut cookies, jam sandwiches, almond crescents, and amaretti. We ventured away from Italian cookies and began baking the cookies that were published every December in *Gourmet* magazine and special holiday issues of *Martha Stewart Living*, *Fine Cooking*, and other magazines—chewy chocolate ginger crinkles, coconut macaroons, Linzer hearts, pecan butter balls. The three of us—Mom, Maria, and

I—would bake deep into the night, long after Dad had gone to bed, making dozens and dozens of cookies while watching old Fred Astaire and Ginger Rogers movies, mesmerized by Astaire's debonair agility and Rogers's gracefulness as she swirled around in her ostrich feathers and high heels.

Eventually, as an adult, I pivoted back toward the traditional Italian cookies I had grown up with. I developed a new appreciation for the ingredients: almonds and hazelnuts, candied orange peel and dried figs, the use of honey, olive oil, anise, and wine in cookie dough. They were as far from your basic chocolate chip cookies as you could get, but the more I learned about them, the more I wanted to know. When I traveled to Italy, whether for work or vacation, I took note of the cookies I came across in fancy *pasticcerie* (pastry shops) and in rustic *forni* (bread bakeries), especially their inventive and curious names: Occhi di Santa Lucia (the eyes of Saint Lucy, named for a third-century martyr whose eyes were gouged out); Brutti ma Buoni (ugly but good); Pân di Mòrt (bread of the dead), and more.

Many cookies were tied to holidays or feast days, such as Quaresimali, spiced Lenten biscotti from Naples. Some were the inspiration of a single baker. Such was the case of *cantucci*, the famous twice-baked sliced almond cookies from Tuscany. Antonio Mattei opened his *biscottificio* in Prato in 1858, and his cookies won accolades in Florence and Paris. The small shop is still there, and the crunchy cookies, perfect for dipping in wine or coffee, are still made according to his recipe.

In Saronno, Lombardy, the Lazzaroni family has been making its crunchy amaretti even longer, since the eighteenth century. The company archives, which are stored in the fourteenth-century Franciscan cloisters in the center of town, include a breathtaking collection of decorated cookie tins that date to the 1700s.

More recently, in the charming medieval town of Scanno, deep in the wilds of Abruzzo, Ilario Notarmuzzi mans the cookie shop that his mother Liliana Rosati opened in 1990. It's one of the smallest *biscotterie* in Italy, but the cookies that Ilario produces—amaretti, mostaccioli, tender chocolate and almond slices—are oversize and beautifully rustic.

How could one—especially a cookie lover—not be transported by such places and the treasures that emerge from these artisans' ovens?

Anyone who has stepped into an Italian bakery, in Italy or elsewhere, knows the temptation that awaits—buttery piped S cookies and wreaths decorated with sprinkles and candied cherries; chewy, pine nut-studded cookies; fried pastry ribbons showered with powdered sugar; iced lemon rings and fig rolls; delicate ladyfingers, and airy, peak-tipped meringues. I knew there were many more sweet stories out there, so I set out to find them. The result is this book.

Thank you for joining me on this nut-studded, chocolate-dipped, anise-spiked, lemon-iced, sugar-dusted journey.

Domenica

How to Use this Book

Given the clear regionality of Italy's cookies, it made sense to organize the recipes similarly, in broad regional chapters: Cookies of the North, Cookies of Central Italy, Cookies of the South, and Cookies of the Islands. But you should feel free to start baking from whichever region, chapter, or recipe that appeals to you. Have you been wanting to learn how to make classic Cuccidati—spiced and iced fig- and chocolate-filled cookies from Sicily? The recipe is on page 183. Maybe you'd like to pull your pizzelle iron out of storage, in which case I suggest you try either the anise-scented OG version on page 164 or the chocolate-hazelnut variation on page 167.

In addition to the four central chapters, there is a final chapter, Basics and Embellishments, where you'll find recipes for Pasta Frolla (page 206), the classic butter-rich shortcrust dough that is the foundation of many Italian cookies; preserves for filling sandwich cookies; flourishes such as candied orange peel; and other essential recipes.

Whichever region you decide to dip into first, you'll find that most of the recipes are easy to make and require no special equipment. There are a few challenges and labors of love sprinkled here and there, like the Ventaglie (palmiers) on page 123 and the Celli Ripieni (stuffed bird-shaped cookies) on page 150. I believe that it is important for home bakers to try recipes that will improve our skills and knowledge of this deeply satisfying pursuit. It's rewarding, and it's fun!

ESSENTIALS OF ITALIAN COOKIE BAKING

There are, broadly speaking, three types of dough in Italian cookie baking:

Pasta frolla This is the Italian equivalent of shortcrust pastry, or dough enriched with fat, usually butter. I've included a basic recipe for both pasta frolla and chocolate pasta frolla in the Basics and Embellishments chapter, but many recipes throughout the book use variations on this theme. There are as many recipes for pasta frolla as there are bakers. While typically butter based, you will also find pasta frolla made with lard or even olive oil.

Olive oil dough Shiny olive oil dough is satisfying to work with. It is the foundation for many traditional cookies of southern Italy, where olive oil is plentiful and an important pantry staple. Some olive oil doughs also include wine (a delicious duet).

Almond-based dough Cookies made with ground almonds or almond paste, such as amaretti, are found throughout Italy. Many of these doughs are made with just three ingredients: ground almonds or almond paste, sugar, and egg whites. And yet, the variations these three ingredients produce is astounding. Almond doughs are especially important to the baking of Sicily and Sardinia, as well as Puglia, the heel of Italy's boot. Almonds called Mandorla Romana are especially suited to baking; they are sweet, with an unmistakable true almond flavor (see page 186).

There are exceptions, like the Meringhe di Assisi—oversize meringues—on page 120. And there is a subcategory I want to mention because it is too delicious not to: Biscotti da Inzuppo, a.k.a. the *dunking cookie*. These are generously sized cookies that are perfect for dunking in your morning cappuccino, a glass of milk, or whatever your morning beverage is. Try the Biscotti della Nonna (page 92), the Cantuccioni (page 101), or the chocolate-studded Biscotti da Inzuppo (page 142).

When it comes to ingredients, it's important to keep in mind that quality matters. If you make amaretti with stale almonds, your cookies will taste stale. Use good-quality butter, fresh eggs, and jam and preserves that taste like fruit, not a mix of sugar and pectin. I've included several recipes for preserves in the Basics and Embellishments chapter.

Before you bake, please read the Ingredients and Equipment sections that follow, as well as Essential Techniques. This step will go a long way toward making your foray into Italian cookie baking successful from the start.

INGREDIENTS

An alphabetical list of key ingredients:

Chocolate

Bittersweet chocolate Numerous recipes call for bittersweet chocolate. It contains more cacao and less sugar than semisweet chocolate and pairs well with many other ingredients common in Italian cookies, such as almond and anise. In recipes, it is grated into fillings or melted and used for dipping or drizzling on top of cookies. Semisweet chocolate, which has more sugar, may be substituted.

Cocoa powder Used to flavor cookie doughs and fillings, cocoa powder is made by grinding cocoa beans to a powder and removing the cocoa butter. Cocoa powder is naturally acidic, with an appealing fruity note. Dutch-processed cocoa powder is treated to neutralize the acidity and has a smoother flavor. Either can be used in the recipes in this book.

Milk chocolate With more sugar and milk mixed in, milk chocolate is lighter and sweeter than bittersweet. It is used for drizzling over cookies such as Cantuccioni del Bar (page 102).

Coffee

I use espresso-roast beans and freshly brewed espresso for the recipes in this book. The beans are roasted at length at high temperatures to concentrate their flavor.

Eggs

All recipes in this book call for large eggs (or yolks or whites from large eggs). If you can, buy fresh eggs from a local farm where chickens are allowed to roam. These have the best flavor.

Extracts And Flavorings

Many recipes in this book call for flavor in the form of an extract, mostly almond or vanilla, and occasionally anise. Use pure extracts rather than artificially flavored ones, which are manufactured from chemicals designed to mimic the aroma and taste of an ingredient but never taste like the real thing. Pure almond extract is a great stand-in for the bitter almonds or apricot kernels that traditional Italian bakeries use in their almond desserts but that aren't readily available in the U.S. due to their potential toxicity (see Nuts, page 21, for more information). Some recipes call for whole vanilla beans. Split the bean open lengthwise, scrape out the seeds, and add them to the cookie dough or batter.

Fats

Fat, in the form of butter, lard, or oil, enriches dough, adding flavor and contributing to the flaky, crumbly, and tender texture of cookies.

Butter All recipes in this book were tested using American butter, which typically contains 80% fat. By contrast, European butter contains 82 to 86% fat. If substituting European or European-style butter, know that it may affect the outcome of the recipe.

Lard Some traditional Italian cookies, especially in the south, are made with lard, which is rendered pork fat. The best lard for baking is leaf lard, a clean-tasting premium fat that surrounds the kidneys of the pig. It produces cookies with a rich, redolent undertone and a more flaky-crumbly texture than either butter or oil (see Sources on page 225 for purchasing leaf lard online).

Oil Many southern Italian cookie recipes call for oil rather than butter or lard. Both olive oil and sunflower oil are abundant and commonly used. I use olive oil when I want its rich, buttery flavor to shine through in a cookie. It's important to use good oil, preferably one that is not produced by a multinational conglomerate that might be using low-quality olives that have been sitting in storage containers growing rancid (it happens). At the same time, you don't want to use expensive, freshly pressed oil either. Find a brand you like and trust, look for important information on the label of the bottle, such as the harvest or bottling date, the date of expiration, the type of olives, and where the oil was pressed and produced.

When I want a lighter, more neutral flavor, I use sunflower oil. Look for sunflower oil that is expeller pressed rather than solvent-extracted. This means that a mechanical press is used to extract the oil rather than chemicals. I tend to avoid canola oil, which I find often has an unpleasant, fishy aftertaste.

Flour

Most of the recipes in this book call for unbleached all-purpose flour—a blend of hard and soft wheat that works in many baking preparations, from breads and cakes to pie crusts and cookies. Several recipes call specifically for pastry flour, finely milled soft-wheat flour that has a low protein content. Cookies

made with pastry flour have a fine, tight crumb and are more tender (less chewy) than other cookies. Other flours used in this book include corn flour and fine cornmeal, which are common in the baked goods of northern Italy; farro flour, made with emmer, an ancient form of wheat that grows in several regions of Italy, including Tuscany and Abruzzo; and whole wheat flour, which gives cookies a pleasing nutty flavor and slightly grainy texture. (For almond and other nut flours, see Nuts, page 21.)

Fruit

Fruit—fresh, dried, zested, candied, and preserved—plays a starring role in many Italian cookies.

Candied orange and lemon peels are used to flavor and garnish a variety of cookies. The recipe for how to make them is on page 220.

Dried fruit like apricots, figs, dates, and golden raisins, sometimes steeped in wine or liquor, bring texture and concentrated flavor to cookies such as Cuccidati (page 183), Settembrini (page 118), Pabassinas (page 191), and Zaleti (page 77).

Freshly grated lemon and orange zest perfumes dough and adds a bright note to fillings and icings.

Jams and preserves make a colorful filling for sandwich cookies such as Occhi di Bue (page 72) and Baci di Dama Calabresi (page 141). You'll find several recipes for homemade jam and preserves in the Basics and Embellishments chapter.

Wine grapes are found in a small handful of recipes that call for products made from them. Celli Ripieni (page 150), a jam-filled cookie from Abruzzo, is made with Scrucchjata (page 214), a rustic grape jam that is a pantry staple in the region. And the recipe for Mostaccioli (page 160)—chocolate-coated spice cookies—contains Mosto Cotto (page 215), cooked-down grape must syrup. There are vineyards and winemakers in most U.S. states. Contact them directly and ask about purchasing grapes or grape must. There are also options for buying online in the Sources section at the end of the book (page 225).

Leavening Agents

In short, leavening agents make baked goods rise. Several different types are used for the recipes in this book.

Baker's ammonia, also known as ammonium bicarbonate, is an old-fashioned raising agent that predates baking powder and baking soda. Many traditional Italian cookie recipes, particularly those from the south, still call for it. It produces cookies that are deliciously crispy and light, like the Biscotti di San Pellegrino Terme (page 45). However, as its name might suggest, baker's ammonia has a strong odor. If you take a whiff straight from the jar, it will make your eyeballs shrivel. The good news is that the ammonia smell dissipates during baking, and once the cookies come out of the oven, there should be no trace of it left. If you would rather not use it, simply substitute baking powder or a mix of baking powder and baking soda. If, on the other hand, you are an intrepid baker and want to get that supremely crispy texture, see page 225 for where to source baker's ammonia.

Baking powder is what is called for in most of the recipes. It gives lift to cookies, causing them to expand, and lightens their texture.

Baking soda, often used together with baking powder, also adds lift, but is employed in recipes that contain an acidic ingredient, such as lemon juice or wine. Cookies with baking soda tend to be crispier than those made with just baking powder.

Cream of tartar is a white crystalline powder that is used to stabilize egg whites and help them hold their peaks when beaten. If you don't have any on hand, simply substitute twice the amount of lemon juice (for example, if a recipe calls for ⅛ teaspoon cream of tartar, use ¼ teaspoon lemon juice).

Instant yeast is called for in the recipe for Torcetti di Saint-Vincent (page 84). This type of yeast is typically used in breads and yeast-leavened pastries such as croissants. And, in fact, torcetti have a yeasty flavor and bread-like quality to them. Unlike active dry yeast, instant yeast does not need to be activated by mixing it with warm liquid; it can be added directly to dry ingredients in a recipe, which makes it slightly more convenient to work with. (Instant yeast should not be confused with rapid-rise yeast, which will not work in this recipe.)

Liqueurs and Wine

We are talking about Italian baking, after all. Here is a list of wines and liqueurs that are used in recipes in this book.

Alchermes Also spelled Alkermes, this bright red liqueur dates back to medieval times, when it was used for medicinal purposes. Now, it is brushed onto sponge cakes and added to other baked goods. Alchermes is made by infusing spirits with cinnamon, cloves, nutmeg, and other spices. Its scarlet hue originally came from a small insect called cochineal, though many commercial brands now use artificial coloring. Alchermes is what gives the Tozzetti all' Alchermes on page 128 their pink hue. A dash of red food coloring may be substituted.

Amaretto This sweet almond liqueur originated in Saronno, where crunchy amaretti cookies also originated (see page 38). Like the cookie, amaretto liqueur has a touch of bitterness, imparted by either bitter almonds or by apricot or peach kernels.

Cognac I use a splash of cognac—brandy produced in the Cognac region of France—in my Fig and Chocolate Preserves with Cognac (page 212).

Limoncello Now world-famous, this lemon liqueur is produced in Sorrento and other towns along the Amalfi Coast. The area is famous for its large, bumpy-skinned lemons; their oil-rich peel is used to infuse the liqueur.

Malvasia Malvasia wines from the Veneto region can be smooth or sparkling and are bright in flavor, with notes of citrus. The wine is called for in the recipe for Zucherancici—Istrian wedding cookies (page 86). Jamaican rum can be substituted.

Punch Abruzzo This sweet, potent liqueur is made from caramelized sugar and the zest of lemons and oranges. It is a popular after-dinner *digestivo* but I sometimes think its true purpose is for drizzling over vanilla ice cream, adding a splash to French toast batter, or flavoring cookies. See page 225 for online sources. If you are unable to find it, substitute dark or Jamaican rum (mixed with a little orange and lemon zest, if you like).

Ratafia A cherry liqueur made from sour cherries, red wine, and alcohol, Ratafia is popular in Abruzzo, where it is made with Montepulciano d'Abruzzo wine and, sometimes, the leaves of the cherry tree rather than the fruit itself. Substitute any good cherry brandy or regular brandy.

Rum Several recipes call for rum, a popular ingredient in Italian baking. Recipes specify whether white, dark, or Jamaican rum is called for. But honestly, whatever rum you have in your liquor cabinet will work for all of them.

Sambuca and other anise liqueur Sambuca is one of Italy's most well-known liqueurs. The clear, viscous liqueur is sweet and strong, with a pronounced anise flavor. Other anise liqueurs include anisette, pastis, and Pernod.

Wine Both red and white wine are common ingredients in southern Italian cookies. I've suggested specific regional wines in several of the recipes in this book, but you can use any inexpensive—but still drinkable—wine in cookie dough.

Nuts

Because nuts are such an important ingredient in Italian cookies, it's important to use high-quality ones that taste fresh. Look for a good bulk purveyor that restocks its bins often, or a good online source (see page 225). Don't use nuts that smell or taste sour or rancid or stale, as the unpleasant flavor will affect the taste of your cookies.

Almonds are one of the most important ingredients in this book. Many cookie doughs and fillings from north to south and out to the islands include these sweet and bitter nuts, either whole, chopped, finely ground into flour, or pounded into a paste. Sicilian almonds are among the best, for they actually taste like almonds, rather than just earthy and "nutty," like many supermarket almonds. If your budget allows it, splurge on a bag the next time you bake almond cookies like Amaretti di Saronno (page 38) or Amarettus (page 179). You will taste the difference. (See page 225 for an online source.)

The bitter note in many Italian almond-based cookies comes from bitter almonds, a variety of the nut that contains prussic acid, which can be toxic when consumed even in moderate quantities. The toxin is neutralized when the nut is cooked. (The same bitter flavor can also be obtained from apricot and peach kernels, which are also used in Italian baking.) Bitter almonds are not available in the U.S. The best substitute is pure almond extract, which has all of the flavor and none of the toxicity.

Almond flour Some recipes in this book call for grinding your own almonds to make almond flour. Others use store-bought almond flour. Store-bought almond flour has less oil than freshly ground, and for some cookies, this is the better option. There are several types of flour that are made from finely ground almonds. They differ in composition, taste, and texture. Almond meal is made from ground skin-on almonds; it is flecked with tiny specks of brown from the almond skins and slightly coarse in texture. Almond flour is made from blanched almonds, or almonds from which the skin has been removed. The flour is fluffier in texture and lighter in color than almond meal. Superfine almond flour is simply blanched almond flour that has been ground more finely. I used superfine almond flour for the recipes in this book. You may substitute almond meal or regular almond flour but be aware that it may affect the texture and color of your cookies.

Almond paste is made from ground almonds, sugar, and water (or sometimes egg whites). You can find it at well-stocked supermarkets and online (see page 225). But you can also make it at home in a food processor. I've included a recipe on page 219.

Hazelnuts are a key ingredient in the cookies of Italy's north, especially Piedmont, where they are cultivated. The nuts are small and round, delicate and crunchy, with a sweet, buttery flavor. You can find them online (see page 225). They make Baci di Dama (page 42), the bite-size button hazelnut cookies sandwiched with bittersweet chocolate, over-the-top delicious.

Pine nuts are the star ingredient of Pinolate (page 80)—classic pine nut and almond cookies from Liguria. Ligurian pine nuts—the ones traditionally used in pesto—are long and slim, rather than short and squat, and they have a pronounced, sweet and nutty flavor. Look for them in specialty groceries and online (see Sources, page 225).

Pistachios are prominent in Sicilian baking, used as a garnish for cannoli, cooked with sugar into nut brittle, and ground into flour for cookies such as Paste di Pistacchio (page 199). Commercial pistachio flour is available online, and though it is expensive, it is worth the occasional splurge for its rich green color and fine texture (see Sources, page 225).

Walnuts have a tender texture and a buttery, slightly bitter flavor. They are richer in oils than other nuts, which means they can turn rancid quickly—within a few weeks or months, depending on how fresh they are when you buy them. If they smell or taste "off"—sour or extra-bitter or just stale—don't use them.

Spices

The spice trade had a big impact on Italian cooking and baking during the Middle Ages and the Renaissance. Spices were expensive, a status symbol available only to nobility and the wealthy. They turned up in both savory and sweet dishes, including cookies. Be sure the spices you use are fresh and not past their expiration date so that you get their full impact. Some recipes call for toasting a spice before adding it to a recipe. This step helps to release and deepen the spice's flavor. Here is a list of spices—both whole and ground—used in the recipes in this book.

- Anise and star anise
- Black peppercorn
- Caraway
- Cinnamon
- Cloves
- Coriander
- Ginger
- Nutmeg

Sugar and Other Sweeteners

Granulated sugar is the most-used sweetener in the recipes in this book. A few recipes call for superfine sugar, also known as caster sugar. Its fine texture allows it to dissolve more quickly than granulated sugar. Confectioners' sugar is used both in cookie doughs and to coat baked cookies as a finishing touch. Demerara sugar is minimally processed cane sugar with large crystals and light caramel color. I use it to decorate the otherwise rustic Biscotti del Pescatore (page 94). Pearl sugar is made by compressing sugar crystals into small white pellets that don't melt when baked. They add a pretty finish to cookies such as Amaretti di Saronno (page 38) and Cantuccioni (page 101) .

Before sugar was commonplace in Italian baking, many recipes called for honey or other natural sweeteners. One recipe that showcases honey in the dough is Pupazze Frascatone (page 112), a traditional spiced holiday cutout cookie from Frascati, outside of Rome. Mosto cotto, a cooked-down syrup made from the juice of freshly pressed grapes, is another natural sweetener. Also known as saba or sapa, it is a key ingredient in many old-fashioned and traditional recipes, including Mostaccioli, spiced chocolate diamond cookies from Abruzzo (page 160). The recipe for making mosto cotto at home is on page 215.

EQUIPMENT

Angled spatula for transferring cookies from baking sheets to wire racks.

Baking sheets I keep 3 rimmed 11 x 17-inch (28 x 43-cm) baking sheets on hand for making cookies.

Bench scraper This flat, rectangular tool is great for scooping up chopped nuts, grated chocolate, and other ingredients.

Biscotti pan USA Pan makes a special pan that is the perfect size for large coffee bar-style biscotti. It's not essential, but it does come in handy (see Sources, page 225).

Cookie cutters I use an assortment of round, rectangular, and flower-shaped cookie cutters to stamp out cookies, some with smooth edges, others with pretty fluted borders.

Cookie press This cylindrical tube punches stiff cookie dough through patterned plates to make flowers, stars, wreaths, and other shapes. I use one to make Biscotti Ricci del Gattopardo (page 185), Sicilian almond cookies.

Cookie scoop A small (1 tablespoon) spring-loaded cookie scoop is useful for measuring out equal portions of cookie dough.

Deep-fry thermometer This comes in handy for measuring the temperature of oil for frying Calcionelli (page 148) and Chiacchiere (page 156).

Food processor Essential for finely chopping and pulverizing nuts—I can't imagine doing all that by hand! I also use a food processor to make many cookie doughs.

Hand mixer An electric handheld mixer is useful for whipping egg whites or yolks and for mixing small batches of cookie batter.

High-side skillet or frying pan I use a well-seasoned cast iron skillet with 2¼-inch (5½-cm) high sides to fry calcionelli and chiacchiere.

Mixing bowl A large ceramic, glass, or stoneware mixing bowl works well for doughs that are mixed by hand.

Mortar and pestle If you like unplugged tools (as I do), a mortar and pestle is a good tool to have. It works well for chopping or pounding small quantities of nuts or spices.

Parchment paper Precut sheets of parchment are essential for lining baking sheets (see Sources, page 225).

Pastry brush A brush with natural (boar's hair) bristles works well for painting egg wash or thin icing onto the surface of cookies, as well as for brushing off excess flour.

Pastry wheel I use a fluted pastry wheel to cut out and trim the edges of cookies before baking.

Piping/pastry bags and tips I use both disposable and reusable pastry bags to pipe out cookie dough and batter. Sturdy reusable bags work best for stiff dough, as they don't burst or leak. I have a basic set of tips that includes both plain (smooth) tips as well as open and closed star tips. See individual recipes for specifics on which tips to use.

Pizzelle iron You'll need a pizzelle iron to make the classic Pizzelle (page 164), as well as Pizzelle alla Gianduia (page 167). The iron can also be used to make Brigidini di Lamporecchio (page 95). I have several pizzelle irons, including an electric one and several old-fashioned manual ones originally meant for the hearth—they work beautifully on my gas range. See page 225 for information on where to buy pizzelle irons.

Rimmed baking sheets Most of the cookies in this book are baked on 11 x 17 inch (28 x 43 cm) rimmed aluminum baking sheets.

Rolling pin I use a standard wood handled rolling pin to roll out cookie dough.

Sifter A stainless-steel flour sifter helps to aerate and remove lumps from flour and other dry ingredients.

Silicone spatulas I have several for mixing cookie doughs and batters.

Spice grinder An electric spice grinder works well for pulverizing toasted (and non-toasted) spices. It can also blitz granulated sugar into superfine sugar or even powdered sugar within seconds.

Stand mixer I have a thirty-year-old KitchenAid stand mixer that still works well. I use both the whisk attachment and the paddle attachment for mixing ingredients and doughs.

Storage tins I prefer to store cookies in aluminum tins with tight-fitting lids, though any airtight container will do.

Water bath canning equipment If you make any of the jam or preserve recipes in this book, you may want to process them in a water bath for long keeping. For this you'll need canning jars, lids and rings, a jar lifter, and a canner (large pot) with a jar rack. See Essential Techniques (page 26) for more information on water-bath canning.

Waxed paper I often wrap dough that needs to chill in waxed paper (or plastic wrap). And I use sheets of waxed paper to separate iced cookies into layers when placing them in storage tins.

ESSENTIAL TECHNIQUES

Read through this section to familiarize yourself with techniques used throughout this book. As with any baking process, the more you do it, the better you will get.

Grinding Spices

Several recipes call for grinding whole spices such as anise and star anise, cloves, and coriander seeds. The quantities are too small for a standard food processor, so I use a spice grinder. If you have a mortar and pestle, you can pound the spices by hand.

Prepping Nuts

Many recipes call for toasted and/or peeled or skinned nuts. To toast nuts, spread them out on a rimmed baking sheet and bake at 350° F (180° C) for 5 to 8 minutes, tossing once halfway through, until lightly browned and fragrant. You can buy peeled or skinned nuts, but if you're starting with skin-on, follow these instructions to remove the skins from almonds, hazelnuts, and pistachios.

Almonds Place raw, skin-on almonds in a heat-proof bowl and pour boiling water over them. Let sit for a minute or two to loosen the skins. Drain and rinse and use your fingers to pop the almonds out of their skins.

Hazelnuts Preheat the oven to 350° F (180° C). Spread the shelled nuts on a rimmed baking sheet and bake for 10 minutes, or until the skins start to crackle. Wrap the hot hazelnuts in a clean kitchen towel and let stand about 1 minute. Roll the nuts back and forth in the towel to loosen and rub off the skins. Not all the skins will come off, which is fine.

Pistachios I rarely peel pistachios because, frankly, it is fussy and tedious. However, buying peeled pistachios is very expensive. If you want the nuts' vibrant green hue to be visible in your cookies, you may want to take the time to peel them. Place the nuts in a heat-proof bowl and pour enough boiling water over them to cover. Let them sit for 2 minutes and then drain. Don't let the nuts sit longer in the water or they will soften. You can either peel the skins off with your fingers or wrap the nuts in a clean kitchen towel and roll them back and forth to remove the skins. I find the towel method removes some, but not all, of the skins, so I use my fingers.

Melting and Tempering Chocolate

Several recipes call for dipping or coating cookies in melted chocolate. Tempering the chocolate produces a glossy finish that won't "bloom" as it dries—meaning no white streaks or crystals forming on the surface. Once dry, tempered chocolate has an appealing snap.

Tempering chocolate in the microwave Chop the chocolate into small pieces. Place ⅔ of it into a microwave-safe bowl. Melt on 50% power at 1-minute intervals, stirring between each interval, until the chocolate is melted. Use a digital thermometer to check the temperature of the chocolate. It should be 100° to 110° F (38° to 43° C). Stir in the remaining chocolate a little at a time, making sure it is melted before adding more (this is called "seeding" the chocolate). The chocolate will thicken and become glossy. The chocolate is ready when it has cooled to between 85° and 90° F (29° to 32° C). If necessary, reheat the chocolate in the microwave in short bursts to maintain that temperature range.

Tempering chocolate on the stovetop Chop the chocolate into small pieces. Place ⅔ of the chocolate in a heat-proof bowl. Set the bowl over a pan of barely simmering water, making sure that the bottom of the bowl does not touch the water. Start stirring when the chocolate starts to melt and keep stirring until it is nearly melted. Remove the bowl from the pan and keep stirring until all the chocolate is melted. Use a digital thermometer to test the temperature. It should be 100° F to 110° F (38° C to 43° C). Add the remaining chocolate to the bowl a little at a time, making sure it melts before adding more (this is called "seeding" the chocolate). The chocolate will thicken and become glossy. Keep stirring until the temperature has cooled to between 85° F and 90° F (29° C and 32° C). If necessary, return the bowl to the pan of hot water to maintain that temperature range.

Whipping Egg Whites and Meringue

Several recipes for amaretti (almond cookies) and the recipe for Meringhe di Assisi (page 120) call for whipping egg whites to soft or stiff peaks. Here are tips to successfully whip egg whites:

- Fresh egg whites are more stable than older whites, so use fresh eggs if you have them.
- Use a stand mixer, especially if you are beating the whites to firm or stiff peaks. A mixer makes quick work of the process.

- Use a very clean stainless-steel bowl that has no trace of greasy residue. Fat of any kind will prevent egg whites from whipping properly. Make sure your whisk attachment is also clean, with no greasy residue.
- Separate the whites from the yolks while the eggs are still cold but bring the whites to room temperature before beating them. Room-temperature eggs whip more quickly and to a higher volume.
- Start beating the whites on low to break up the strands of protein. Once the whites are foamy, beat in cream of tartar or lemon juice, if called for in the recipe. These ingredients help to stabilize the egg whites so they retain their volume.
- Increase the speed and beat until the whites are sufficiently whipped. "Soft" peaks means peaks that droop or curl over. "Firm" peaks keep their shape without drooping. And "stiff" peaks stand up straight without drooping even if you turn the bowl upside down. Take care not to overbeat, or you will end up with dry, grainy whites that will clump when you try to incorporate them into other ingredients.

Making meringues If you are adding sugar to make meringues, use superfine (caster) sugar instead of granulated. The fine crystals will dissolve more readily in the egg whites. Start adding the sugar when the egg whites have been whipped to foamy white, adding it gradually—1 to 2 tablespoons at a time—and making sure it is well incorporated before adding more. Keep adding sugar on medium-high to high speed until you have added it all. Continue beating until the meringue is light, glossy, and voluminous, with no trace of graininess from the sugar. It should hold firm peaks that barely droop at the tip.

WATER-BATH PROCESSING FOR PRESERVES

In the Basics and Embellishments chapter, you'll find several recipes for homemade preserves, which can be used in cookie recipes. The preserves can be refrigerated but processing them in a water bath will extend their shelf life. Here are basic water bath canning instructions.

HERE'S WHAT YOU NEED FOR BASIC WATER BATH PROCESSING:

Ball glass jars (½ pint; 250 ml) If you are reusing jars, be sure to inspect them for cracks or chips.

Canner and rack a large pot with a rack that fits on the bottom.

Lids and rings Standard Ball jars are capped with a flat metal lid and screw-on band. The lids have a ring of rubber on the underside that sits flush with the rim of the glass jar. Softening the rubber in simmering water helps to create a good seal (see steps below).

Other useful canning tools Silicone spatulas or wooden spoons, for stirring; a clean ladle to fill jars; a plastic wide-mouth funnel to guide the preserves neatly into jars; a jar lifter to place jars into and lift them out of boiling hot water; a small, magnetic wand called a lid lifter to lift lids and rings out of hot water; a long plastic bubble remover or a clean plastic chopstick to dislodge any air bubbles that may form in a filled jar.

Start with clean equipment Make sure your canner and canning tools have been washed in hot soapy water and dried. Spread a clean kitchen towel near the canner (large pot). Fill the canner halfway with water and bring to a boil. The level of water will rise when you add your filled jars.

Sanitize your jars and lids Wash them with hot soapy water, rinse, and dry. Place the lids and rings in a small pot and heat to simmering. Turn off the heat and let the lids and rings sit in the hot water until ready to cap the jars.

Fill the clean jars with hot preserves Use a clean wide-mouth funnel to ladle the preserves into the jars, taking care to leave about ¼ inch (6 mm) headspace–the space between the top of the food and the rim of the jar. Gently run a bubble remover or clean plastic chopstick around the inside of the jar to dislodge any bubbles.

Carefully wipe the rims of the filled jars Use a damp paper towel to remove any drips. Set the lids on top of the jars and screw on the rings, taking care not to tighten them too much (air needs to escape during processing).

Place the jars in the canner Use a jar lifter to arrange the jars on the rack. The jars should be submerged by 1 to 2 inches (2½ to 5 cm).

Process the jars Place the lid on the canner and return the water to a boil. Process for 10 minutes. When time is up, turn off the heat under the canner and let the jars sit until the bubbling stops. Use the jar lifter to remove the jars and set them on the kitchen towel to cool. Within a few minutes, you should hear that satisfying "ping" signifying that the jars have sealed, though not all jars will make noise. Let the jars cool for 12 to 24 hours.

Test the seal When the jars are cool, remove the rings around the lids and test the seal by pressing your finger into the center of the lid. It should remain concave and not flex back up. Lift the jar by the edge of the lid. If the lid stays on, you have a good seal. If a jar has not sealed properly, store it in the refrigerator and use that jar first.

FOR MORE INFORMATION ON HOME CANNING: *Visit the National Center for Home Food Preservation (nchfp.uga.edu) and Ball Corporation (freshpreserving.com).*

COOKIES
OF THE NORTH

Recipes and stories from

EMILIA-ROMAGNA, FRIULI-VENEZIA GIULIA, LIGURIA, LOMBARDY, PIEDMONT, TRENTINO-ALTO ADIGE, VALLE D'AOSTA, VENETO

A great diversity exists among the eight regions that stretch from the Alps to the Apennines and from the Italian Riviera, where the Mediterranean coast of Liguria meets France, to Trieste and its Adriatic border with Croatia and Slovenia.

Northern Italy covers 40% of the Italian republic (46,452 square miles; 120,311 square km) and is home to 46% of the population (27.4 million as of 2022). Its cities include Milan, Italy's commerce and fashion capital; elegant Torino, home to the headquarters of Alfa Romeo, Fiat, and Lancia; color-splashed Genoa, a densely populated port city built on steep hills that rise up from the Mediterranean Sea; Venice, overcrowded with tourists, yet forever romantic and beguiling; Trieste, a city of both medieval and neoclassical splendor; and Bologna, where the world's oldest university still operates and where you'll find iconic dishes such as Lasagne alla Bolognese and Tortellini in Brodo.

In landscape, northern Italy ranges from the Mediterranean microclimates of Liguria and Lombardy's Lakes District to the alpine meadows and peaks of the Aosta Valley, and from the magnificent slopes of the Dolomites to the cultivated fields of the Po Valley.

The cookies in this chapter reflect the range of ingredients that come from these eight diverse regions. Among them: alpine butter; bittersweet chocolate and fresh hazelnuts from Piedmont; buttery pine nuts from Liguria; soft wheat and cornmeal from the Po Valley. Fine yellow cornmeal is what gives Venetian Zaleti (page 77) their delicate crunch; Baci di Dama al Caffè (page 42) owe their tender crumble and deep toasty flavor to Piedmont's crispy hazelnuts. And good butter, perfectly whipped with fresh eggs, is the defining feature of Canestrelletti di Torriglia (page 50), the flower-shaped cookies from Liguria that inspired this book.

Although almonds are more closely associated with southern Italy and the islands of Sicily and Sardinia, they have also been cultivated for centuries in Liguria and lower Piedmont, which is one reason there are many types of amaretti—cookies made with ground almonds—both soft (pages 35 and 37) and crunchy (page 38), sprinkled throughout the north. The cookies of northern Italy are both elegant and rustic, a sweet homage to the lands they represent.

AMARETTI DI GALLARATE *(Lombardy)*

Amaretti from Gallarate

Among the wide variety of almond cookies that I came across while researching this book, I found this one to be among the most intriguing. It has the same ingredients as most amaretti—ground almonds, sugar, and egg whites. But the way the batter is mixed and the cookies shaped yields a completely different and unique result. They have a pronounced almond taste and an almost powdery, meringue-like texture, with a slightly chewy center, and craggy peaks that rise up like tiny Alps. Perhaps their aspect is intentional; Gallarate, the city where the cookies were invented, is located northwest of Milan, with the Alps as a distant backdrop.

Pasticceria Bianchi has been turning out amaretti di Gallarate since the 1930s. The lore accompanying their version is that the cookies obtained their uneven, cracked appearance by accident; one night, after trays of unbaked cookies were set out to dry before being put in the oven—a key step in making these sweets—a cat found its way into the kitchen and trampled over them, leaving them misshapen. The truth is less charming, but still clever: bakers pinch the piped cookie batter with the thumbs and first two fingers of each hand to create an uneven pattern and give the cookies their cracked peaks. Before going into the oven, the cookies are dusted with a mixture of confectioners' sugar and flour, which creates their signature Alpine look.

You'll need a food processor to properly mix the batter for these cookies.

MAKES ABOUT 20 COOKIES

Scant 1 cup (125 g) blanched almonds

1¼ cups (250 g) granulated sugar

2 large (60 g) egg whites

2 teaspoons honey

Pinch of fine salt

½ teaspoon pure almond extract

TO FINISH

4 tablespoons confectioners' sugar

1 tablespoon pastry flour or unbleached all-purpose flour

1. Place the almonds and sugar in the work bowl of a food processor fitted with the metal blade. Process until the nuts are finely ground and the mixture looks sandy.

2. In a bowl, lightly whisk the egg whites with the honey, salt, and almond extract. With the machine running, pour this mixture through the feed tube and process for several minutes, until you have a thick, smooth creamy batter. Scoop the batter into a piping bag fitted with a ½-inch (¾-cm) plain tip.

3. Line two rimmed baking sheets with parchment. Pipe 2-inch (5-cm) circles onto the parchment, 12 per sheet. Leave the baking sheets uncovered overnight, or for 12 hours, to allow the batter to dry slightly and form a "skin."

4. To finish: Preheat the oven to 375° F (190° C). Sift together the confectioners' sugar and flour and use a fine-mesh sieve or a sugar shaker to coat the cookies. With the thumbs and first two fingers of both hands, pinch the circles of batter, lifting your fingers slightly as you go, to give the cookies an elongated shape with some height and cracks. Bake, one sheet at a time, in the middle of the oven for about 9 minutes, until the cookies are golden-brown. Transfer the baking sheets to wire racks to cool completely. These cookies are best eaten within a few days of baking. They will keep in a tightly lidded container for up to 1 week, though they will begin to dry out after about 3 days.

0,70
CAD.
AMARETTO
CAVO
€ 1,00 CAD.

AMARETTI DI GAVI *(Piedmont)*

Almond Cookies from Gavi

Gavi is a picturesque medieval town nestled in the countryside where Piedmont meets Liguria. Although it is probably best known for the crisp, dry white wine produced in the area, Gavi is also where you will find these tender, two-bite almond cookies. Every coffee bar and *pasticceria* in town sells them, piled enticingly on trays in display cases or tidily wrapped in cellophane packets. My favorite place to buy them is at Antico Caffè del Moro, right on the main street in Gavi's historical center. The café has been producing them by hand since 1938, according to fifth-generation owner Enrica Bassano.

Like other amaretti, amaretti di Gavi are made with few ingredients—primarily almonds, sugar, and egg whites. But they are notable for their rounded triangular shape, made by pinching small balls of almond dough with your thumb and two fingers. The cookies are rolled in confectioners' sugar, and when they bake, they puff just enough to form a beautifully crackled surface. They are delicately crisp on the outside, with a soft, yielding center.

In my version here, I've added a touch of honey to ensure that tender center, and I've used almond flour in place of ground almonds for its finer texture. See the Baker's Note below for an Amaretti di Voltaggio variation.

MAKES ABOUT 32 COOKIES

2½ cups (250g) blanched superfine almond flour

1 cup (200g) granulated sugar

2 large (60 g) egg whites

2 tablespoons honey

½ teaspoon pure almond extract

½ teaspoon pure vanilla extract (optional)

About 1 cup (120g) confectioners' sugar, for coating

1. Preheat the oven to 325° F (165° C). Line two or three baking sheets with parchment.

2. Measure the almond flour and sugar into a bowl and whisk well to combine. In a separate bowl, whisk together the egg whites, honey, and extracts. Pour this mixture into the flour and sugar and mix thoroughly with a sturdy spatula. The dough will be soft and somewhat sticky but should hold its shape. Use your hands to knead it briefly in the bowl. Cover and let rest 30 minutes.

3. Pour the confectioners' sugar into a shallow bowl. Pinch off walnut-size pieces of dough (about 1 tablespoon) and roll them into balls. Coat them well with confectioners' sugar and place them on the baking sheets, 1 to 2 inches apart. You should be able to fit 16 cookies onto each sheet. With your thumb and two fingers, pinch each ball of dough to give it a rounded triangular shape with three indentations, sort of like a tricorner hat.

4. Bake, one sheet at a time, in the middle of the oven, for 17 to 18 minutes, until the cookies have puffed and are softly set and barely golden in color. Transfer the baking sheets to wire racks and let the cookies cool completely on the sheets. Store in an airtight container for up to 1 week.

BAKER'S NOTE: *Here's a variation to try. Nine miles south of Gavi, the town of Voltaggio boasts a similar cookie, known (not surprisingly) as amaretti di Voltaggio. Created and patented by pastry chef Attilio Cavo at the end of the nineteenth century, these amaretti likely predate those of Gavi. They are slightly larger, flavored with fresh lemon zest, and also baked a couple of minutes longer, just enough to give them a crispy golden exterior. To make amaretti di Voltaggio at home, omit the vanilla extract and add the finely grated zest of 1 lemon to the dough. Roll the balls slightly larger than you would for amaretti di Gavi, then proceed with the recipe. Bake for 18 to 20 minutes, until golden.*

AMARETTI DI SARONNO *(Lombardy)*

Crunchy Almond Cookies

Surely these crunchy bite-size almond cookies are one of Italy's most iconic sweets. They come individually wrapped in pastel tissue paper or packaged in colorful tins festooned with cherubs, flowers, maidens, and pastoral scenes. They are sometimes topped with pearl sugar, and they are redolent with the aroma and distinctive sweet and bitter taste of almonds. If biting into one doesn't satisfy your sweet tooth, nothing will.

While visiting Saronno, where the cookies have been made for centuries, I stopped in at the headquarters of Paolo Lazzaroni & Figli, one of the preeminent producers of amaretti. The company markets its amaretti under the label Chiostro di Saronno (Cloister of Saronno).

Paolo Lazzaroni, the family patriarch who runs Chiostro di Saronno with his son Luca, is elderly but hale and trim, with piercing blue eyes and silver-white hair. In addition to cookies, the company makes amaretto liqueur, panettone, and a range of other sweets. I interviewed him at the company's headquarters; a sprawling production facility located in the industrial outskirts of the city.

The amaretto's story, Paolo Lazzaroni said, began in the eighteenth century in the Valtellina, an alpine valley in the northern reaches of Lombardy near the Switzerland border. One Giuseppe Lazzaroni, together with his beloved wife, Osolina, devised an early version of the cookie to satisfy the sweet tooth of cardinals and other religious and noble figures. A roving poet took to calling the almond confections *amarette di Lazzaron* from the word *amaro*, meaning "bitter." Giuseppe's grandson, Carlo, moved the artisanal baking operation to Saronno in the nineteenth century, passing it on to sons Davide and Paolo—great-grandfather and namesake of the Paolo Lazzaroni with whom I spoke. As we paged through an album of Art Deco print ads, he mused that the unnamed roving poet's declaration might be a double entendre.

"It is possible there was a play on words, between the word *amaro*, which means 'bitter' and refers to the bitter character of the almonds, and the word *amare*, which means 'to love.'"

This recipe is my own version of amaretti di Saronno. The originals are said to be made with a mix of almonds and apricot kernels. It is the apricot kernel—the small seed inside the fruit's hard pit—that gives the cookies their stealthy bitter notes. However, these seeds are considered toxic when ingested in large quantities, and you can't buy them in the U.S. I have occasionally resorted to hoarding apricot pits in summer, then hammering them open to retrieve the seed, a task for which the idiom "a tough nut to crack" was surely created. A few drops of pure almond extract produces the same result with none of the exertion.

MAKES ABOUT 100 COOKIES

Scant 1 cup (125 g) blanched and toasted almonds, cooled (see page 26)

1¼ cups (250 g) granulated sugar

2 large (60 g) egg whites, at room temperature

½ to 1 teaspoon pure almond extract

Pearl sugar, for sprinkling

1. Preheat the oven to 375° F (190° C). Line two or three rimmed baking sheets with parchment. You will need to reuse the sheets to bake all the cookies.

2. Place the cooled nuts and half the sugar in the work bowl of a food processor fitted with the metal blade. Pulse until the nuts are coarsely chopped. Add the rest of the sugar to the bowl and pulse again until the mixture resembles sand. With the motor running, pour the egg whites and almond extract through the feed tube and process for several minutes, until the batter is smooth and dense.

3. Scoop the batter into a large piping bag fitted with a ½-inch (12-mm) round or French star tip and pipe 30 to 35 rounds per sheet, spacing them about 1 inch (2½ cm) apart. Each round should be about ¾ to 1 inch (2 to 2½ cm) in diameter. Sprinkle the tops of the amaretti with a pinch of pearl sugar, just a few granules per cookie.

4. Bake the cookies, one sheet at a time, in the middle of the oven for 5 minutes. Increase the heat to 400° F (200° C) and bake an additional 4 to 5 minutes, until the

cookies are puffed and browned, with cracked, domed tops. Transfer the baking sheet to a wire rack to cool for 10 to 15 minutes, then transfer the cookies to racks to cool completely. Remember to return the oven to 375° F (190° C) before baking the next batch of cookies. This is inconvenient but starting the cookies at a slightly lower temperature and finishing with a burst of extra heat toward the end of baking yields perfectly crunchy amaretti without the risk of overbrowning.

Store the amaretti in a tin for up to 1 month. You can also freeze them for up to 3 months.

BAKER'S NOTE: *This recipe makes a lot of cookies. Although they keep for a long time, there are lots of ways you can use them in other desserts. They are a key ingredient in the* Pân di Mòrt *cookies on page 74. They can also be used in bonet, a chocolate-amaretto flan from Piedmont, as a base for trifles and parfaits, and crumbled into cake batter or on top of ice cream.*

BACI DI ALASSIO *(Liguria)*

Alassio Kisses

Alassio is a color-splashed town along the Italian Riviera—the northern Mediterranean coast of Liguria, where the boot of Italy fans out. For generations, its sandy beaches and pretty, historic old town have attracted luminaries and celebrities, from poet Gabriele D'Annunzio to Ernest Hemingway and Salvador Dalí. Once an important fishing and trade center, Alassio is now a lively resort, its main street lined with shops, seafood restaurants, coffee bars, and bakeries.

Wherever you go in Alassio, you'll find these chocolate-hazelnut kisses for sale. They are as much an emblem of the city as the gold and orange stucco buildings with their green shutters and trompe l'oeil painted facades. The cookies—two piped stars sandwiched with dark chocolate ganache—were created in 1919 by confectioner Rinaldo Balzola, whose family bakery, Caffè Balzola, has been in operation since 1902.

The dough for these cookies is fairly stiff, so that they hold their shape during baking. Be sure to use a durable, reusable piping bag rather than a disposable plastic one. I use a ½-inch (12-mm) star tip.

MAKES 20 SANDWICH COOKIES

BACI

1 rounded cup (140 g) blanched and toasted hazelnuts, cooled (see page 26)

½ cup (100 g) superfine sugar

3½ ounces (⅓ cup; 100 g) almond paste, cut into ½-inch (12 mm) cubes (see page 219)

3 tablespoons cocoa powder

Pinch of fine salt

1 large egg white

1 tablespoon mild honey

GANACHE FILLING

4 ounces (113 g) bittersweet chocolate, finely chopped

½ cup (125 ml) heavy cream

1 tablespoon salted butter

1. For the baci: Place the hazelnuts and sugar in the work bowl of a food processor fitted with the metal blade. Pulse to form a fine, sandy grind with some coarse bits–50 to 60 pulses. Scatter in the almond paste and pulse to break it up, then add the cocoa powder and salt and pulse until the mixture is finely ground.

2. In a small bowl, whisk the egg white and honey just enough to combine them. Pour this into the food processor and pulse until a dense dough comes together. Scoop the dough into a durable piping bag fitted with a ½-inch (12 mm) star tip.

3. Line two rimmed baking sheets with parchment. Pipe 20 stars, about 1 inch (2½ cm) in diameter, onto each sheet. Let rest, uncovered, for 30 minutes.

4. Preheat the oven to 350° F (180° C) while the cookies rest. Bake them, one sheet at a time, in the middle of the oven for 8 to 10 minutes, until they are barely set. Take care not to overbake or the cookies may be tough or taste burnt. Transfer the baking sheet to a wire rack to cool for 5 minutes; then slide the parchment off the baking sheet onto the rack to cool completely.

5. For the ganache: Place the chopped chocolate in a heat-proof bowl. Heat the heavy cream in a small, heavy-bottomed saucepan just until tiny bubbles begin to form around the edges and you can see steam rising from the pot. Pour the hot cream over the chocolate and gently stir with a heat-proof spatula until the chocolate is completely melted. Stir in the butter until melted and thoroughly mixed in. Let the ganache cool until it is just stiff enough to pipe or spread without dripping. It will continue to harden after you sandwich the cookies, fusing them together.

6. Scoop the ganache into a piping bag fitted with a small (⅜-inch; 5-mm) star tip. Arrange half the cookies upside down on a parchment-lined baking sheet and pipe a small amount of ganache onto them, about ½ teaspoon. Sandwich each cookie with another cookie and let them sit until the ganache has set. Transfer the cookies to an airtight container, where they will keep for up to 2 weeks. The cookies will soften and become slightly fudgy as the days go by (a good thing!).

BACI DI DAMA AL CAFFÈ *(Piedmont)*

Lady's Kisses

Among their many attributes, these dainty sandwich cookies have one of the greatest names in the Italian cookie name hall of fame: Lady's Kisses. Two buttery almond or hazelnut buttons fused together with melted dark chocolate. What could be more romantic or delicious?

There are differing origin stories about Baci di Dama. They are said to have come from the town of Tortona, near the Ligurian foothills, east of Torino. But there are also claims that they were invented in 1852 by a pastry chef in the House of Savoy for King Vittorio Emanuele II, so that he could gift them to a woman he fancied. Some old recipes note that the cookies were originally made with ground almonds and that hazelnuts were substituted when almonds became too expensive. And other recipes claim the opposite.

In any case, they are quintessentially *Piemontesi*, for their use of both chocolate and hazelnuts, two ingredients that are historically important in this region and its elegant capital, Torino. The area's small round hazelnuts are a protected ingredient, prized for their delicate crunch. Torino, meanwhile, has been renowned for centuries for its chocolate confections and its chocolate and coffee culture.

Now I've given these *baci* my own little spin. I opted for hazelnuts over almonds for their robust flavor, and I've spiked my kisses with finely ground espresso as my personal little tribute to the city of Torino. If you would like to stick with tradition, replace the ground coffee with an equal amount of flour.

MAKES 50 COOKIE SANDWICHES

1 rounded cup (140 g) toasted and skinned hazelnuts (see page 26)

½ cup (100 g) granulated sugar

2 teaspoons very finely ground espresso, optional

⅛ teaspoon fine salt

1 cup plus 2 tablespoons (140 g) unbleached all-purpose flour

½ cup (1 stick; 113 g) unsalted butter, at cool room temperature (65° F; 18° C), cut into cubes

2 ounces (57 g) bittersweet (65 to 70%) chocolate, coarsely chopped

1. Line two baking sheets with parchment and set aside.

2. Pour the nuts and sugar into the work bowl of a food processor and process until the nuts are finely ground and the mixture looks like sand. Add the espresso (if using) and salt and pulse to combine. Pulse in the flour until thoroughly combined. Distribute the butter around the work bowl and process until the dough starts to clump together.

3. Turn the dough out onto a clean, very lightly floured work surface and press it into a smooth disk. Pinch off marble-size pieces of dough and roll them into balls. (If you want to be precise, weigh the pieces on a kitchen scale; each little ball should weigh ⅛ ounce (5 g.) Place them on the baking sheets, 1 to 2 inches (2½ to 5 cm) apart. You should be able to fit 50 on each sheet. If not, use a third parchment-lined sheet.

4. Set the baking sheets in the freezer to chill while you preheat the oven to 325° F (165° C). If you can't fit both sheets in the freezer, chill one and then chill the second while the first is in the oven. Chilling is an important step, as it will prevent the cookies from flattening out while they bake. You are aiming for beautifully domed little cookie buttons.

5. Bake the baci, one sheet at a time, in the middle of the oven for 20 minutes, or until they are lightly browned and set. Transfer the baking sheets to wire racks and let the cookies cool completely on the sheets. When they are cool, turn half of them bottom up.

6. Melt the chocolate in a microwave-safe bowl in the microwave or in a small heat-proof bowl or pan set over gently simmering water. Let the melted chocolate cool until thick enough to dollop or pipe onto the cookies (if you try to sandwich the cookies while the chocolate is still too hot, the tops will slide off). To dollop: Using a small coffee or teaspoon, dollop a drop of melted chocolate onto the upturned bottom of a cookie and sandwich it with another cookie. To pipe: Transfer the cooled melted chocolate to a small plastic sandwich bag. Cut a tiny hole in a corner and pipe dollops of chocolate onto the cookie bottoms. Gently place the "kiss" on a parchment-lined baking sheet and allow the chocolate to harden. Once set, transfer the cookies to an airtight container, where they will keep for up to 2 weeks.

BISCOTTI DI SAN PELLEGRINO TERME (Lombardy)

Crescent Moon Cookies from San Pellegrino Terme

One day, while staying in Bergamo, I got in my car and headed to San Pellegrino Terme, a half-hour drive north into the foothills of the Alps. I had got wind of a cookie that originated there, and I wanted to learn more.

I am of course referring to *that* San Pellegrino, the San Pellegrino of green-bottled spring water and *limonata* and other sparkling drinks. Driving into the town is like driving onto a movie set. As I headed up the Via de Medici, the main street, I passed the bottling plant, a vast, partially open steel structure with vaulted roofs and a fleet of red delivery trucks.

Farther along, the tree-lined boulevard was dotted with shops and bars and bakeries and small hotels. To my right, the river Brembo, swollen from recent rain, was churning ferociously, drowning out all other noise. The river cuts right through the center of town, and on the far bank stood a palatial brick and stone belle epoque building, the Grand Hotel, currently closed but on track to be renovated and reopened in the near future.

I admit, I was dazzled by this dreamlike spa town, with its Art Deco flourishes and air of nostalgia, and momentarily forgot about the cookie. But eventually, walking along the boulevard, I found the bakery I was looking for—Pasticceria Bigio, named for Luigi "Bigio" Milesi, the baker who invented the Biscotto di San Pellegrino back in 1934.

The cookie, it turns out, is everything the town is not—no gilt or flourishes—just a plain brown biscuit shaped like a crescent moon. It is described in the bakery's literature as *quotidiano* (plain), but also *ammaliante* (bewitching), and it is. Its rich flavor comes from butter and vanilla and a deep browning in the oven, and it has a super crunchy texture that stands up to a good dunking, whether in cappuccino, milk, or wine. Bigio's granddaughter Roberta Milesi, who now runs the café-bakery with her siblings, told me that her grandfather—who was also a traveling puppeteer—created the cookies to hand out to the families and children who attended his shows. If you stop in at Bigio, you'll see his puppets displayed on the bakery walls.

MAKES ABOUT 42 COOKIES

4 ounces (1 stick; 113 g) unsalted butter, softened to room temperature (65° F to 72° F; 18° C to 22° C)

3/4 cup (150 g) granulated sugar

1/3 cup (80 ml) whole milk

2 large egg yolks

1 teaspoon pure vanilla extract

1 teaspoon honey

2 1/2 cups (300 g) unbleached all-purpose flour

1/2 teaspoon baking soda

1/2 teaspoon ammonium bicarbonate (see page 17)

Continued >>

1. Combine the butter, sugar, and milk in a heavy-bottomed saucepan and heat on low, just until the butter begins to melt and the milk is slightly warm. With a hand mixer or a whisk, break up the softening butter and stir everything together to form a raggedy half-melted mix. Transfer this to the bowl of a stand mixer fitted with the whisk attachment.

2. Add the egg yolks, vanilla extract, and honey, and mix on low speed until the ingredients are combined. Add the flour, baking soda, and ammonium bicarbonate and mix on low until incorporated and a soft, sticky dough forms. Scrape it onto a sheet of reusable wrap or plastic wrap, wrap tightly, and refrigerate overnight.

3. Preheat the oven to 375° F (190° C). Line two rimmed baking sheets with parchment. Remove the dough from the refrigerator and let it rest for about 30 minutes to soften slightly, then knead it gently to soften it further. On a lightly floured surface, roll the dough into a large circle about 1⁄4 inch (6 mm) thick. The traditional way to cut these cookies is with a round cutter, about 2 1⁄2 inches (6 cm) in diameter. After cutting out the first circle, cut a "bite" out of it with the cutter it to remove a portion of the dough so that you are left with a crescent moon shape. Now position the cutter over the dough so that it overlaps a little with the space left by first cookie, to give you a crescent moon shape rather than a full circle. Continue to cut out crescent moons with this overlapping method, arranging the cookies on the baking sheets as you go and spacing them about 1 inch (2 1⁄2 cm) apart. If you have a crescent moon cookie cutter, you can use that. But it's much quicker (and clever) to use the traditional trick. Gather up the scraps and reroll more cookies. You should end up with about 42 total, 20 to 22 per baking sheet.

4. Bake, one sheet at a time, in the middle of the oven, for 15 to 18 minutes, until the cookies are deep golden brown and set. Transfer the baking sheets to wire racks to cool for 10 minutes, then use an angled spatula to transfer the cookies from the baking sheets to the racks to cool completely.

5. Possibly the best feature of Biscotti di San Pellegrino, beyond their satisfying crunch, is how long they last. Stored in an airtight container (I use an aluminum tin) they will maintain that crunch and keep indefinitely–at least 2 months, though I suspect they won't hang around that long.

BRUTTI MA BUONI *(Piedmont, Lombardy, Tuscany and beyond)*

Ugly but Good Cookies

In spite of their name, which translates to "ugly but good," these classic cookies from Piedmont—or Lombardy or Tuscany, depending on whom you believe—are truly lovely and irresistible, with contrasting textures: crispy meringue, crunchy toasted nuts, and a soft center.

The story goes that they were created in 1869 by a pastry chef named Viganotti from Varese, in Lombardy, who had moved west to Borgomanero, in neighboring Piedmont, to open a bakery. One morning the chef "inadvertently" knocked some egg whites into a bowl of sugar, or sugar into a bowl of almonds, or almonds into egg whites. In order not to waste the ingredients, he mixed them and baked them and these cookies were born. Honestly, I've heard so many of these "accidental" creation stories that I believe none of them, but they are kind of endearing. In any case—and this part is true—in 1905, Sig. Viganotti and his cookies were awarded a gold medal at a prestigious international culinary exhibition in Paris.

The traditional technique for making brutti ma buoni is unusual in that after you have whipped up a glossy, billowy meringue and folded in your chopped nuts, you then do something counterintuitive, which is to cook the meringue on the stovetop, turning it into a sort of sticky nougat, before scooping the mixture into little mounds on a baking sheet and baking them. The stovetop step accomplishes two things: it "dries" out the meringue, which gives the cookies a crispier shell and prevents them from turning gummy; and it deepens their color and flavor by lightly caramelizing the sugar in the meringue.

During my research, I found that older recipes tended to include a bit of spice in the batter, while newer ones used only vanilla for flavoring, or, even more minimally, no flavoring at all. I chose to venture toward the medieval with two spiced versions, one flavored with cocoa powder and cinnamon, the other with Pisto Napoletano (page 217) or French *Quatre Épices*, a blend of cloves, ginger, nutmeg, and white pepper.

You can make these cookies with just hazelnuts or almonds, or both, as I do. Just make sure the total weight of the nuts is 7 ounces (200 grams). Also, keep in mind that the amount of time the cookies spend in the oven will determine whether they will be crisp throughout or crispy on the outside with a slightly soft center, which is my preference.

MAKES 12 TO 20, DEPENDING ON SIZE

MERINGUE BATTER

3/4 cup (105 g) blanched and toasted almonds (see page 26), cooled

3/4 cup (100 g) toasted and skinned hazelnuts (see page 26), cooled

About 3 (90 g) large egg whites, at room temperature

1/8 teaspoon cream of tartar

1/8 teaspoon fine salt

1 cup (200 g) granulated sugar

SPICE MIX 1

1/2 teaspoon Pisto Napoletano (page 217); or *Quatre Épices* (see Sources, page 225)

SPICE MIX 2

1 tablespoon unsweetened cocoa powder

1/4 teaspoon ground cinnamon

1/2 teaspoon pure vanilla extract, optional

Continued >>

1. For the meringue batter: Preheat the oven to 300° F (150° C). Line a rimmed baking sheet with parchment. Coarsely chop the toasted, cooled almonds with a sharp chef's knife. Hand-chopping will give you some unevenness in the size of the pieces, but this is a good thing. Chop the hazelnuts in the same way. Scoop the nuts into a bowl and set aside.

2. Pour the egg whites into the clean metal bowl of a stand mixer fitted with a clean whisk attachment. Add the cream of tartar and begin whipping on medium-low speed. When the whites are foamy, add the salt and beat on high until the mixture is creamy white and growing in volume. With the mixer running, gradually add the sugar, a few tablespoons at a time. It's important to add the sugar gradually rather than all at once to prevent the meringue from collapsing.

3. Beat until medium-soft peaks form—the peaks should curl at the top. Sprinkle in the spices (either Spice Mix 1 or Spice Mix 2) and beat a few seconds more to incorporate. The meringue should be glossy; it will look like marshmallow or soft-serve ice cream. Gently fold in the nuts by hand with a silicone spatula.

4. Scoop the meringue into a heavy-bottom stainless-steel (not nonstick) saucepan (1½ to 2 quarts; 1.4 to 2 L). Set the pan over low heat and cook, stirring continuously, for 8 to 10 minutes. You may think to yourself: What am I doing? Why did I make a glorious, glossy meringue only to watch it become a sticky mess? This is exactly what you want. As you cook and stir, the meringue will first loosen, and a film of egg may develop on the bottom of the pan. This is fine. After 5 or 6 minutes, the meringue will begin to stiffen and look slightly "thready" when you stir it—sort of like the threads of marshmallow that form when you make Rice Krispies Treats. Essentially, the mixture is now a soft nougat. Continue to cook until it has turned a couple of shades darker—a sort of pale caffè latte, or soft-serve chocolate if you've added cocoa powder—and has begun to pull away from the bottom and sides of the pan. Remove it from the heat and stir in the vanilla extract (if using).

5. Working quickly, lightly wet a clean surface with cold water and scrape the batter onto it, spreading it out a bit to stop the cooking process. Using a small (1 tablespoon) ice cream scoop or a metal spoon, drop mounds of meringue onto the prepared baking sheet. For jumbo-size cookies, use just under 2 tablespoons. You should end up with 12 to 20 total. For standard-size cookies, I make five rows, four mounds per row. For jumbo cookies, I make four rows of three.

6. Bake for 20 to 25 minutes, checking at the 20-minute mark. For cookies with a slightly soft center, remove from the oven when the outside is crispy and the inside is still slightly jiggly. For cookies that are crispy throughout, bake a few minutes more until they no longer jiggle. Keep in mind that the baking time will also depend on the size of your cookies. They will continue to crisp up as they cool so don't overbake. Once out of the oven, let them cool right on the cookie sheet before gently lifting them off the parchment. Once cool, store the cookies in an airtight container for up to 2 weeks.

CANESTRELLETTI DI TORRIGLIA *(Liguria)*

Flower-Shaped Butter Cookies from Torriglia

Here it is—the cookie that inspired this book and prompted me to follow a path of sweet crumbs from the north of Italy's boot to the south, from east to west, and out to the islands.

At its core, this is a simple butter cookie composed of just four ingredients: butter, sugar, eggs, and flour. The original recipe does not even contain salt, though I add a pinch to round out the flavor. What sets it apart is its texture, which manages to be both dense and airy, crispy, crumbly, delicate, butter-rich, and melt-in-your-mouth tender. From the moment I took my first bite of this flower-shaped cookie from Torriglia, in the hills north of Genoa, I was smitten.

The canestrelletto's origins date to the fifteenth century, but only in the last few decades has it become popular beyond the confines of Torriglia and even Liguria. So popular, in fact, that there are now many recipes floating around on the internet and in baking books. Most of them rely on a variety of tricks to achieve that singular texture and rich flavor, from adding cornstarch or potato starch to substituting hard-boiled egg yolks in place of raw because they have less moisture. Some doughs are enhanced with vanilla or rum or grated lemon zest to improve their flavor. None of these modifications would pass muster with the bakers of Torriglia. Instead, follow these two simple rules: Use high-quality ingredients, and mix them properly, according to the method below. I learned the technique from Maria Paola Rosazza Battore, whose family has been making canestrelletti in their Torriglia shop for more than a century (see Cookie Story, page 52).

The cookie's rise in popularity has spawned many variations, which you will find even in the bakeries of Torriglia—cookies dipped in dark chocolate or white chocolate, with chocolate chips in the dough, or with chestnut flour or whole wheat flour mixed in. Sure, they're all good. But the OG remains my favorite.

MAKES 24 CANESTRELLETTI

3 large eggs

½ cup (100 g) granulated sugar

8 ounces (2 sticks; 227 g) unsalted butter, cut into ½-inch (12 mm) cubes, at cool room temperature (65° F; 18° C)

2½ cups (300 g) pastry flour, plus more for the work surface

¼ teaspoon fine salt (optional)

1. Separate the eggs and return the whites to the refrigerator. You will need them when you bake the cookies. Place the egg yolks and the sugar in the bowl of a stand mixer fitted with the whisk attachment. Beat, first on medium-low, then on high, for 4 to 5 minutes, until the mixture is very pale and fluffy. Drop in cubes of butter, two at a time, beating to incorporate them well before adding more. This will take several minutes, but don't rush the process, or the mixture won't whip properly. You are aiming for the texture of a soft, emulsified buttercream.

2. When all the butter has been incorporated, switch to the paddle attachment. Add the flour and salt all at once and mix on low speed to incorporate without kicking up any flour. Once the flour is mixed in, beat on medium high for 10 to 20 seconds to make sure everything is thoroughly combined. Scrape the dough onto a sheet of reusable wrap or plastic wrap, wrap tightly, and refrigerate overnight.

3. Remove the dough and the egg whites from the refrigerator and let them sit at room temperature for about 30 minutes to warm up slightly. Preheat the oven to 325° F (165° C). Line two rimmed baking sheets with parchment.

4. Lightly flour a clean work surface and lay the dough on it. Lightly flour the top of the dough and your rolling pin. Roll the dough out to a thickness of ⅜-inch (5-mm), in other words, just under ½ inch (12 mm). Use a 2½ inch (6 cm) six-petal flower cookie cutter with a hole in the center to stamp out canestrelletti. If you don't have a cookie cutter with a hole in the center, use a solid one and then use a zucchini corer or even the wide end of a stainless-steel piping tip to cut out the hole. Place the cookies on the

prepared baking sheets, leaving about 1 inch (2½ cm) between them. You should be able to fit 12 per sheet. Gather up the scraps and the punched-out centers and roll out more cookies, for a total of about 24.

5. Lightly beat the egg whites and brush the tops of the cookies. Bake the canestrelletti, one sheet at a time, in the middle of the oven, for 25 to 30 minutes, until they are set and golden, but not too brown. Transfer the baking sheets to wire racks to cool for 20 minutes, then transfer the cookies to the racks to cool completely. Serve them as is or with a dusting of confectioners' sugar. Store canestrelletti in an airtight container for up to 2 weeks.

COOKIE STORY

HOW A BUTTER COOKIE REVIVED A LIGURIAN TOWN

Maria Paola Rosazza Battore spends her days immersed in butter and sugar. To a cookie lover like me, this sounds like a dream, but—of course—it is hard work. She wakes before dawn, and by 6 a.m. when I meet her at her bakery one chilly day in late September, she has already stamped out hundreds of flower-shaped cookies and arranged them on large baking sheets. She brushes their surfaces with egg white, the last step before they go into the oven.

"We make them the way we have always made them, with eggs, butter, sugar, and flour. That's all," she says. In spite of the early hour, her tight, silver-gold curls are tidy and her eyes are bright behind her red-framed glasses.

I came to visit Paola, as she is known, in Torriglia, a small town tucked amid the chestnut and beech forests of the Val Trebbia, north of Genoa. This pretty Ligurian locale not far from the Piedmont border has long been a summer vacation spot for Genoese looking to escape the heat of the city. These days, it is also known for its rich butter cookies, called canestrelletti, which are produced by seven bakeries, including Paola's. That's a lot of bakeries for a town of 2,000 souls, whose main street extends for about a kilometer before it disappears into the green hills of the Antola Park natural preserve. But it works and this is by design.

Like so many Italian hill and mountain towns, Torriglia saw its population dwindle during the second half of the twentieth century, as residents left for Genoa and parts beyond in search of work. Among the hardest-hit businesses were the small bakeries and bread shops that had fed residents for generations but, at the turn of the twenty-first century, were in danger of falling into irrelevance.

"These shops had their legs cut from beneath them," Mario Casale, a former vice mayor, told me when I visited Torriglia for the first time seven years ago. In 1997, he and a handful of business leaders and bakers formed the Canestrelletto di Torriglia Cultural Association, with a mission to revive the flagging local economy by attracting visitors and, hopefully, new business to Torriglia's bakeries. They researched the history of the canestrelletto, tracing it back to the fifteenth century. The cookie's distinctive six-petal shape was found to be even older, turning up on thirteenth-century coins from the Republic of Genoa as a symbol of abundance. The origin of the canestrelletto's name remains something of a mystery (it translates to "little basket") but the association speculates that it could refer to a basket in which freshly baked cookies were set to cool.

The association devised a strict set of criteria for the canestrelletto: the cookie must contain only flour, butter, sugar, eggs. Flavoring such as lemon or rum was allowed, but no added leavening, such as baking powder, could be used to achieve its signature delicate, crumbly texture. They created an official logo for participating bakeries to use on their packaging to differentiate their product from impostor cookies. And they started an annual festival, held in early June, in which bakers set up stalls along Torriglia's streets and offer free samples of canestrelletti, accompanied by glasses of white wine.

The cookie is pretty, if plain-looking. But its looks belie its incomparable texture and flavor. Biting into it is, as Mario Casale described it, a revelatory experience. "As it begins to crumble and melt in your mouth you feel the softness of the flour, the rough consistency of the sugar, the silkiness of the egg, the way the ingredients work together in harmony." In recent years, piggybacking on the cookie's growing popularity, Torriglia's bakers have come up with variations, such as canestrelletti dipped in chocolate or made with chocolate chips, and canestrelletti made with whole wheat or chestnut flour.

The bakery in Paola's family is among the oldest in town, opened by her great-grandfather in 1898. The shop is actually an alimentari, a small grocery and sundries shop that sells fresh produce, olive oil, canned and bottled foods, and the cookies and other baked goods she makes in the small, professionally outfitted kitchen across the street.

Before 7:30 a.m., the cookies baked and cooling, Paola walks over to the shop to help her eighty-seven-year-old mother, Novella, open the alimentari. Later, she'll return to the bakery and prepare another large batch of dough, which will rest in the refrigerator until the morning. Then, she will feed cold chunks of it through a laminator to create large, thick sheets, from which she will stamp out hundreds more fresh cookies. Who eats all these cookies that she and Torriglia's other bakers produce? Thanks, in large part, to the consortium's PR campaign, canestrelletti are now popular throughout the region. The booming tourism scene in the city of Genoa has further fueled demand. Once or twice a week, Paola's husband, Graziano, leaves the house even before Paola awakens and drives to Genoa, to distribute orders of canestrelletti to coffee bars, alimentari, focaccia shops, and other retailers.

"In the end, yes, we are talking about a simple butter cookie," Paola tells me. "But for us, it's more. If we had just the store, it wouldn't be enough. So, for us, the canestrelletto is more than a cookie."

CAPORALI | SAVOIARDI LIGURI *(Liguria)*

Fat Ladyfingers from Liguria

I have not been kind to ladyfingers. In the past, I have maligned them as "weightless batons of dried sponge cake that hold little flavor and even less appeal."

I've changed my mind. After all, a cookie that has lasted for more than 700 years must be doing something right. There are various accounts (of course!) of the history of savoiardi, but most seem to agree that the cookie was created in the mid-fourteenth century by a chef in the House of Savoy for a banquet in honor of French royalty. The biscuit's popularity was immediate and lasting. In Italy, you can find savoiardi and numerous regional variations at most bakeries and supermarkets.

In Liguria, they are known as *caporali*, corporals. I first had these at an inn in Torriglia, where the proprietor set them out on the breakfast table in a large glass jar. They immediately caught my attention—they are about twice the width of a standard ladyfinger, and, when I lifted one out of the jar, I found it was as soft as an angel's pillow, the perfect morning treat to dip into my cappuccino.

When I baked my first batch it was revelatory, as baking often can be. By going through the process—beating egg yolks at length to create volume, whipping the whites to stiff, but still creamy, peaks, adding just enough vanilla and lemon zest to achieve that unmistakable flavor, folding everything together ever so gently and then piping out the airy oblong "fingers" onto a baking sheet—I finally and truly came to understand and appreciate the cookie's qualities: its delicate structure and gentle perfume, its impossible lightness, the way it holds air.

MAKES 20 COOKIES

6 large eggs, separated and at room temperature

Zest of 1 lemon, plus 1 teaspoon freshly squeezed juice

¼ teaspoon fine salt

1 cup (200 g) superfine sugar, divided

½ teaspoon pure vanilla extract

1½ cups (180 g) unbleached cake flour

Confectioners' sugar, for dusting

1. Preheat the oven to 325° F (165° C). Line two rimmed baking sheets with parchment.

2. Place the egg whites in the bowl of a stand mixer fitted with the whisk attachment. Mix briefly on medium until foamy, then add the lemon juice and beat until white and frothy. Increase the speed to high, and with the mixer running, beat in the salt. Slowly beat in ½ cup (100 g) of the superfine sugar, 1 to 2 tablespoons at a time, waiting a few seconds after each addition before adding more. Continue to beat until you have added the full ½ cup (100 g) of sugar and the meringue is dense and glossy and holds upright peaks. Take care not to overbeat, or the meringue will become dry and grainy.

3. In a separate large bowl, combine the yolks and the remaining ½ cup (100 g) superfine sugar, the vanilla, and the lemon zest. Beat on high with a hand mixer, or transfer the mixture to the bowl of a stand mixer fitted with the whisk attachment and beat, for several minutes, until the mixture has tripled in volume and is fluffy and pale.

4. Using a sturdy, flexible spatula, gently fold a third of the meringue into the yolk mixture. Sift the flour over this mixture and fold gently until fully incorporated. Carefully fold in the rest of the meringue until fully incorporated.

5. Scoop the batter into a piping bag fitted with a ½ inch (1 cm) plain tip. Position a parchment-lined baking sheet horizontally and pipe two rows of batons, each about 2 inches (5 cm) wide and 4 inches (10 cm) long. You should be able to fit 4 to 5 batons per row. Pipe the remaining batter onto the second sheet in the same way, for a total of 20 batons. If you have leftover batter, pipe it onto a third parchment-lined sheet, or wait until you have baked the first batch and reuse the baking sheet, with a fresh sheet of parchment.

6. Sprinkle a light coating of confectioners' sugar over the caporali and bake, one sheet at a time, for 10 to 15 minutes, until they are set and are the palest gold in color.

Transfer the baking sheets onto wire racks and let the caporali cool completely. Once cooled, gently lift them off the parchment and transfer them to an airtight container, where they will keep for up to 2 weeks. To serve, shower the caporali with a fresh coating of confectioners' sugar.

BAKER'S NOTE: *To make classic savoiardi, pipe fingers that are about 1 inch (2½ cm) wide, or half the width of the caporali. Bake as directed, but check after 10 minutes, as they will be done sooner than their fatter siblings.*

CAVIADINI *(Lombardy)*

Rhombus Butter Cookies

Northwest of Bergamo and east of Lake Como lies the Valsassina, a lush valley in the Alps of Lombardy. The area offers hiking and biking trails and breathtaking views of snowcapped mountains. The valley is sprinkled with cheese dairies and rustic alpine *trattorie*. These rhomboid or diamond-shaped butter cookies are typical of this area. A sprinkling of pearl sugar gives them a pretty finish. Their flavor is pure and sweet, their texture light and crisp in spite of their richness. Use the best butter your budget allows to do these cookies justice.

MAKES ABOUT 32 COOKIES

4 ounces (1 stick; 113 g) unsalted butter, at cool room temperature, cut into ½-inch (1-cm) cubes

½ cup (100 g) granulated sugar

1 large egg, at room temperature

1 teaspoon pure vanilla extract

2 cups (240 g) pastry flour

¼ teaspoon fine salt

1 teaspoon baking powder

3 tablespoons milk

Pearl sugar, for decorating

1. Place the butter and sugar in the bowl of a stand mixer fitted with the paddle attachment. Beat briefly on low to break up the cubes of butter. Increase the speed to high and beat until the butter and sugar are well combined and fluffy. Add the egg and vanilla to the bowl and beat on high until thoroughly incorporated. Pour in the flour, salt, and baking powder, and mix on low just until the dry ingredients are worked in.

2. Scrape the soft dough onto a sheet of reusable wrap or plastic wrap, cover tightly, and refrigerate for at least 2 hours—overnight is best.

3. Remove the dough from the refrigerator and let it soften slightly—about 30 minutes. Preheat the oven to 350° F (180° C). Line three rimmed baking sheets with parchment. (If you don't have three, use two. You can reuse one after baking the first batch of cookies.)

4. Lightly flour a clean work surface and a rolling pin and roll the dough out into a large circle or rectangle about ¼ inch (6 mm) thick. Use a 2 x 3-inch (5 x 8-cm) fluted rectangular or diamond-shaped cookie cutter to cut out as many caviadini as possible. Gather up the scraps of the dough, reroll once more, and cut out more cookies. You should end up with about 32, depending on the size of your cutter. If you don't have a fluted cutter, you can use a fluted pastry wheel to cut out 2 x 3-inch (5 x 8-cm) diamonds or rhombuses. Transfer the cookies to the prepared baking sheets.

5. With a fluted pastry wheel, make a vertical 1-inch (2½-cm) cut in the center of the cookies. Gently pull the cookies apart slightly to widen the gap in the center just a bit. Brush the surface of each cookie with a little milk and sprinkle lightly with pearl sugar. Bake, one sheet at a time, for 10 to 12 minutes, until set and lightly browned. Let the caviadini cool for 5 minutes on the baking sheets, then transfer them to a wire rack to cool completely. Once cooled, the caviadini will keep in an airtight container for about 2 weeks.

BUSSOLAI | BURANELLI *(Veneta)*

Venetian Butter S- or Ring-Shaped Cookies

Burano, an island in Venice's lagoon, is known for the brightly colored houses that line its canal and for the intricate lacework that has been produced there since the 1500s. For centuries, the island has also produced these ring- or S-shaped butter cookies. Before home ovens were commonplace, Burano's women would make and shape the dough at home, then bring trays of unbaked cookies to be baked at one of a handful of *forni* (bread bakeries) in town.

Bussolai, also known as Buranelli, were originally mariner cookies; Burano's wives would bake large batches with which to send their fishermen husbands off to sea. Over time, they morphed into an Easter cookie, and now they've become so popular that bakeries offer them all year long. Bussolai are easy to make at home; they are a good morning cookie to dunk into coffee or hot chocolate, and are just as good enjoyed on their own or in the evening with a glass of sweet wine.

While it's not traditional, I like to decorate bussolai by dipping the ends in melted bittersweet chocolate (see Baker's Note). It pairs really well with the cookie's buttery, orange-scented flavor.

MAKES 18 COOKIES

4 ounces (1 stick; 113 g) unsalted butter, cut into ½-inch (¾-cm) cubes, at cool room temperature

⅔ cup (130 g) granulated sugar

3 large egg yolks

1 teaspoon pure vanilla extract

Finely grated zest of 1 lemon

Finely grated zest of ½ orange

¼ teaspoon fine salt

2 cups (240 g) unbleached all-purpose flour

1. Place the butter and sugar in the bowl of a stand mixer fitted with the paddle attachment. Mix on low to break up the butter, then beat until the mixture is light and fluffy, 3 to 4 minutes. Drop in the egg yolks, one at a time, beating well after each addition. Beat in the vanilla, lemon and orange zests, and salt. Add the flour to the bowl and mix on low just until incorporated. Pat the dough into a disk, wrap it in reusable wrap or plastic wrap, and refrigerate until thoroughly chilled, at least 2 hours and up to overnight.

2. Preheat the oven to 350° F (180° C). Line a rimmed baking sheet with parchment. Divide the dough into 18 equal pieces—they should weigh about 1 ounce (30 g) each. Roll each piece into a rope about 5 inches (13 cm) in length and as thick as a pinkie finger. Form the rope into a ring or an S—your choice; I usually do half and half.

3. Bake the cookies in the middle of the oven for 15 to 17 minutes, until they are lightly golden and set. Transfer the baking sheet to a wire rack to cool for 20 minutes; then use an angled spatula to transfer the cookies from the baking sheet to the rack to cool completely. Store the cookies in an airtight container for up to 2 weeks.

BAKER'S NOTE: *To decorate the cookies with melted chocolate, wait until they are completely cool. Then follow the instructions for melting and tempering chocolate on page 27. You'll need about 4 ounces (113 g) for this recipe. Once the chocolate is melted, dip each end of the S-shaped cookies, and about ⅓ of each ring cookie, into the chocolate. Transfer the dipped cookies to a parchment-lined baking sheet and let the chocolate set completely before serving. Dipped cookies will last about 1 week stored in an airtight container.*

CHIFFERI ALLA NOCCIOLA *(general)*

Hazelnut Crescents

This is the cookie that made me fall in love with Italian cookies when I was a child. My mother made them every Christmas when I was growing up, along with her Calcionelli (page 148). But these were my absolute favorite, butter-rich and redolent with the toasty perfume of hazelnuts. Dipped in powdered sugar while still warm, the delicate cookies crumbled, then melted in my mouth when I took a bite. There was nothing better.

Except . . . they weren't actually Italian. The recipe had been given to my mom by a German neighbor, and the original cookies contained ground walnuts. My mother adapted them to her own preferences, substituting hazelnuts for the walnuts. While they may not be strictly Italian, to me they have all the characteristics of a great northern Italian cookie—crescent-shaped, sumptuously buttery, and toasty with ground nuts. She started with whole raw hazelnuts in the shell, and it was my sister's and my job to crack them open, a mildly tedious task that we did at the kitchen table and complained about more than we actually minded. Afterward, Mom toasted the nuts in the oven, then rolled them vigorously in kitchen towels to remove their papery brown skins (see page 26).

Now, when I make these crescents, I splurge and use hazelnuts from Piedmont (page 22), which I buy online through Gustiamo, a New York–based purveyor of Italian foods (see Sources, page 225). The nuts have a light, crispy texture and they taste earthy and buttery and sweet, with just a hint of bitterness. And they come vacuum sealed, already toasted and skinned. There's really no excuse not to make these.

MAKES ABOUT 4 DOZEN COOKIES

1 rounded cup (140 g) toasted and skinned hazelnuts (see page 26)

½ cup (100 g) granulated sugar

¼ teaspoon fine salt

8 ounces (2 sticks/227 g) unsalted butter, cut into pieces and slightly softened

2 cups (240 g) unbleached all-purpose flour

1 cup (120 g) confectioners' sugar, for coating

1. Pour the hazelnuts and granulated sugar in the work bowl of a food processor and pulse until the nuts are coarsely ground. Add the salt and process until the nuts are very finely ground but not pasty.

2. Scatter the butter around the bowl and pulse until well incorporated and the mixture is nearly smooth. Sprinkle in the flour and pulse just until incorporated. The dough will be soft. Scrape it onto a piece of reusable wrap or plastic wrap, form it into a disk, wrap, and refrigerate until well chilled, at least 2 hours and up to overnight.

3. Preheat the oven to 325° F (165° C). Line two rimmed baking sheets with parchment. Sift the confectioners' sugar into a bowl and set aside.

4. Divide the dough into quarters. Divide each quarter into 12 equal pieces. Roll each piece into a ball and then roll each ball between your palms to make a cylinder with tapered ends, about 3 inches (8 cm) long. Bend the cylinders to form crescents and place them, 1 inch (2½ cm) apart, on the parchment-lined baking sheets.

5. Bake the crescents, one sheet at a time, in the middle of the oven for 15 to 20 minutes, until set and just beginning to brown around the edges. Transfer the baking sheets to wire racks and let the cookies cool for 5 to 10 minutes. With an offset metal spatula, lift a cookie and gently dip it in the bowl of powdered sugar, taking care to coat it on all sides. Dip all the cookies while they are still warm and place them on the wire racks to cool completely. Store the chifferi in an airtight container in layers between sheets of waxed paper for up to 2 weeks.

FAVETTE TRIESTINE *(Friuli-Venezia Giulia)*

Little Fava Beans from Trieste

More confection than cookie, these diminutive tricolor sweets are a specialty of Trieste, in northeastern Italy. Made with an almond flour base, the dough is divided into three pieces and each portion given a separate color and flavor: white (rum), pink (Alchermes liqueur), and brown (cocoa powder).

Why are they named fava beans? For one thing, their shape is vaguely reminiscent of the legume. But it's also about lore. This is but one of many versions of *fave dei morti* or "beans of the dead" that you'll find throughout Italy, especially in fall. At one time, fava beans were thought to be a way to communicate with the dead because the plant's long roots extended deep into the earth. Today, bean-shaped cookies are an important part of All Souls' Day (November 2) celebrations commemorating the departed.

The colors of the favette Triestine aren't just for decoration but rather symbolic: white is said to symbolize birth, pink represents life, and brown death. Alchermes (page 18), the red-hued liqueur that gives the pink beans their color, is not easily found outside of Italy. You can substitute a few drops of red food coloring and a splash of almond extract or rum.

MAKES ABOUT 60 COOKIES

2½ cups (250 g) superfine blanched almond flour (see page 21)

¾ cup (90 g) unbleached all-purpose flour

1 cup (200 g) granulated sugar

¼ teaspoon fine salt

2 tablespoons white rum, divided

1½ teaspoons pure vanilla extract, divided

3 large (90 g) egg whites, lightly beaten to a froth, at room temperature

¼ teaspoon pure almond extract

2 teaspoons Alchermes (see page 18), optional

A few drops of red food coloring

2 teaspoons unsweetened cocoa powder

1. In a large bowl, whisk together the almond flour, all-purpose flour, sugar, and salt. Sprinkle in 1 tablespoon rum, 1 teaspoon vanilla extract, and enough egg whites to bring together a dense, cohesive dough.

2. Divide the dough evenly into three portions; for accuracy, weigh the whole piece, then divide it and weigh each portion. Place each portion in a separate bowl. To the first, add the almond extract, working it in with a sturdy spatula or your hands. To the second portion, add the Alchermes or 1 tablespoon of rum and 1 to 3 drops of red food coloring. Gently knead the piece of dough until the color is a uniform pink. Add the 2 teaspoons cocoa powder and ½ teaspoon vanilla extract to the third piece, working the ingredients in as you did for the other two pieces.

3. Preheat the oven to 325° F (165° C). Line two rimmed baking sheets with parchment. Pinch off small pieces of the dough—about the size of a hazelnut in the shell—and roll them into ovals. Set them on the baking sheets, about 30 per sheet. Bake, one sheet at a time, in the middle of the oven, for about 15 minutes, until they have puffed up slightly and are just set. Pinch one gently; it should give slightly under the pressure of your fingers. Let the favette cool completely on the baking sheets before serving. Store them in an airtight container, where they will keep for up to 2 weeks.

FROLLINI AL BURRO *(Piedmont and elsewhere)*

Piped Butter Cookies

These are the cookies you see not only in pasticcerie throughout Italy, but also in just about every Italian American bakery. You know the ones: pretty little piped cookies in various shapes—wreaths, stars, S's, ridged batons—dipped in chocolate and festooned with sprinkles, or topped with a candied cherry.

In Italy, these cookies are known as *biscotti di frolla montata*, because they are made with an extra buttery variation of classic Pasta Frolla (page 206) that is whipped to lightness in the mixer before being piped onto baking sheets.

Although you can find *frolla montata* cookies in pretty much every region of Italy, I have placed this recipe in the north, where butter is the baking fat of choice, and where the influence of Viennese baking traditions is still evident.

MAKES ABOUT 36 COOKIES, DEPENDING ON SIZE AND SHAPE

8 ounces (2 sticks / 227 g) unsalted butter, cut into ½-inch (1-cm) cubes, at cool room temperature

1¼ cups (150 g) confectioners' sugar

1 large egg plus 2 yolks

1 teaspoon pure vanilla extract

¼ teaspoon pure almond extract

2 cups (240 g) unbleached all-purpose flour, plus more as needed

⅓ cup (40 g) pastry flour

½ teaspoon fine salt

TO DECORATE

Glacé cherries, optional

6 ounces (170 g) melted bittersweet or semisweet chocolate (see page 27)

Rainbow sprinkles

1. Place the butter and sugar in the bowl of a stand mixer fitted with the whisk attachment. Beat on high speed until the mixture is thoroughly combined, light, and fluffy, 3 to 4 minutes. Use a spatula to scrape down the bowl as you go.

2. Beat in the egg and yolks, vanilla, and almond extract on low speed, then increase the speed to high to fully incorporate the ingredients.

3. In a bowl, sift together the all-purpose flour and pastry flour. Sprinkle these into the mixing bowl, along with the salt. Switch to the paddle attachment and mix in the flours on low to medium-low just until incorporated.

4. Line two to three rimmed baking sheets with parchment. Scoop the doughs into sturdy reusable piping bags fitted with ½-inch (12-mm) star nozzles. Pipe the shapes of your choice–stars, S's, horseshoes, batons, wreaths–onto the baking sheets, leaving 1½ to 2 inches (4 to 5 cm) between them. If you're decorating stars or wreaths with glacé cherries, press a half or whole cherry into the center. Place the baking sheets in the refrigerator for 30 to 60 minutes or in the freezer for 15 to 20 minutes.

5. Preheat the oven to 350° F (180° C). Bake the cookies, one sheet at a time, in the middle of the oven for about 15 minutes (begin checking after 10 minutes), until they are set and lightly browned, with golden edges. Set the baking sheets on wire racks and let the cookies cool completely.

6. To decorate: Dip the ends of the cookies in melted chocolate, letting the excess drip off. Set the cookies on parchment-lined baking sheets and decorate with rainbow sprinkles. Let the chocolate set completely set before serving. Store the cookies in an airtight container for up to 1 week.

BAKER'S NOTE: *For chocolate frollini, add cocoa powder to some of the dough: Transfer one-half of the dough to a separate bowl and stir in 3 tablespoons cocoa powder with a spatula until thoroughly mixed in. Scoop the dough into a sturdy reusable piping bag fitted with a ½-inch (12-mm) star tip and proceed with the recipe. For bicolor cookies, pipe a half circle with basic dough and the other half with chocolate dough to create a bicolor wreath.*

IMPERIALINE DI OMEGNA *(Piedmont)*

Little Imperial Cookies from Omegna

The first time my daughter tasted one of these dainty sandwich cookies, she likened it to Pepperidge Farm's perennially popular Milano cookies. And she's exactly right. Two crisp-tender wafer-like cookies are fused together by a dark chocolate center. In this version, the bite-size cookie sandwiches are round rather than oblong. Plus, there is almond flour in the cookie dough, which gives it extra flavor and tenderness, and a ganache filling of chocolate and finely chopped hazelnuts, which adds a touch of luxury.

Imperialine are said to date to 1937 and originated in Omegna, in northern Piedmont. The town is perched on the north shore of Lago di Orta, the smallest of the lakes that comprise northern Italy's Lake District. It may be less famous than Bellagio and Como but no less *mozzafiato*—Italian for "breathtaking." Bisected by the Nigoglia Canal that runs through its center, Omegna is surrounded by lush green mountain forests, giving it a fairy-tale quality.

Not surprisingly, there are numerous variations of this cookie and they go by several names, *reginette di Omegna* and *damiani* being two of them. Some versions contain ground hazelnuts in the dough rather than the filling, and some versions are sandwiched only with melted chocolate rather than ganache. No matter what they are called, you will find these cookies in every pasticceria in town. In fact, if you visit and take a stroll through the historic center, it's a good bet you will be accompanied by the perfume of chocolate and butter. Those same sweet aromas will perfume your kitchen if you make your own.

MAKES ABOUT 25 COOKIE SANDWICHES

COOKIES

- 4 ounces (1 stick; 113 g) unsalted butter, at cool room temperature (65° F; 18° C)
- 1/2 cup (100 g) sugar
- 1 teaspoon pure vanilla extract
- 2 large (60 g) egg whites, at room temperature
- 3/4 cup (75 g) superfine blanched almond flour (see page 21)
- 3/4 cup (90 g) unbleached all-purpose flour
- 1/4 teaspoon fine salt

GANACHE

- 4 ounces (113 g) bittersweet or semisweet chocolate, finely chopped
- 1/2 cup (125 ml) heavy cream
- 1/4 cup (35 g) finely chopped toasted and skinned hazelnuts (see page 26)

Continued >>

1. Preheat the oven to 375° F (190° C). Line two rimmed baking sheets with parchment.

2. For the cookies: Place the butter, sugar, and vanilla in the bowl of a stand mixer fitted with the whisk attachment and beat briefly on medium to combine, then on high until the mixture is light and fluffy, 3 to 4 minutes.

3. With the mixer on high speed, dribble in the egg whites in three additions, beating well after each addition. The mixture might separate but keep beating and it will come together again. Ultimately, it should be pale in color and light and fluffy in texture.

4. In a separate bowl, sift together the almond flour, all-purpose flour, and salt. Scatter this over the butter mixture and beat on low to medium-low just until combined. Spoon the batter into a piping bag fitted with a plain ½-inch (12-mm) tip. Pipe circles about 1½ inches (4 cm) in diameter onto the baking sheets, 18 to 20 per sheet.

5. Bake the cookies, one sheet at a time, in the middle of the oven for 10 to 12 minutes, or until they are browned around the edges and pale gold and set in the center. Set the baking sheets on wire racks to cool completely.

6. For the ganache: Place the chopped chocolate in a heat-proof bowl. Pour the cream into a small saucepan and heat on medium until it is nearly boiling—there will be small bubbles around the edge of the pan and steam rising up. Pour the hot cream over the chocolate. Let it sit briefly, then stir until the chocolate is completely melted. Stir in the finely chopped hazelnuts. Let the ganache cool to a spreadable consistency.

7. Spread a little ganache onto the bottom (flat) sides of half the cookies. You can transfer the ganache to a piping bag with a small star tip and pipe on the filling, if you prefer. Sandwich the bottoms with the remaining cookies, pressing lightly to secure the sandwiches. Store the imperialine in an airtight container for up to 1 week.

LINGUE DI GATTO *(Piedmont)*

Cat's Tongues

It's likely that these delicate, wafer-like cookies made their way to Italy from France, where they are known as *langues de chat*. You'll find them in bakeries throughout Europe. In Italy, they are not exclusive to the North, but they are most prevalent in Piedmont. The batter is easily mixed, by hand or with a mixer. But they can be a little fussy to pipe, as the loose batter tends to spread. Pipe slowly and deliberately and keep them on the small side; they will expand as they bake.

Serve these elegant cookies with afternoon coffee or tea, or as a light dessert. You can also dip the ends in melted chocolate to give them an elegant finish.

MAKES 40 TO 48 COOKIES

3½ ounces (7 tablespoons; 100 g) unsalted butter, at cool room temperature

1 cup (120 g) confectioners' sugar

3 large (90 g) egg whites

½ teaspoon pure vanilla extract

Pinch of fine salt

¾ cup (100 g) plus 1 tablespoon unbleached all-purpose flour

1. Preheat the oven to 350° F (180° C). Line two rimmed baking sheets with parchment.

2. Place the butter and confectioners' sugar in the bowl of a stand mixer fitted with the paddle attachment. Mix on medium-low until the sugar is completely blended with the butter. Beat in the egg whites, a little at a time, taking care to incorporate them fully. Add the vanilla and salt and mix briefly to combine. Sprinkle the flour over the batter and beat until it is fully incorporated.

3. Scoop the batter into a piping bag fitted with a ¼-inch (6-mm) plain tip. Pipe 3-inch- (8-cm-) long fingers about ¾ inch (2 cm) wide onto the baking sheets, about 12 per sheet, leaving 2 inches of space between them. Bake the cookies in batches, one sheet at a time, in the middle of the oven for about 10 minutes, until they are nicely browned around the edges and pale gold in the center. Transfer the baking sheets to wire racks to cool for 10 minutes, then lift them off with an angled spatula and set them on the racks to cool completely. Store the cookies in an airtight container for up to 1 week.

BAKER'S NOTE: *To make curved cookies, shape them as soon as they come out of the oven, while still warm and pliable. Use an angled spatula to remove the cookies one at a time, and carefully drape them over a cylinder-shaped object, like a rolling pin or a bottle. Let the cookies cool to set the shape.*

KRUMIRI *(Piedmont)*

Crunchy Butter Cookies from Casale Monferrato

When I visited the town of Casale Monferrato, on the banks of the Po River, every pasticceria and coffee bar was selling the town's most famous product: buttery Krumiri cookies, known for their toasty brown color, ridged exterior, and crescent shape. I bypassed them and went straight to the source: Krumiri Rossi, the bakery where the cookies were invented in the late 1800s by owner Domenico Rossi. The official story is that Rossi created the cookies on the fly one evening for friends who had stopped by his café. Their shape was either an homage to—or spoof of—the exceedingly bushy mustaches of Umberto I, king of a newly unified Italy. The cookies, dense and crumbly in texture and tasting of fresh butter, sugar, and vanilla, were immediately popular and won multiple accolades in the succeeding decades.

Krumiri Rossi is a small operation in the heart of Casale Monferrato's historic center. Proprietor Anna Portinaro, whose grandparents bought the bakery in 1953, showed me the three small rooms at the back of the shop that comprise the kitchen: a mixing room, where dough is made; the oven room, where the cookies are baked; and a packaging room, where they are packed by hand into the shop's signature red rectangular tins. With great pride, Signora Portinaro told me that while the cookie dough is extruded into logs by machine, each one is bent by hand into a crescent by one of the small staff of the bakers. She believes that this human touch is why Krumiri Rossi's cookies are still so prized.

This version veers slightly from traditional krumiri in that I use a piping bag and star tip to pipe the cookies. And I put a little cornmeal in my dough to give it that bit of roughness characteristic of Rossi's extruded krumiri.

MAKES 30 COOKIES

5 ounces (11 tablespoons; 150 g) unsalted butter, cut into ½-inch (1-cm) cubes, at cool room temperature (65° F; 18° C)

½ cup (100 g) sugar

2 large egg yolks

1 teaspoon pure vanilla extract

¼ teaspoon fine salt

1 cup (120 g) unbleached all-purpose flour

¾ cup (113 g) fine cornmeal

1. Place the butter and sugar in the bowl of a stand mixer fitted with the paddle attachment. Beat on medium, then high, until the mixture is fluffy, about 3 minutes. Add the yolks, one at a time, beating well after each addition. Beat in the vanilla and salt.

2. Sift together the flour and cornmeal and pour this into the mixing bowl. Mix on low just until the flours are incorporated. Cover and let the dough rest for 30 to 60 minutes.

3. Preheat the oven to 375° F (190° C). Line two rimmed baking sheets with parchment. Scoop the dough into a sturdy, reusable piping bag fitted with a wide (½ inch; 1 cm) French star tip and pipe 15 (3 inch; 8 cm) logs onto each sheet. With your fingers, slightly bend each log into a "mustache." Place the baking sheets in the refrigerator to chill for 30 minutes. If you can't fit both sheets in the refrigerator, chill one, then chill the other while the first is baking.

4. Bake the krumiri, one sheet at a time, in the middle of the oven for 12 to 15 minutes, until they are set and golden-brown. Transfer the baking sheet to a wire rack to cool for 10 minutes; then use an angled spatula to transfer the cookies from the baking sheet to the rack to cool completely. Store them in a tightly covered container for up to 2 weeks.

NOCCIOLINI DI CHIVASSO *(Piedmont)*

Hazelnut Buttons from Chivasso

If there were a contest for cutest cookie, surely these tiny buttons would win. A sort of variation of crunchy amaretti, *nocciolini* resemble the star ingredient—hazelnuts—both for their warm color and diminutive size.

Nocciolini were invented in Chivasso, a small city northeast of Torino, in 1810 by a baker named Giovanni Podio. They were originally called *Noasèt*, or "Noisettes," a nod to the close connection between Piedmontese and French culinary and pastry traditions stretching back to the seventeenth and eighteenth centuries. The name was changed to "nocciolini" during Mussolini's fascist reign, when non-Italian words were officially struck from the vocabulary.

I stopped in at Caffè Pasticceria Bonfante, one of the primary producers of *nocciolini di Chivasso*, to see how the cookies are made. It's a simple process, one that ultimately comes down to the human touch. The batter is mixed, then fed through a machine that quickly extrudes row upon row of tiny circles onto parchment-lined trays. After they come out of the oven, a baker examines each tray and picks off any that are not perfectly round. The nocciolini are then packaged into the bakery's signature pink and blue cellophane bags.

While I enjoy it, I realize that piping out dozens upon dozens of hazelnut-size buttons might not be everyone's idea of fun in the kitchen. I've given instructions and yields for both the traditional tiny version and for larger, amaretti-size nocciolini. Either way, these are well worth making, both for their satisfying crunch and for the buttery, sweet taste of hazelnuts. Serve a plate or shallow bowlful of these cookies with an after-dinner espresso, or as an accompaniment to a spoon dessert such as zabaglione or simple custard.

MAKES 250 OR MORE TINY NOCCIOLINI, OR ABOUT 100 AMARETTI-SIZE COOKIES

1 scant cup (125 g) toasted and skinned hazelnuts (see page 26)

1¼ cups (250 g) granulated sugar

2 large (64 g) egg whites, at room temperature, lightly beaten

1. Preheat the oven to 350° F (180° C). Spread the hazelnuts out on a rimmed baking sheet and bake for 6 to 7 minutes, until they are fragrant and have turned a couple of shades darker. Let them cool completely. (Make sure you toast the nuts at home, even if you have bought nuts that have already been toasted.) Turn up the oven temperature to 425° F (220° C). Line two or three rimmed baking sheets with parchment.

2. Place the cooled nuts and half the sugar in the work bowl of a food processor fitted with the metal blade. Pulse until the nuts are coarsely chopped. Add the rest of the sugar to the bowl and pulse again until the mixture is sandy. With the motor running, pour the egg whites through the feed tube and process for several minutes, until the batter is smooth and dense.

3. To make traditional hazelnut-size nocciolini, scoop the batter into a piping bag fitted with a small (3/8-inch; 1-cm) round or star tip. Pipe rows of ½-inch (12-mm) buttons,

about 10 per row, onto the baking sheets. You should end up with 90 to 100 per sheet. Bake the cookies, one sheet at a time, in the middle of the oven for 5 to 6 minutes, until they are puffed, with beautifully browned, lightly cracked dcmes. Transfer the baking sheets to wire racks to cool completely.

4. To make larger, amaretti-size cookies, lower the oven heat to 375° F (190° C). Fit the piping bag with a ½-inch (12-mm) round or French star tip and pipe 30 to 35 rounds per sheet. Each round should be about ¾ inch to 1 inch (2 to 2½ cm) in diameter. Bake the cookies, one sheet at a time, in the middle of the oven for 5 minutes. Increase the heat to 400° F (200° C) and bake an additional 4 to 5 minutes, until the cookies are puffed with browned, lightly cracked domes. Transfer the baking sheets to wire racks to cool completely.

5. Store the cookies in airtight containers for up to 2 weeks. For longer keeping, freeze leftover cookies in an airtight container for up to 6 months.

OCCHI DI BUE *(Trentino-Alto Adige)*

Bull's-Eye Jam Cookies

These classic jam-filled butter cookies are by no means exclusive to Italy. But they are ubiquitous in Italian pastry shops, especially in Alto Adige, where alpine butter is essential to baking. There, they are also known as *Spitzbuben*, a nod to the region's bilingual status and its proximity to Austria. The dough is one of many variations of *pasta frolla*—basic shortcrust pastry—that you'll find throughout the book. This version contains a pinch of baking powder, which gives the dough a little lift, but feel free to substitute the basic Pasta Frolla recipe on page 206, the Canestrelletti dough on page 50, or even the dough for Ciambelline Sarde (page 188), the Sardinian version, which is made with lard.

Be sure to use a good-quality jam—homemade if you have it. Two of my favorites are Vanilla Apricot Jam (page 209) and Sour Cherry Preserves (page 210). Raspberry and strawberry jam are also delicious in these rich cookies. If you want to go all out, try filling them with Nutella or pistachio cream.

MAKES 20 (2-INCH/5-CM) SANDWICHES OR 30 (1½-INCH / 4-CM) SANDWICHES

2 cups (240 g) unbleached all-purpose flour

½ to ⅔ cup (65 to 85 g) confectioners' sugar, depending on the sweetness you prefer; plus more for dusting

1 teaspoon baking powder

¼ teaspoon fine salt

Zest of 1 small lemon

4½ ounces (9 tablespoon; 125 g) cold unsalted butter, cut into cubes

1 large egg plus 1 yolk

½ teaspoon pure vanilla extract

About 1¼ cups (375 g) jam or preserves, homemade (see page 209) or store-bought

1. Measure the flour, confectioners' sugar, baking powder, salt, and lemon zest in the work bowl of a food processor and pulse to combine. Distribute the butter inside the bowl and pulse to incorporate it, taking care not to overprocess. In a separate small bowl, whisk the egg and yolk with the vanilla and pour it into the food processor through the feed tube. Pulse until the mixture begins to clump together.

2. Turn the dough out onto a clean surface, gather the clumps together, and pat them into a disk. Cover tightly with reusable wrap or plastic wrap and refrigerate until thoroughly chilled, at least 2 hours and preferably overnight.

3. Remove the dough from the refrigerator. Preheat the oven to 350° F (180° C). Line two rimmed cookie sheets with parchment.

4. Roll the dough out on a lightly floured surface to a little less than ¼ inch thick (4 to 5 mm). Using a fluted round 1½- to 2-inch (4-to 5-cm) cookie cutter, cut out as many circles as possible. With a ¾-inch (2-cm) cutter, cut a hole in the center of half the rounds. If you don't have a tiny cutter, use a round object from your kitchen, such as a zucchini corer. Arrange the circles onto the cookie sheets. Gather up the scraps of dough, including the leftover punched-out circles, knead briefly to bring them together, then roll out and cut out more. You should end up with forty 2-inch (5 cm) cookie halves or sixty 1½-inch (4-cm) cookie halves.

5. Chill the unbaked cookies for 30 minutes in the refrigerator or 10 minutes in the freezer. If you don't have space for both sheets, chill one first, then chill the second while the first batch is baking.

6. Bake, one sheet at a time, in the middle of the oven for 18 to 20 minutes, until very lightly browned (begin checking at 16 minutes). Transfer the sheets to wire racks and let the cookies cool on the baking sheets for 10 minutes; then transfer them to the wire racks to cool completely.

7. To finish, dollop each cookie bottom (the one with no hole) with about ½ teaspoon of jam (or other spread), spreading it slightly but not all the way to the edge.

8. On a separate parchment-lined baking sheet, shower all the top cookies—the ones with a "bull's-eye"—with confectioners' sugar. Sandwich them on top of the filled cookies. Store the cookies in a tightly lidded container, separating the layers with parchment or waxed paper, for up to 1 week.

PÂN DI MÒRT *(Lombardy)*

Day of the Dead Cookies

One recent October in Bergamo, I was drawn to a window displaying trays of large oval cookies. They looked like soft gingerbread, with cracked surfaces and a scattering of sliced almonds on top. They were *pân di mòrt*, or "bread of the dead." Like other regions, Lombardy has a cookie specifically to commemorate November 2, the Day of the Dead. It's a day when families head to the cemetery to visit their departed loved ones. Bringing along these large, spiced cake-like cookies is a way to break bread together, both literally and symbolically. It's not meant to be a macabre ritual, but rather a contemplative, even uplifting, one.

Nowadays, pân di mòrt is enjoyed not only on November 2, but throughout fall, and for no particular reason beyond the fact that it is delicious. When you read the recipe, you'll notice that the dough for these cookies is composed in part by other cookies. There are other such recipes I came across during my research for this book. Although this has not been confirmed to me, I'm convinced this was a practical and clever way for both home bakers and professional bakeries to use up cookie leftovers, pieces and crumbs.

MAKES 10 LARGE OR 20 MEDIUM COOKIES

1/3 cup (50 g) skin-on or blanched almonds

4 ounces (113 g) spiced crunchy cookies, such as Biscoff or Speculaas cookies, broken into pieces

4 ounces (113 g) Caporali | Savoiardi Liguri (page 54) or store-bought ladyfingers; about 12, broken into pieces

2 ounces (57 g) Amaretti di Saronno, homemade (page 38) or store-bought; about 6 total, broken in half

1/2 cup (70 g) golden raisins

4 (70 g) soft dried figs, cut into pieces

1 cup (120 g) unbleached all-purpose flour

3/4 cup (150 g) sugar

1/2 teaspoon baking powder

1/2 teaspoon fine salt

1/2 teaspoon ground cinnamon

1 tablespoon unsweetened cocoa powder

Pinch of freshly grated or ground nutmeg

3 (90 g) large egg whites, lightly beaten

1/4 cup (60 ml) dry white wine

TO FINISH

3 tablespoons whole milk or half-and-half

1/2 cup (50 g) sliced almonds, optional

Confectioners' sugar, optional

Continued >>

1. Place the almonds in the work bowl of a food processor fitted with the metal blade and pulse until they are coarsely chopped. Distribute the cookies, savoiardi, and amaretti around the bowl and pulse until the mixture is mostly ground–a little texture is fine. Pour the mixture into a large bowl.

2. Drop the golden raisins and figs into the food processor and pulse until they are coarsely ground. In a separate bowl, whisk together the flour, sugar, baking powder, salt, cinnamon, cocoa powder, and nutmeg. Pour ⅓ of this mixture into the food processor with the dried fruit and pulse until combined. Add another third of the dry ingredients and process again to combine, then add the remaining dry ingredients and process one more time until everything is thoroughly mixed together. Scrape this mixture into the bowl with the pulverized almonds and cookies.

3. Stir in the egg whites and white wine and fold everything together with a sturdy spatula. Then use your hands to form a ball of dough (it will be sticky but should hold its shape). Wrap the dough in reusable wrap or plastic wrap and refrigerate it overnight. This is an important step as it gives all of the ingredients a chance to meld.

4. Line two rimmed baking sheets with parchment. Preheat the oven to 350° F (180° C). To make large cookies, pinch off pieces of dough about the size of a lemon and form them into 3 x 5-inch (8 x 13-cm) ovals. They should be about ½ inch (12 mm) thick. Arrange them on the baking sheets, 5 per sheet.

5. To make medium-size cookies, pinch off pieces of dough about the size of a lime and form them into 2 x 3-inch (5 x 8-cm) ovals. They should be about ½ inch (12 mm) thick. Arrange them on the baking sheets, 10 per sheet. For either size, brush the tops lightly with milk and sprinkle with sliced almonds. If you like, you can omit the sliced almonds and dust the cookies with confectioners' sugar after they are baked.

6. Bake the cookies one sheet at a time. For large cookies, bake for about 20 minutes; they should be set with cracked tops, but still somewhat soft. Bake medium-size cookies for 13 minutes, until set and cracked on top, but still somewhat soft. Transfer the baking sheets to wire racks to cool for 20 minutes; then lift the cookies off with an angled spatula and place them onto the wire racks to cool completely. For cookies that aren't garnished with sliced almonds, give them a generous dusting of powdered sugar before serving. Store the pân di mòrt in an airtight container for up to 1 week.

ZALETI *(Veneta)*

Golden Polenta Cookies

Recipes for this beloved Venetian cornmeal and raisin cookie, known also as *zaeti* and *zaletti* in Venetian dialect, and *gialletti* in proper Italian, date back to at least the 1700s. They are so named for their sunny yellow hue, imparted by cornmeal in the dough.

In his seminal nineteenth-century compendium *La Scienza in Cucina e l'Arte di Mangiar Bene* (Science in the Kitchen and the Art of Eating Well), author Pellegrino Artusi included a recipe for these tender cookies, cautioning: "Mothers, delight your children with these gialletti, but don't taste them yourselves, unless you wish to hear your babies cry because they get only crumbs." Though they look deceptively plain, once you bite into one, you'll see just what he meant. Artusi's recipe called for fresh yeast and both butter and lard in the dough. Modern recipes use baking powder and only butter, which is what I use here.

MAKES ABOUT 32 COOKIES

½ cup (70 g) golden raisins

¼ cup (60 ml) grappa or Jamaican rum

1¼ cups (150g) unbleached all-purpose flour

½ cup (75 g) fine cornmeal

¾ cup (75 g) corn flour (may substitute more fine cornmeal)

1 teaspoon baking powder

¼ teaspoon fine salt

Zest of 1 lemon

5 ounces (11 tablespoons; 150 g) unsalted butter

1 large egg plus 1 yolk

½ cup (100 g) sugar

1 teaspoon vanilla extract

Confectioners' sugar, optional

1. Place the raisins in a bowl. Cover them with the grappa and let them soak for at least 1 hour (I often soak them overnight before making the cookies).

2. Preheat the oven to 350° F (180° C). Line two rimmed baking sheets with parchment. In a large bowl, whisk together the flour, cornmeal, corn flour, baking powder, salt, and lemon zest.

3. Melt the butter in the microwave or in a small saucepan on the stovetop and let it cool for about 10 minutes. Stir it into the dry ingredients; you'll end up with a thick paste.

4. In a stand mixer fitted with the paddle attachment, beat the egg and yolk with the sugar until the mixture is lightened and the sugar is mostly dissolved. Beat in the vanilla. Scrape in the cornmeal mixture and beat on medium-low until thoroughly combined. Pour in the raisins and any liqueur remaining in the bowl and mix on low speed just until incorporated.

5. Pinch off 1 tablespoon-size pieces of dough—they should weigh 20 to 22 grams, slightly less than 1 ounce. Roll the pieces into batons about 1 by 2 inches (2½ by 5 cm) and place them on the baking sheets, 15 to 16 per sheet. Bake, one sheet at a time, in the center of the oven, for 15 to 20 minutes, until golden and puffed and just set, with a few cracks on the surface. Transfer the baking sheets to wire racks to cool for 10 minutes, then lift the cookies off the sheets and set them on the racks to cool completely.

6. Serve the zaleti plain or dusted lightly with confectioners' sugar. Not surprisingly, they are delicious with grappa, as well as coffee or tea. Store them in an airtight container for up to 2 weeks.

PASTE DI MELIGA *(Piedmont)*
Cornmeal Butter Cookies

These piped golden wreaths are from the Cuneo province, in southern Piedmont. They are made with a variation of *pasta frolla*—classic Italian butter pastry. The word *meliga* is Piedmontese dialect for *mais*, the Italian word for corn, and in fact fine cornmeal gives these cookies a little crunch. The lore around *paste di meliga* is that the cookies were created at a time of rising wheat prices. To lower costs, bakers began substituting cornmeal for wheat flour in their cookie dough.

It is traditional to serve paste di meliga with zabaglione, the popular Piedmontese dessert of whipped egg custard spiked with wine, or a small glass of Moscato. I like them with my morning cappuccino.

MAKES 36 COOKIES

2 cups (240 g) unbleached all-purpose flour

1 cup (150 g) fine cornmeal

½ cup (100 g) sugar

¼ teaspoon fine salt

Finely grated zest of 1 lemon

8 ounces (2 sticks; 227 g) cold unsalted butter, cut into ½-inch (12-mm) cubes

1 large egg plus 1 yolk

1 teaspoon pure vanilla extract

1. Pulse together the flour, cornmeal, sugar, salt, and lemon zest in the work bowl of a food processor fitted with the metal blade. Scatter the butter cubes around the bowl and pulse until the butter is broken up into small pieces and evenly distributed throughout the flour.

2. In a small bowl, lightly whisk the egg and yolk with the vanilla extract. Pour this through the feed tube of the processor and pulse until a soft, sticky dough comes together. Scoop the dough into a sturdy, reusable piping bag fitted with a ½-inch (12-mm) open star tip.

3. Line three rimmed baking sheets with parchment–use two baking sheets if you don't have three; you can reuse one after baking the first batch of cookies. Pipe 12 wreaths about 2¼ inches (5½ cm) in diameter onto each baking sheet. Set the baking sheets in the refrigerator to chill for 30 minutes. (If you don't have enough space, chill the piped cookies one sheet at a time.) Preheat the oven to 350° F (180° C) while the cookies are chilling.

4. Bake, one sheet at a time, in the middle of the oven for 15 to 17 minutes, until they are set and lightly browned around the edges and on the bottom. Transfer the baking sheets to wire racks to cool completely. Store the cookies in an airtight container for up to 2 weeks.

PINOLATE GENOVESI *(Liguria)*

Pine Nut Cookies from Genoa

Pinolate, or *pignolate*, the OG version of pine nut cookies, come from Liguria, the region that forms Italy's northwest Mediterranean coast. Here, the pine nut is a key ingredient in the region's food, most notably in Genovese pesto. The nuts are the fruit of the Mediterranean stone pine tree (*Pinus pinea*), easily recognizable by its tall trunk and umbrella-shaped canopy top. They have a slightly elongated oval shape, and are prized for their creamy color and sweet, resinous flavor. Look for them in specialty grocery stores or online (see Sources, page 225).

Most recipes for these cookies are made from ground almonds or almond paste, plus egg white and sugar. They are, essentially, soft amaretti with a scattering of pine nuts on top. However, it is my contention that if you are making pine nut cookies, there should be pine nuts *in* the cookies as well as on top of them. So that's what I've done.

MAKES 20 COOKIES

1½ cups (225 g) pine nuts, preferably Italian or Mediterranean (see Sources, page 225), divided

7 ounces (200 g) almond paste, cut into cubes or slices (see page 219)

¾ cup (150 g) sugar

¼ teaspoon pure almond extract

¼ teaspoon fine salt

2 large (60 g) egg whites

¼ to ½ cup (25 to 50 g) superfine blanched almond flour, plus more as needed

1. Place ½ cup (75 g) pine nuts in the work bowl of a food processor fitted with the metal blade. Pulse a few times to grind them coarsely. Distribute the pieces of almond paste around the interior of the work bowl and pulse until well combined with the nuts. Pulse in the sugar, almond extract, and salt and process until the mixture is more or less a smooth paste.

2. In a small bowl, lightly whisk the egg whites and pour them into the food processor through the feed tube, processing until thoroughly combined. Check the consistency of the dough. Sprinkle in about ¼ cup (25 g) almond flour and pulse to combine. You are aiming for a stiff, sticky paste that can be rolled into balls. If the mixture is still too loose, add more almond flour, 1 tablespoon at a time, to reach the right consistency. Transfer the dough to a container or bowl, cover tightly, and refrigerate for at least 2 hours and up to overnight.

3. Preheat the oven to 325° F (165° C). Line a rimmed baking sheet with parchment. Put the remaining 1 cup of pine nuts in a small bowl. Using a small scoop or tablespoon, scoop out 20 balls of dough, each slightly less than 1 ounce (30 grams). Roll the balls in the pine nuts and set them on the baking sheet in five rows of four. Bake, one sheet at a time, in the middle of the oven for about 20 minutes, until the cookies are puffed and just set and the pine nuts are lightly browned.

4. Transfer the baking sheet to a wire rack to cool for 5 minutes. Using an angled spatula, transfer the cookies from the sheet to the rack to cool completely. The pinolate will keep in an airtight container for up to 1 week.

SBRISOLONA *(Lombardy and Emilia-Romagna)*

Big Crumbly Cookie

This giant crumbly cookie is a specialty of Mantua, in Lombardy. But I first tasted it at a cooking class at the home of a chef from Parma, in Emilia-Romagna, where it is also popular. This makes sense, as Parma is just about an hour south of Mantua, and popular cookies tend to travel beyond their place of origin.

Also known as *torta sbrisolona*, the name of this cookie roughly translates to "crumbly cake." It comes from the verb *sbricolare*, which means "to crumble." The cookie was once upon a time prepared by farmers using simple ingredients that they were likely to have on hand—flour, cornmeal, sugar, a little lard or butter, and almonds. It was eaten as a snack to revive them after a long morning of work.

When assembling your *sbrisolona*, resist patting the sandy dough into the pan too firmly. It needs to be loosely packed in order to yield that fall-apart texture that makes it so irresistible. Once baked, is customary to break this cookie into irregular pieces for serving, though you can cut it with a knife for a neater presentation.

MAKES 1 LARGE COOKIE, TO SERVE 8 TO 10

3/4 cup (105 g) whole raw almonds, plus a handful more for decorating

1/2 cup (100 g) sugar, plus 1 tablespoon for sprinkling

3/4 cup (100 g) unbleached all-purpose flour

2/3 cup (100 g) fine cornmeal (do not use coarse cornmeal or polenta or your cookie will be grainy and tough)

Finely grated zest of 1 lemon

3 1/2 ounces (7 tablespoons; 100 g) cold unsalted butter, cut into 1/2-inch (12-mm) cubes

1 large egg yolk

1 teaspoon pure vanilla extract

1/4 teaspoon fine salt

1. Preheat the oven to 350° F (180° C). Line an 8-inch (20-cm) springform pan or cake pan with parchment. The easiest way to do this is to crumple up the parchment with your hands and then insert it into the pan; once crumpled, it's easy to make the parchment fit.

2. Reserve 10 of the 3/4 cup (105 g) almonds and put the rest into the work bowl of a food processor fitted with the metal blade. Add the 1/2 cup (100 g) sugar and process until the nuts are very finely ground, almost like almond flour. Take care not to overprocess or you will release the oils from the almonds. Pulse in the flour, cornmeal, and lemon zest.

3. Distribute the butter around the inside of the work bowl and pulse briefly to break it up into small pieces. In a small bowl, whisk the egg yolk with the vanilla and salt and pour this in through the feed tube of the food processor. Pulse until the mixture begins to look like damp sand. Pinch a small handful; it should clump together lightly. Toss in the reserved 10 almonds and pulse briefly to break them up a bit.

4. Remove the blade from the food processor. Scoop up handfuls of the almond mixture, lightly clumping it together, and spread it evenly into the parchment-lined pan. You can pat it lightly, but resist the urge to pack it in. Once it's all in the pan, sprinkle with the 1 tablespoon sugar and decorate it with the handful of whole almonds.

5. Bake the sbrisolona for 30 to 35 minutes, until the center feels firm and it is lightly browned on top and around the edges. Set the pan on a wire rack to cool completely. Once cooled, remove the sbrisolona from the pan by unlatching the ring (if using a springform pan), carefully lifting out the parchment (the edges will crumble easily), and transferring the sbrisolona to a plate. Break or cut into pieces and serve. Store leftovers in an airtight container for up to 1 week.

TORCETTI DI SAINT-VINCENT *(Aosta Valley)*

Saint-Vincent Twists

My family and I spent Christmas 2018 in Aosta. The Alpine city is the capital of the Valle d'Aosta, Italy's smallest region, tucked up in the northwest corner of the peninsula. Aosta is a charming town, notable for its grand central piazza and the ruins of a Roman theater that rise up against the backdrop of the Alps. One afternoon, at the Christmas market, I bought a packet of these twisted, sugar-dipped ring cookies, which I was told originated in the nearby town of Saint-Vincent. They were like nothing I had ever had before, crunchy and flaky and buttery, with slightly caramelized undersides from the sugar. They reminded me a bit of *ventaglie* (see page 123), those buttery fans made with puff pastry, but more bread-like, almost like sweet, flaky breadsticks. They were said to be a favorite of Italy's Queen Margherita.

The cookies began to make sense once I started reading about them. The dough contains yeast rather than baking powder or baking soda as its leavening agent. They puff up as they bake and perfume your kitchen with caramelized sugar and yeast. I used two recipes as road maps to eventually come up with my own here: one is from the book *Cucina della Val D'Aosta*, by Emilia Valli; and the other is from *I Dolci della Cucina Regionale Italiana*, by Fernada Gosetti.

Since my first encounter with *torcetti*, I have seen them in bakeries in various parts of northern Italy, especially in Piedmont, where they seem to be especially popular in Barolo wine country. And, in fact, since they aren't too sweet, they make an excellent accompaniment to a glass of red wine or, in keeping with Piedmontese tradition, hot chocolate.

MAKES ABOUT 36 COOKIES

2 generous cups (250 g) unbleached all-purpose flour

1 tablespoon sugar, plus about 3/4 cup (150 g) more for coating

1/2 teaspoon fine salt

1 teaspoon instant yeast (not rapid-rise)

1/2 to 2/3 (120 to 160 ml) cup water

4 ounces (1 stick; 113 g) unsalted butter, cut into 1/2-inch (12-mm) cubes and softened to room temperature

1/2 cup (125 ml) honey, for glazing, optional

1. Combine the flour, 1 tablespoon of sugar, salt, and instant yeast in the bowl of a stand mixer fitted with the paddle attachment. Mix briefly on low speed. Drizzle in 1/2 cup (120 ml) water and mix, first on low, then on medium, until a ball of dough forms. If the dough seems dry or is not coming together, drizzle in additional water, 1 tablespoon at a time, and continue to beat on medium until it comes together. Switch to the dough hook and knead for a couple of minutes until the dough is smooth and compact. Cover the bowl and let the dough rest and rise for 1 to 1 1/2 hours, until nearly doubled in size.

2. Switch back to the paddle and begin to work in the butter on medium-low speed, adding one or two pieces of the softened butter at a time and making sure the butter is incorporated before adding more. Continue until all the butter has been added and the dough is smooth, silky, and elastic. Cover the bowl and let the dough rise in a warm spot for 1 hour.

3. Preheat the oven to 400° F (200° C). Line two to three rimmed baking sheets with parchment. Fill a small bowl with about 3/4 cup (150 g) sugar and have it nearby.

4. Turn the dough out onto a clean work surface. You shouldn't need to flour it, as the buttery dough should not stick. Flatten the dough into a loaf. Cut off a slice about 3/4 inch (2 cm) thick and roll it into a thin rope, about the width of a pencil and 7 to 8 inches (18 to 20 cm) long. Bring the ends together to form a teardrop shape, crossing one end over the other very slightly and pinching them so they adhere. Dip the torcetti in the sugar, coating on both sides, and place them on parchment-lined baking sheets. You should be able to fit 12 to 16 torcetti per sheet. Bake, one sheet at a time, for 15 to 17 minutes, until golden brown and cooked through.

5. This step is optional, but it does give a glossy finish to the torcetti. While they are baking, heat the honey in a small pan until it is loose. Brush the torcetti lightly with the runny honey as soon as they come out of the oven. Let them cool on the baking sheet for 10 minutes, then transfer them to a wire rack to cool completely. Store the cookies in an airtight container in a cool spot, where they will keep for 2 or more weeks.

ZUCHERANCICI *(Friuli Venezia-Giulia, Croatia)*

Istrian Wedding Cookies

These pinwheel-shaped butter cookies are among the prettiest in the book. I first came across them in my friend Paola Bacchia's cookbook *Istria: Recipes and Stories from the Hidden Heart of Italy, Slovenia, and Croatia*. The Istrian peninsula, located northeast of Venice and just south of Trieste, once belonged to Italy but was ceded to Yugoslavia at the end of World War II. The majority of Istria is now part of Croatia, with a sliver split between Italy and Slovenia. The food and baking of the peninsula reflect its complex past.

According to Paola, zucherancici, or *cukerančići* in Croatian, are traditionally made to celebrate weddings and baptisms. To achieve the cookie's pinwheel shape, the dough is cut into strips, which are then notched with small incisions. The ends of the strips are brought together to form a circle, giving the cookies their signature spokes. This is my slightly adapted version of Paola's recipe.

MAKES 32 TO 36 COOKIES

Rounded ½ cup (115 g) superfine sugar

4 ounces (1 stick; 113 g) unsalted butter, at cool room temperature

2 large eggs, at room temperature

2 tablespoons whole milk

2 teaspoons Malvasia or Jamaican rum (see Baker's Note), plus 2 tablespoons for brushing

Zest of 1 lemon

3 cups (360 g) unbleached all-purpose flour, plus more for the work surface

1 teaspoon baking powder

¼ teaspoon fine salt

Confectioners' sugar for dusting

1. Combine the sugar and butter in the bowl of a stand mixer fitted with the paddle attachment and beat on medium-high speed until fluffy, about 3 minutes. Beat in the eggs, one at a time, on medium, then high speed, until thoroughly combined. Beat in the milk, Malvasia, and lemon zest.

2. In a medium bowl, whisk together the flour, baking powder, and salt. Pour the dry ingredients into the butter-and-egg mixture and mix on low just until incorporated. Take care not to overbeat or your cookies will be tough. Pat the dough into a disk, wrap it in reusable wrap or plastic wrap, and refrigerate for at least 2 hours or preferably overnight.

3. Remove the dough from the refrigerator and let it soften slightly. Lightly flour a clean work surface. Lightly flour the dough and a rolling pin and roll the dough out into a large rectangle, about 10 x 12 inches (25 x 30 cm) and ⅓ inch (8 mm) thick. Trim the edges to straighten them. With a bench scraper or knife, cut the rectangle crosswise into 16 strips, each about ¾ inches (2 cm) wide.

4. Line two rimmed baking sheets with parchment and have them nearby. Preheat the oven to 350° F (180° C). Place a strip in front of you and cut it in half so that you have two strips, each 5 inches (13 cm) long. Cut four or five diagonal incisions along the length of each strip, taking care not to cut all the way through. Take the ends of one strip and bring them together so that the strip forms a small wheel with spokes pointing outwards. Arrange the wheels on the baking sheets, 16 per sheet. You should have a total of 32. You may end up with a few more, depending on the exact size of your strips. If you have extras, arrange them on a third sheet or set them aside and reuse one of the baking sheets once the first batch has baked.

5. Bake the cookies, one sheet at a time, in the middle of the oven, for 10 to 12 minutes, until set and barely browned on top and slightly golden underneath.

6. Place the reserved 2 tablespoons of Malvasia in a small bowl. As soon as the cookies are out of the oven, lightly brush their tops with the wine, then sprinkle with

confectioners' sugar. Let the cookies cool on the baking sheets, then transfer them to an airtight container, where they will keep for about 1 week. Give them a fresh coating of confectioners' sugar right before serving.

BAKER'S NOTE: *Malvasia is a wine produced in various parts of Italy and beyond. It can be either white or red, dry or sweet. For this recipe, choose sweet white Malvasia. If you are not able to find it, you can substitute another sweet wine, such as Vin Santo (an expensive alternative), or Jamaican or white rum.*

COOKIES
OF CENTRAL ITALY

Recipes and stories from

LAZIO, LE MARCHE, TUSCANY, UMBRIA

When the nineteenth-century French novelist Stendhal visited Florence in 1817, he was so moved by the beauty and significance of what he saw that he nearly had to be carted off. "I was in a sort of ecstasy," he later wrote. "I had palpitations of the heart. . . . Life was drained from me. I walked with the fear of falling."

Such a phenomenon has come to be known as Stendhal syndrome, and I totally get it. I'm exaggerating only a little when I tell you that I have felt similarly when traveling, not just in Florence, but anywhere in central Italy, whether I was gazing at Botticelli's High Renaissance masterpiece, *The Birth of Venus*, at Uffizi Gallery, looking up through the oculus of the Pantheon in Rome, taking in the view of the Valle di Assisi from the grounds of St. Francis's Basilica, or walking through the medieval splendor of Urbino, the hilltop city in Le Marche where the painter Raphael was born.

I feel the same way toward the cookies of these lands. Renaissance spice. Ancient grains. Olive oil. Wine. Almonds. These are among the ingredients that define the cookies of central Italy. How can you not swoon over them?

Think of the Renaissance glamour of Ricciarelli (page 114), a fourteenth-century diamond-shaped almond cookie perfumed with orange zest and coated in confectioners' sugar. Or *Cantucci*, far more rustic but just as iconic, the OG double-baked and sliced almond cookies that were born more than 150 years ago in a small bakery in Prato and are still produced there today. In Assisi, pastry shop windows are filled with giant cloudlike meringues (page 120), as lofty as the Basilica honoring the city's patron saint. Nearby, in the fields of the Valley of Assisi, one family mill uses its own grains to make a variety of appealingly rustic cookies like Frollini al Farro (page 104). And at Biscottificio Innocenti, in the heart of Rome's Trastevere neighborhood, owner-baker Stefania Innocenti turns out dozens of types of cookies, from rustic wine rings to plate-size ventaglie—puff pastry fans, also known as elephant ears. You'll find my version of crisp, buttery puff pastry fans on page 123 and more about Stefania's bakery on page 90.

BISCOTTI DELLA NONNA *(Umbria and other regions throughout Italy)*

Nonna's Cookies

So many cookies in Italy go by the name Biscotti della Nonna that it's impossible to say where they originated. There are as many recipes as there are nonnas, which is to say—a lot! But most recipes have two defining qualities: they are perfect for dunking in milk or cappuccino; and they are oversize, just like a nonna's hug.

Biscotti della Nonna are generally big and round or oblong, though you'll also find them shaped into twists, or large slices, like Cantuccioni (page 101). They can be soft and tender, or more on the crumbly side. These are a bit of both. The cinnamon sugar coating is not traditional, but it goes beautifully with the orange zest in the cookie.

MAKES 10 LARGE OR 20 MEDIUM COOKIES

1/3 cup (70 g) granulated sugar

1 large egg

1/3 cup (75 ml) extra-virgin olive oil, plus more to coat your hands

1/4 cup (60 ml) whole milk

1 teaspoon pure vanilla extract

Zest of 1 small orange, about 2 teaspoons

2 cups (240 g) unbleached all-purpose flour

1 teaspoon baking powder

1/4 teaspoon baking soda

1/4 teaspoon fine salt

CINNAMON SUGAR

1/4 cup (50 g) granulated sugar

1/2 teaspoon ground cinnamon

1. Combine the sugar, egg, olive oil, and milk in a large bowl and mix well with a whisk or a hand mixer. Whisk in the vanilla extract and orange zest.

2. In a separate bowl, whisk together the flour, baking powder, baking soda, and salt. Pour this into the egg mixture and fold everything together with a large spatula until thoroughly combined. The dough will be soft and sticky. Cover the bowl and let it rest briefly.

3. Preheat the oven to 350° F (180° C). Line a rimmed baking sheet with parchment.

4. To make the cinnamon sugar: In a small bowl, mix together the 1/4 cup (50 g) sugar and the cinnamon.

5. Lightly coat your hands with a little olive oil. Pinch off golf ball-size pieces of dough and roll them into ovals or circles. Pat them down to flatten them a bit; they should be about 1/2 inch (12 mm) thick. If you want to weigh for accuracy, each piece should weigh slightly under 2 ounces (about 50 g). Coat both sides of each oval or circle in cinnamon sugar and place them on the baking sheet, taking care to leave about 1 inch (2 1/2 cm) of space between them.

6. Bake the cookies in the middle of the oven for 15 minutes, or until they are lightly browned. They should be puffed and set, with some light cracking on the surface. Transfer the baking sheet to a wire rack to cool for 5 minutes; then transfer the cookies from the baking sheet to the rack to cool completely. Store the cookies in an airtight container for up to 1 week.

BISCOTTI DEL PESCATORE *(Le Marche)*

Fishermen's Cookies

Le Marche, on the north-central Adriatic coast, is still an under-the-radar region in Italy. Those who know it love it, for it contains much to love: Apennine mountains and green forests, splendid hilltop towns crowned with castles and fortresses, vineyards and olive groves, and a swath of cliffs overlooking the blue Adriatic coast. The baking in this region tends toward the rustic, and these cookies are a good example. They are called fisherman's cookies because of their high-energy and nutritious contents—almonds, pine nuts, walnuts, and golden raisins. Their long shelf life made them a good and practical provision for seafaring travelers.

I hope the words "nutritious" and "long shelf life" haven't put you off; these really are delicious cookies; dense and packed with the warm flavor of toasted nuts and the winey sweetness of brandy-soaked raisins. Sprinkling the cookies with Demerara (raw) sugar before baking is not traditional, but I like the extra crunch.

MAKES 24 TO 28 COOKIES

½ cup (70 g) golden raisins

¼ cup (60 ml) Ratafia or cherry brandy (see page 18)

4 ounces (1 stick; 113 g) unsalted butter, cut into ½-inch (12-mm) cubes, at cool room temperature (65° F; 18° C)

1 cup (200 g) sugar

3 large eggs, at room temperature

½ teaspoon fine salt

2 teaspoons baking powder

¼ cup (30 g) farro flour (see page 16); or ¼ cup (45 g) unbleached all-purpose flour

3 cups (360 g) unbleached all-purpose flour

½ cup (50 g) toasted walnut halves or pieces, cooled (see page 26)

⅓ cup (50 g) blanched and toasted almonds, cooled (see page 26)

¼ cup (40 g) toasted pine nuts, cooled (see page 26)

TO DECORATE

¼ cup (60 g) Demerara or raw sugar

24 to 28 walnut halves

1. Place the golden raisins and brandy in a small bowl and steep for at least 1 hour and up to overnight–the longer, the better.

2. Preheat the oven to 325 F (165° C). Line two rimmed baking sheets with parchment.

3. Place the butter and sugar in the bowl of a stand mixer fitted with the paddle attachment. Beat on medium-low, then on high, until well blended and fluffy, 3 to 4 minutes. Drop in the eggs, one at a time, beating well after each addition. Beat in the salt, baking powder, and farro flour. Add the all-purpose flour and nuts and mix on low to medium-low just until the ingredients incorporated. Finally, mix in the golden raisins and any brandy remaining in the bowl until the raisins are evenly dispersed.

4. Use a small cookie scoop or a tablespoon to scoop out walnut-size balls of dough. If you're weighing them, each scoop should weigh about 1¼ ounces (35 grams). Place them on the baking sheets, 12 per sheet. Sprinkle with Demerara sugar and press a walnut half into the top of each cookie.

5. Bake the cookies for 18 to 20 minutes, or until they are set and golden-brown on the bottom. Set the baking sheets on wire racks to cool for 10 minutes; then use an angled spatula to transfer the cookies to the racks to cool completely. Store the cookies in an airtight container, where they will keep at least 2 weeks.

BRIGIDINI DI LAMPORECCHIO *(Tuscany)*

Crispy Anise Wafers from Lamporecchio

Passaparola—word of mouth—has always been the best way to find hidden gems in Italy. If it had not been for my friends' Giulia and Tommaso's recommendation, I might not have contacted Massimiliano Lunardi, whose bakery outside of Pistoia I wrote about on pages 96 and 108. And it if it had not been for a tip from Massimiliano, I likely would have missed these addictive cookies.

Brigidini are thin, crunchy wafers made with eggs, sugar, flour, and ground aniseeds. Although they are round, they tend to be haphazardly folded and somewhat misshapen. In texture they remind me a bit of fortune cookies, though their crunch is more delicate, almost like potato chips. And just like potato chips, it's hard to stop at one.

The cookies are a specialty of Lamporecchio, a town on the western slope of Monte Albano, south of Pistoia. Centuries ago, they were made by nuns who were devotees of St. Brigid of Sweden, a fourteenth-century nun and mystic. Hence their name. According to *La Scienza in Cucina e l'Arte di Mangiar Bene*, Pellegrino Artusi's nineteenth-century book on Italian cooking, the nuns' primary task was to make communion wafers. But for Carnival and other festivals and celebrations, they would turn the wafers into sweet treats by adding anise and honey to the batter.

You'll need a pizzelle iron with shallow grates or a tortilla press to make these wafers. I use a small pizzelle iron with a shallow stamped design and round plates that are about 5 inches (13 cm) in diameter. My brigidini are not as thin as those from Lamporecchio, but they are still crunchy and delicious. See page 25 for details on pizzelle irons.

MAKES ABOUT 24 COOKIES, DEPENDING ON THE SIZE AND TYPE OF IRON OR PRESS

2 teaspoons whole aniseeds

Rounded ½ cup (115 g) superfine sugar

3 to 4 tablespoons sunflower or other neutral oil, plus more as needed to grease the iron

2 large eggs, at room temperature

1 tablespoon anise liqueur, such as Meletti or sambuca

¼ teaspoon fine salt

1¼ to 1½ cups (150 to 180 g) unbleached all-purpose flour

Confectioners' sugar, optional

1. Spread the aniseeds out in a small dry skillet set over medium heat. Toast the seeds, stirring them now and again, for 2 to 3 minutes, until they turn a shade or two darker and you can smell their warm chamomile-like scent. Transfer them to a small bowl or plate to cool completely. Grind them to a powder in a spice grinder. You can use ground aniseeds if you want to save time, but the anise flavor won't be as bright.

2. Combine the sugar, ground aniseeds, oil, eggs, liqueur, and salt in a large bowl and beat with a whisk or a hand mixer until thoroughly combined. Add in enough flour to make a thick sticky batter that can be scooped with a cookie scoop or a tablespoon.

3. Heat a waffle or pizzelle iron or a tortilla press according to the manufacturer's instructions and oil the plates if needed. Dollop a scant 1 tablespoon of the batter onto the hot plate and close the iron. Cook for about 20 to 30 seconds, until golden brown. Lift the cookie off the iron with a small, angled spatula and set it on a plate or baking tray. If you like, you can fold it in half, but do this quickly before it has a chance to set. The brigidini will become crispy as they cool. Keep on going until you have used all the batter. You should end up with about 20 brigidini. To serve, pile them onto a plate and dust with confectioners' sugar if you like, or try the chocolate-dipped variation below.

BAKER'S NOTE: *Pasticceria Carli, a Lamporecchio bakery that has been making brigidini since the 1870s, also sells a chocolate-dipped version. To make them, just dip the ends of cooled brigidini in melted tempered dark chocolate (see page 27) and let the chocolate harden. The combination of anise and chocolate is dreamy.*

BISCOTTI GIRANDOLA *(Tuscany)*

Black and White Spirals

I assigned these buttery chocolate and vanilla spirals to the Central Italy chapter primarily because I first spied them at Fratelli Lunardi, a wonderful bakery run by two brothers in Quarrata, a suburb of Pistoia, north of Florence. The eye-catching spirals of vanilla and chocolate pasta frolla (basic pastry dough) are a sort of best-of-both-worlds cookie, as they satisfy your craving for both rich vanilla and deep, dark chocolate. See the Baker's Note at the end of the recipe for other black and white configurations. And head to page 108 for more on Fratelli Lunardi bakery and their recipe for Hazelnut and Jam Bar Cookies.

MAKES 30 COOKIES

½ batch Basic Pasta Frolla (page 206), chilled

½ batch Chocolate Pasta Frolla (page 206), chilled

Unbleached all-purpose flour for the work surface

1. Remove both doughs from the refrigerator and let them sit for about 30 minutes, to soften a bit–not too much; they should be rollable but still firm. Line a rimmed baking sheet with parchment.

2. Have a sheet of parchment at the ready. Lightly flour a work surface and roll out one piece of dough into a large square, about 11 x 11 inches (25 x 25 cm) and about ¼ inch (6 mm) thick. Lay the square on top of the parchment. Roll out the other piece of dough to the same measurements and lay it directly on top of the first piece of dough. Gently roll over the stacked doughs to help them stick together. Then, using the parchment to help you, roll the two doughs together into a tight spiral log. Work slowly to avoid cracking the dough. If you see cracks forming, press your hands lightly to the dough to warm it slightly and help it roll up smoothly. Twist the ends of the parchment and tie them tightly with cooking string. If you have a concave vessel, like a corncob holder, set the log on it–this will keep the bottom of the log from flattening out. Place the log in the refrigerator to chill for 1 hour.

3. Preheat the oven to 350° F (180° C). Line two rimmed baking sheets with parchment. Remove the log of dough from the refrigerator and unwrap it. Use a sharp knife to trim the uneven ends. Cut the log into ¼-inch (6-mm) slices to make 30 spirals. Arrange them on the baking sheets, leaving a little space between. Bake, one sheet at a time, in the middle of the oven for 12 to 15 minutes, until they are set and the vanilla dough is light gold in color. Transfer the baking sheets to wire racks to cool for 10 minutes; then use an angled spatula to transfer the cookies from the baking sheets to the rack to cool completely. Store the cookies in an airtight container for up to 2 weeks.

BAKER'S NOTE: *Since this recipe calls for a half batch each of vanilla and chocolate pasta frolla, you will likely have leftover dough. You can freeze it for up to 3 months; or you can bake more cookies. There are lots of clever ways to combine the two doughs to make black and white cookies:*

COOKIE CUTTER BLACK AND WHITES: *Roll out both pieces of dough as directed in the recipe. Cut out an equal number of small shapes from each sheet–stars, for example. Fit the vanilla stars into the chocolate dough and the chocolate stars into the vanilla dough. Then use a larger cutter–a circle, heart, or a square, for example–to cut out cookies. Don't worry about keeping the smaller star shapes intact. Each cookie should have some vanilla and chocolate in it. Bake as directed.*

TWISTS: *Roll pieces of each dough into long thin ropes and twist them together. Then, cut the ropes crosswise into 3-inch (7-cm) twists. Bake as directed.*

CHECKERBOARDS: *Alternate strips of black and white dough and stack them together, then cut them into patterned squares. Bake as directed.*

CANTUCCI DI PRATO *(Tuscany)*

Classic Twice-Baked Cookies from Prato

One of life's little pleasures is sitting down to a glass of Vin Santo, Tuscan dessert wine, accompanied by a cantuccio. This is *the* classic twice-baked cookie, cut on the bias and studded with nuts. It is dry and crunchy and tremendously satisfying, especially when dipped into that glass of wine.

We have pastry chef Antonio Mattei to thank for these now iconic cookies. In 1858, Mattei opened a bakery in Prato, north of Florence, and started producing cookies based on a centuries-old recipe. His original ingredients were flour, sugar, eggs, and pine nuts or almonds from nearby groves. The soft, nut-studded dough was shaped into loaves, baked, sliced, and baked again into crunchy oblongs. Mattei's cantucci won prizes at food expos in Florence in 1861 and Paris in 1867. To this day, Biscottificio Antonio Mattei continues to turn out thousands upon thousands of its founder's sweet, crunchy creations, packaged in its signature blue waxed-paper bags.

These famous cookies, meanwhile, have traveled far beyond the confines of Prato. In the U.S. and elsewhere, they are known as biscotti rather than cantucci. This is slightly confusing to Italians, for whom the word 'biscotti' is a catchall term for any kind of cookie. The cookies themselves have morphed into all sorts of iterations: cranberry-pistachio, fig and fennel, lemon and ginger, drizzled with icing, or dipped in chocolate. They are big, small, thin, fat. The variations are endless. Here is my slightly embellished version of the classic.

MAKES 40 TO 42 COOKIES

1 cup (200 g) plus 2 tablespoons sugar, divided

3 large eggs, 1 separated

1 teaspoon pure vanilla extract

½ teaspoon pure almond extract

Zest of 1 small lemon, optional

½ teaspoon baking powder

2 cups (240 g) unbleached all-purpose flour, plus more for the work surface

1 cup (150 g) raw almonds

1. Combine 1 cup of sugar, 2 whole eggs, and 1 egg yolk in the bowl of a stand mixer fitted with the whisk attachment. Add the vanilla and almond extract and the lemon zest (if using) and beat until the mixture is light and airy, about 3 minutes. Switch to the paddle attachment and sprinkle in the baking powder and flour. Mix on low or medium-low just until the flour is worked in. Pour in the nuts and mix on low just until incorporated. Scrape the dough onto a sheet of reusable wrap or plastic wrap and refrigerate for at least 1 hour or overnight. The dough is easier to handle when chilled.

2. Preheat the oven to 350° F (180° C). Line two rimmed baking sheets with parchment. Divide the dough into 4 quarters. On a lightly floured surface, roll and shape each piece of dough into a log about 1½ to 2 inches (4 to 5 cm) wide and 9 inches (23 cm) long. Place the logs crosswise on the baking sheet—you should be able to fit all four with 2 inches (5 cm) between them. Press down to flatten them out a bit and make the tops even. Lightly beat the egg white and brush it over the tops of the logs; sprinkle the remaining 2 tablespoons of sugar.

3. Bake for 20 to 25 minutes, until lightly browned on top and just set—the loaves should be springy to the touch and there should be cracks on the surface. Transfer the baking sheet to a wire rack for 5 minutes. Gently slide an offset spatula under each loaf to loosen it from the baking sheet. Transfer the loaves to the rack to cool for 30 minutes. Lower the oven temperature to 300° F (150° C).

4. Place the loaves, one at a time, on a cutting board, and use a santoku knife or a serrated bread knife to cut them into ¾-inch- (2-cm-) thick slices. Arrange the slices standing upright on the baking sheet, in batches if necessary, and bake for 15 to 20 minutes. They will not feel completely firm when touched, but they will crisp up as they cool. Transfer the slices to wire racks to cool completely. Store the cantucci in an airtight container for up to 1 month.

CANTUCCIONI *(Tuscany)*

Oversize Soft Biscotti

I spent a coffee-fueled morning looking for inspiration in the streets of Siena's historic center, stopping in at every café and pasticceria I came across to down a shot of espresso and ogle and taste their selections of ricciarelli (see page 114) and other cookies. At Panificio Il Magnifico I found an unexpected and delightful stand out: cantuccioni. The name means big cantucci, and these oversize sliced cookies do share some similarities with the famous crunchy twice-baked cantucci di Prato (see page 98). But they are also entirely their own thing.

The sugar-coated cookies are first baked as small, fat loaves. Then they are cut into large, oblong slices, fitted back together, and packaged in cellophane bags tied with red raffia string. I bought a package, expecting something like classic crunchy coffeehouse biscotti. Instead, the cookies were soft, tender, and crumbly. I realized they had been baked just once, rather than twice like classic cantucci. They were so good dunked in cappuccino that I resolved to figure out how to make them at home. It took a few tries, but here they are. I know I shouldn't play favorites with the cookies in this book, but these might be among my top five.

By the way, these cookies make an artful holiday or hostess gift packaged in cellophane bags and tied with colorful string, the way Panificio Il Magnifico does it.

MAKES 18 TO 20 COOKIES

4 ounces (1 stick; 113 g) unsalted butter, cut into ½-inch (12-mm) cubes, at cool room temperature (65° F; 18° C)

1 cup (200 g) sugar

3 large eggs, at room temperature

2 teaspoons pure vanilla extract

½ teaspoon pure almond extract

1 tablespoon Punch Abruzzo, or dark or Jamaican rum (see page 18)

2¾ cups (340 g) unbleached all-purpose flour

1½ teaspoons baking powder

½ teaspoon fine salt

TO FINISH

Flour for the work surface

1 large egg

2 tablespoons pearl sugar or granulated sugar

1. Place the butter and sugar in the bowl of a stand mixer fitted with the paddle attachment. Beat on medium, then high, until well incorporated and fluffy, about 3 minutes. Drop in the eggs, one at a time, beating well after each addition. Beat in the vanilla and almond extracts and liqueur until thoroughly mixed in.

2. In a separate bowl, whisk together the flour, baking powder, and salt. Pour this into the butter-and-sugar mixture and mix on low just until incorporated. Scrape the dough out onto a piece of reusable wrap or plastic wrap and pat it into a disk. Wrap tightly and refrigerate until fully chilled—at least 2 hours and up to overnight.

3. Preheat the oven to 350° F (180° C). Line a rimmed baking sheet with parchment. Lightly flour a work surface and your hands. Divide the dough in half and shape each piece into an oval about 7 x 5 inches (18 x 13 cm), and ¾ inch (2 cm) thick. Place the loaves on the baking sheet, taking care to leave at least 3 inches (8 cm) between them.

4. In a small bowl, whisk the egg with 1 tablespoon water. Brush this on the surface of both loaves. Sprinkle the loaves with pearl sugar or granulated sugar—or one of each. Bake for 25 to 28 minutes, until the loaves are golden and set, with cracks on the surface. Transfer the baking sheet to a wire rack to cool for 15 minutes. Then transfer the loaves from the baking sheet to the rack to cool completely.

5. With a sharp santoku or serrated knife, cut the loaves on the bias into 1-inch-(2½-cm-) thick oblong slices. You should end up with 10 slices per loaf, including the ends. Store the cantuccioni in an airtight container for up to 2 weeks. If you want to package them to give away, be sure they are completely cooled before fitting them into cellophane bags and tying with ribbon.

CANTUCCIONI DEL BAR *(general)*

Coffeehouse Biscotti

These oversize biscotti pay homage to the giant cookie slices displayed in jars in coffee houses and fancy bakeries the world over. They come in all flavors—studded with dried fruit and nuts or chocolate chips, dipped in white chocolate, or drizzled with thick icing or salted caramel, and in countless other combinations.

Here, I've opted for toasted hazelnuts in the dough, a generous glug of vanilla, and a double drizzle of bittersweet chocolate and milk chocolate. If ever a cookie was meant for dunking in a glass of cold milk or your morning latte, it is this one.

I use a shallow loaf pan known as a biscotti pan to bake these. Its dimensions are 5½ x 12 inches (14 x 30 cm) and it creates the perfect size loaf that can be neatly cut into thick, oversize slices (see Sources, page 225). If you don't have such a pan, you can easily mold the dough by hand into a single loaf of similar dimensions and bake the loaf on a parchment-lined baking sheet.

MAKES 16 EXTRA-LARGE SLICES

2 cups (240 g) unbleached all-purpose flour

1 cup (200 g) sugar

1 teaspoon baking powder

¼ teaspoon fine salt

1 rounded cup (140 g) skinned and toasted hazelnuts (see page 26)

2 ounces (4 tablespoons; 57 g) unsalted butter, at cool room temperature (65° F; 18° C), cut into cubes

2 large eggs, lightly beaten

1 tablespoon pure vanilla extract

3 ounces (85 g) bittersweet chocolate, melted (see page 27)

3 ounces (85 g) milk chocolate, melted (see page 27)

1. Preheat the oven to 350° F (180° C). Line a 5½ x 12-inch (15 x 30-cm) biscotti pan or a rimmed baking sheet with parchment.

2. Combine the flour, sugar, baking powder, and salt in the bowl of a stand mixer fitted with the paddle attachment. Mix briefly on low speed. Add the hazelnuts and mix on low to combine and break up some of the nuts. Drop in the cubes of butter and beat until they have broken up into little pieces and are well mixed into the flour.

3. In a small bowl, lightly beat the eggs with the vanilla. With the mixer on low, pour in the egg mixture and beat until a soft, slightly sticky mass of dough has formed. Gather the dough into a ball and transfer it to the biscotti pan, if using. Otherwise, scrape it onto the prepared baking sheet. Use your hands and fingers to stretch and pat the dough into a loaf roughly 4 inches x 10 inches (10 x 25½ cm). Press down on the loaf to flatten it out a bit and make the top even.

4. Bake in the middle of the oven for 30 to 35 minutes, or until the loaf is set and lightly browned; it should be springy to the touch and there should be cracks on the surface. Transfer the biscotti pan or baking sheet to a wire rack to cool for 5 minutes, then transfer the loaf to the rack to cool for another 20 minutes. Lower the oven temperature to 300° F (150° C).

5. Place the cooled loaf on a cutting board and, using a santoku knife or a serrated bread knife, cut it crosswise into ¾-inch- (2-cm-) thick slices. Arrange the slices standing upright on a parchment-lined baking sheet and bake for 25 to 30 minutes, until lightly browned and crisped. Transfer the slices to the wire rack to cool completely. The slices may not be completely firm when they come out of the oven, but they will continue to crisp up as they cool. Melt the bittersweet and milk chocolate separately (see page 27), while the biscotti cool.

6. Place a wire rack over a baking sheet lined with waxed paper or parchment. Arrange the biscotti upright on the rack. Dip a fork into the melted bittersweet chocolate and wave it back and forth over the biscotti to create drizzles, droplets, and splotches. Do the same with the melted milk chocolate. Place the baking sheet in a cool spot (I put mine in the garage when it is cold outside) or the fridge for 30 minutes to set the chocolate. Let the biscotti return to room temperature before serving. Store the biscotti in an airtight container for up to 10 days.

FROLLINI AL FARRO *(Umbria and other regions)*

Crispy Farro Cookies

Grocery stores and bakeries across Italy sell packages of *frollini* cookies. The word is a catchall term for crumbly cookies made with pasta frolla—they can be tender, crispy, or crunchy, but they should also leave a little trail of crumbs when you bite into them. There are all sorts of frollini in the world of Italian cookies, some made with all-purpose flour, others with whole wheat or heirloom wheat, and others with cornmeal.

In Umbria, there is a mill and bakery in the Valle d'Assisi that makes some of the best frollini cookies I've ever had. Granarium is a "zero kilometer" family-run operation, in which the grains that produce the bakery's bread, pizza, cookies, and pastries, are all grown and stone-milled right on the property. Everything is made on-site, in a low-slung building flanked by a row of silos painted forest green.

This recipe is my homemade take on Granarium's wonderfully rustic farro cookies. They crunch heartily when you bite into them and, yes, they leave a telltale trail of crumbs. You'll need a thin wooden dowel, such as a kebab skewer, to poke holes into the surface of the cookies before baking. This keeps them from puffing up too much. If you don't have a skewer, use the tines of a fork.

MAKES ABOUT 24 COOKIES

5 ounces (11 tablespoons; 150 g) unsalted butter, cut into ½-inch (12-mm) cubes, at cool room temperature

⅔ cup (130 g) granulated sugar

2 large eggs, at room temperature

Zest of 1 small lemon

1 teaspoon pure vanilla extract

¼ teaspoon fine salt

2 cups (240 g) unbleached all-purpose flour, plus more for rolling

Scant 1 cup (110 g) farro flour (see page 16)

1 teaspoon baking powder

1. Place the butter and sugar in the bowl of a stand mixer fitted with the paddle attachment and beat, first on medium and then on high, until well combined and fluffy. Drop in the eggs, one at a time, beating well after each addition. Beat in the lemon zest, vanilla extract, and salt. Pour in the flours and baking powder and mix on medium-low just until the flour is incorporated. Pat the dough into a disk, wrap it in reusable wrap or plastic wrap, and refrigerate it until thoroughly chilled for at least 2 hours–overnight is best.

2. Remove the dough from the refrigerator and let it sit out for about 30 minutes to warm up. Preheat the oven to 375° F (190° C). Line two rimmed baking sheets with parchment.

3. Lightly flour a work surface. Roll the dough out to a large circle about ¼ inch (6 mm) thick. Use a 2 x 3-inch (5 x 8-cm) rectangular cookie cutter, or a 3-inch (8-cm) round cookie cutter to stamp out cookies. If you have cutters with scalloped edges, all the prettier. Arrange the cookies on the baking sheets, 12 per sheet. With the blunt end of a wooden skewer, such as a kebab skewer, prick a series of holes into each cookie, taking care not to poke all the way through. Docking the dough in this way will keep it from puffing up unevenly during baking.

4. Bake the cookies, one sheet at a time, in the middle of the oven for about 18 minutes, until they are honey brown and set. Set the baking sheets on wire racks to cool for 20 minutes; then transfer the cookies from the baking sheet to the racks to cool completely. Store the cookies in an airtight container for up to 1 month–they really keep well.

GIULIA'S CAVALLUCCI SENESI *(Tuscany)*

Spiced Christmas Cookies from Siena

Cavallucci means "little horses" in Italian, but these cookies look nothing like the noble animal for which they are named. They are slightly misshapen, dense rounds, with some cracking and crevices on the surface, but their appearance is deceptive. Look closer and you'll find hints of the treasure within—glints of candied orange peel, walnut pieces, and flecks of warm spices.

This recipe is courtesy of my friend Giulia Scarpaleggia, an esteemed cookbook author and cooking teacher from the Tuscan countryside outside of Siena.

Giulia grew up with cavallucci; the cookies were a favorite of her grandfather, and they are still an important Christmas tradition in her house. The spice blend used in these cookies is called cavallucci spice, a mix of cinnamon, coriander, nutmeg, and aniseed. It is absolutely beguiling. It's easy to make, too. Look for Cavallucci Spice in the Basics and Embellishments Chapter (page 216).

Cavallucci date to the early sixteenth century. The prevailing origin story is that they were given to travelers on horseback passing through the countryside when they stopped to give their animals a rest. Is that history or lore? I can't say for sure, but I can easily picture it—a weary traveler riding through the soft misty hills, past stands of cypress trees, heading toward a distant light where a warm fire and spiced cookies await.

Like several other traditional cookies in this book, this recipe calls for baker's ammonia, or ammonium carbonate, as its raising agent. It gives cookies a lighter, crunchier crumb, but it has a powerful and unpleasant aroma. This dissipates as the cookies bake, with no lingering traces once they are cool. You can read more about baker's ammonia on page 17.

MAKES 24 COOKIES

2⅔ cups (320 g) unbleached all-purpose flour, plus more for shaping the cookies

2 tablespoons confectioners' sugar

1½ cups (150 g) walnut halves, roughly chopped

¾ cup (100 g) diced mixed candied citrus peel—I use orange and lemon (see page 220)

2 tablespoons Cavallucci Spice (page 216)

1 teaspoon baker's ammonia (see page 17) or baking powder

1 cup (200 g) granulated sugar

⅓ cup plus 1½ tablespoons (100 ml) water

1. Preheat the oven to 350° F (180° C). Line two rimmed baking sheets with parchment.

2. In a large bowl, combine the flour, confectioners' sugar, walnuts, diced citrus peel, cavallucci spices, and baker's ammonia. Mix thoroughly.

3. Combine the granulated sugar and water in a small saucepan and set on medium heat. This next step is crucial: as soon as the sugar has melted into a cloudy syrup, remove the pan from the heat. Make sure the syrup does not boil or you will end up with rock-hard cavallucci.

4. Pour the hot syrup into the bowl of dry ingredients and mix thoroughly with a wooden spoon or sturdy silicon spatula. The dough will be stiff.

5. Generously flour a clean surface and shape the dough into 2 rough logs about 1½ inches (4 cm) thick. Cut each log into 12 equal pieces. Roll each piece into a ball about the size of a small apricot, then gently flatten by pressing each ball with your thumb. Arrange the cavallucci on the baking sheets, leaving at least 1 inch (2½ cm) between them.

6. Bake the cookies, one sheet at a time, in the middle of the oven for about 15 minutes; they should be pale in color and slightly soft to the touch. Transfer the baking sheets to wire racks and let the cookies cool completely. Store the cavallucci in an airtight container for up to 1 week.

MATTONCINI *(Tuscany)*

Hazelnut and Jam Bar Cookies

Massimiliano and Ricardo Lunardi grew up in their parents' bread bakery in Quarrata, a small suburb of Pistoia, north of Florence. Their father turned out rustic loaves and *schiacciata*—Tuscany's version of focaccia—while their mom managed the shop, which sold deli products in addition to bread. Now, the brothers run the show and have turned the humble bakery into an expansive operation called Fratelli Lunardi (Brothers Lunardi), with two charming shops and a new state-of-the-art commercial baking facility, though they continue to use the wood-fired oven for some of their bread.

Massimiliano, who runs the bakery side of the business, creates the recipes himself, among them a range of traditional and inventive cookies. The bakery's cantucci, classic twice-baked Tuscan cookies, in the bakery's eye-catching red, white, and black packaging, are well known far beyond Quarrata. These rich butter-pastry sandwiches filled with coarsely chopped nuts and fig jam, on the other hand, can only be bought in the shop. They were among my favorites. Lucky for us, Massimiliano was kind enough to share his recipe. I made only one minor change, swapping in hazelnuts for walnuts. If you prefer walnuts, you can stick to the original. Either way, you'll be pleased.

Note that it will take a couple of days to prepare these cookies, as the dough needs to be refrigerated twice before baking.

MAKES 36 SANDWICH COOKIES

PASTRY

4 cups (480 g) pastry flour or unbleached all-purpose flour, plus more for the work surface

1½ cups (130 g) confectioners' sugar

½ teaspoon fine salt

Finely grated zest of 1 lemon

8 ounces (2 sticks; 227 g) cold, unsalted butter, cut into ½-inch (12-mm) cubes

2 large eggs, lightly beaten

FILLING

1½ cups (375 g) Fig and Chocolate Preserves with Cognac (page 212) or store-bought fig jam

2 cups (270 g) skinned and toasted hazelnuts, coarsely chopped into big pieces (see page 26)

1. To make the pastry: Combine the flour, confectioners' sugar, salt, and lemon zest in the work bowl of a food processor fitted with the metal blade. Pulse to mix thoroughly. Distribute the butter around the inside of the bowl and pulse to break it up into small pieces. Pour in the eggs and pulse until the mixture begins to clump together. Turn it out onto a sheet of reusable wrap or plastic wrap and pat it into a disk. Wrap tightly and refrigerate for several hours and up to overnight.

2. Line a rimmed baking sheet with parchment. Remove the dough from the refrigerator and let it soften for 30 minutes. Divide the dough into 2 pieces. On a lightly floured work surface, roll each piece out into a 9½-inch (24-cm) square. Trim the edges to make two tidy 9-inch (23-cm) squares. Place one square on the parchment-lined baking sheet. Spread half the preserves over the surface of the dough, spreading it out almost to the edges. Sprinkle the chopped hazelnuts on top. Dollop the rest of the preserves on top. Cover with the second square of dough, pressing down on the top to help it adhere and to prevent rogue hazelnuts from escaping. Wrap the whole thing tightly in plastic wrap, set it on the baking sheet, and refrigerate overnight.

3. Preheat the oven to 375° F (190° C). Line two rimmed baking sheets with parchment. Remove the chilled block of dough from the refrigerator, unwrap it, and set it on a cutting board. With a sharp knife, cut it into 36 even squares, each about 1½ inches (4 cm). Arrange them on the baking sheets, leaving about 1 inch (2½ cm) of space between them. Place one sheet in the refrigerator while you bake the other. Bake the cookie sandwiches in the middle of the oven for 20 to 25 minutes, until they are set and golden brown. Transfer the baking sheets to wire racks to cool for 20 minutes, then transfer the cookies from the baking sheets to the racks to cool completely.

Store the cookies in an airtight container for up to 1 week.

LUNARDI

PASTARELLE DI SAN NICOLÒ *(Umbria)*

Wine and Anise Cookies for the Feast of Saint Nicolò

The town of Bevagna, in Umbria, knows how to put on a party. Every June, the village throws a days-long medieval festival with an extensive crafts market, archery contests, food, and more. In December, the town celebrates its children with the Feast of Saint Nicolò. On the evening of December 6, the "saint" arrives at the gates of town on a cart pulled by a donkey, bearing gifts and packets of these anise-scented cookies.

Pastarelle are traditional wine and olive oil cookies. There is no egg in the dough—just flour, sugar, wine, a pinch each of baking powder and salt, and flecks of aniseeds. And while they look rather plain, they are anything but. Toasting the seeds lightly before adding them to the dough infuses the cookies with the spice's sweet, warm flavor and an aroma that hovers somewhere between licorice and chamomile.

At La Bottega del Forno, a fabulous bakery in town (see Tozzetti all' Alchermes on page 128), owner Dorita Polticchia always has a basketful in her display case because they are so popular. She hand-cuts her pastarelle into rustic squares and rectangles. I sometimes do the same, using a fluted pastry wheel to give the cookies pretty edges. Other times, I use cookie cutters to stamp out shapes. Either method works.

MAKES ABOUT 48 COOKIES

1½ tablespoons whole aniseeds

¾ cup (150 g) granulated sugar

½ cup (120 ml) extra-virgin olive oil

½ cup (120 ml) Umbrian white wine, such as Orvieto, or a similar off-dry wine

¼ teaspoon fine salt

3¼ to 3½ cups (390 to 420 g) unbleached all-purpose flour

1 teaspoon baking powder

1. Preheat the oven to 350° F (180° C). Line two rimmed baking sheets with parchment. Spread the aniseeds out in a small dry skillet set over medium heat. Toast, stirring the seeds now and again, for 2 to 3 minutes, until they turn a shade or two darker and you can smell their warm chamomile-like scent. Transfer them to a small bowl or plate to cool completely.

2. Place the sugar and olive oil in the bowl of a stand mixer fitted with the paddle attachment. Mix on medium-low to medium for 2 to 3 minutes to combine the ingredients and allow the sugar to begin to dissolve a little. Pour in the wine, add the salt and cooled aniseeds, and beat for another minute to incorporate them. Add 3¼ cups (390 g) of flour and the baking powder and mix until just incorporated. The dough should be somewhat soft, shiny, and raggedy, but stiff enough to roll out. If it's too soft, add more flour by the tablespoon. Once the flour is incorporated, pat the dough into a ball and place it on a lightly floured work surface.

3. Lightly flour a rolling pin and roll the dough into a large circle or rectangle about ¼ inch (6 mm) thick. Use cookie cutters or a fluted pastry wheel to cut out cookies that are about 2½ inches (6 cm) in size. You should end up with about 48 cookies. Set them on the baking sheets, about 24 per sheet. You can space them fairly close together as they won't expand much.

4. Bake the cookies, one sheet at a time, in the middle of the oven, for 18 to 20 minutes, until set with browned edges. The cookies will remain pale on the surface. Transfer the baking sheets to wire racks to cool completely. Once cooled, store the pastarelle in an airtight container for 2 weeks.

PUPAZZE FRASCATANE *(Lazio)*

Spiced Honey Dough Dolls from Frascati

Frascati is one of the picturesque hilltop Castelli Romani towns located in the Albian hills east of Rome. It is famous for the Villas of Tusculum, opulent vacation residences that were built for Rome's noble families; and also, for its decidedly more pedestrian, pleasant, dry white wine, named for the town.

Among locals, Frascati is also known for these buxom doll cookies—the word *pupazze* is Roman dialect for "dolls"—made with a traditional spiced honey and olive oil dough. They are a Christmas specialty, and in the weeks leading up to the holiday, bakeries sell them packaged in cellophane. Each bakery has its own particular mix of spices and other ingredients to distinguish its pupazze from others. But the dolls have several attributes in common. They stand on their tiptoes in a ballerina stance with their arms akimbo, and they have three breasts—two for milk, one for wine, so the story goes. The pupazze are said to represent *mammane*—women who looked after babies during the grape harvest. In addition to milk, fussy babies were sometimes given a nip of wine to help calm them down.

They also symbolize fertility, abundance, and the earth's generosity, themes reflected in the dough's ingredients. The original dough yields a rather tough cookie, so I have updated it to make it more tender and appeal to modern tastes—namely mine! You'll need a large gingerbread girl cookie cutter or a homemade stencil to make these dolls. I use a 10 x 4-inch (25½ x 10-cm) parchment stencil drawn by my son's partner, Jenna. It looks just like the traditional pupazze from Frascati. Grazie, Jenna!

MAKES 4 DOLLS

2 cups (240 g) unbleached all-purpose flour, plus more as needed

2 teaspoons ground cinnamon

2 teaspoons ground ginger

½ teaspoon ground cloves

½ teaspoon baking powder

¼ teaspoon baking soda

⅛ teaspoon fine salt

½ cup (170 g) honey

¼ cup (60 ml) extra-virgin olive oil

1 large egg, lightly beaten

TO DECORATE

Silver dragées

Cinnamon red hot candies

Whole cloves

1. Measure the flour, cinnamon, ginger, cloves, baking powder, baking soda, and salt into a large bowl and whisk to combine.

2. Make a well in the center of the bowl and add the honey, olive oil, and egg. Stir everything until the mixture comes together as a sticky dough. It will be soft and fudgy. If it is too soft to hold its shape at all, stir in a little more flour–up to ¼ cup (30 g). Scrape the dough onto a sheet of reusable wrap or plastic wrap, wrap tightly, and refrigerate for 2 hours, or until well chilled.

3. Preheat the oven to 325° F (165° C). Line two rimmed baking sheets with parchment. Lightly flour a work surface, the rolling pin, and the top of the dough. Cut the dough into quarters and set three quarters aside. Roll the remaining piece into a ¼-inch (6-mm) thick oval or rectangle big enough to cut out a 10 x 4-inch (25½ x 10-cm) doll–or whatever the dimensions of your stencil or cookie cutter. If you're using a stencil, place it right on top of the dough and trace around it with a sharp paring knife. Otherwise, cut out shapes with a cookie cutter.

4. Set the doll on one of the prepared baking sheets–you should have enough room for 2 or 3 per sheet. Use the scraps from the rolled-out dough to roll out three chickpea-size breasts and affix them to the doll, using a tiny bit of water if needed to make them adhere. Roll out more scraps to make additional flourishes, such as hair. Use a fluted pastry wheel to make a patterned imprint on the doll's skirt. Press in 2 dragées for the eyes, a cinnamon red hot for the mouth, and whole cloves for nipples (if you want to get anatomical).

5. Roll out, cut, and decorate more dolls and set them on the baking sheets. Bake, one sheet at a time, in the middle of the oven for 10 to 15 minutes, until the cookies are set

and lightly browned. Transfer the baking sheets to wire racks to cool for 10 minutes, then transfer the cookies to the racks to cool completely. Store the pupazze in an airtight container for up to 2 weeks.

BAKER'S NOTE: *These ladies are traditionally enjoyed unadorned. However, this old-fashioned spiced honey dough goes beautifully with lemon icing. Make a batch of the lemon icing on page 173 and use it to frost the pupazze.*

RICCIARELLI *(Tuscany)*

Almond Cookies from Siena

Siena is an exquisite medieval city, built of bricks, sunbaked in color, and crowned by a gilded marble-faced cathedral and *duomo*. Among many attributes, the city is home to one of Italy's most famous piazzas, the fan-shaped Piazza del Campo, with its tall, narrow bell tower. For centuries, the piazza has been the scene of a convivial summer jousting competition known as Il Palio that continues to this day.

Siena is also famous for its Renaissance sweets, such as *panforte*, a dense, nut- and fruit-studded spice cake, and these tender almond cookies. Ricciarelli are made with few ingredients—ground almonds, egg white, sugar, and orange zest. They have a delicate, powdered sugar-coated surface and a tender interior. When you bite into one, you set off a tiny dust storm of sugar. The cookies are said to be named for their passing resemblance to Persian-style curled-toe slippers. They were once a refined treat reserved for the city's nobility, and were available only during the Christmas season. Now, they are sold year-round in all of Siena's pastry shops and cafés, and each version is slightly different than the next.

I've tweaked my own ricciarelli recipe over the years. Most recently, I've added finely chopped candied orange peel to the dough in place of orange zest. You'll find the recipe for candied peel on page 220. It's a bit of a project, but worth the effort. However, if you prefer to keep it simple and in line with tradition, use fresh orange zest instead. Note that the dough for these cookies benefits from an overnight rest in the refrigerator.

MAKES 24 COOKIES

2 lightly packed cups (200 g) superfine blanched almond flour

2 cups (240 g) confectioners' sugar, plus ½ cup (50 g) for coating the cookies

3 tablespoons minced Candied Orange Peel (page 220) or the finely grated zest of 1 large orange

¼ to ½ teaspoon pure almond extract

2 large (64 g) egg whites

½ teaspoon freshly squeezed lemon juice

1. Sift the almond flour into a large bowl, then sift in the confectioners' sugar. Stir in the candied orange peel, working it in well—I use my fingers. Sprinkle in the almond extract and stir to combine.

2. In a clean stainless-steel bowl, beat the egg whites with a hand mixer until they become foamy. Add the lemon juice and beat until the whites billow to soft peaks. Alternatively, you can use a stand mixer fitted with the whisk attachment to beat the egg whites.

3. Scoop the egg whites into the bowl with the almond flour and gently fold them in until you have a stiff, sticky paste. Cover the bowl and refrigerate overnight.

4. Preheat the oven to 325° F (165° C). Line two rimmed baking sheets with parchment. Dust a work surface with some of the remaining ½ cup (60 g) confectioners' sugar. Place the chilled dough on the sugar and roll it into a log about 2 inches (5 cm) in diameter and 10 inches (25½ cm) long. Keep your hands lightly coated with sugar to prevent the dough from sticking to them. Cut the log on the diagonal into ¾ inch (2 cm) thick slices. Shape them into ovals with slightly pointed ends. Set the cookies on a prepared baking sheet, about 12 per sheet, leaving a little space between them.

5. Very lightly moisten your fingers and gently press the tops of the ricciarelli to flatten them slightly. Dust liberally with the remaining confectioners' sugar. Let the cookies sit, uncovered, for 1 to 2 hours to dry out.

6. Bake, one sheet at a time, in the middle of the oven for 12 to 14 minutes, or until the cookies' tops have cracked a bit and they are tinged around the edges with pale gold. They should hardly brown at all. Transfer the baking sheets to wire racks and let the cookies cool completely.

7. Arrange the ricciarelli on a decorative platter and dust with additional confectioners' sugar before serving. They are best enjoyed with a small glass of Vin Santo, a sweet Tuscan dessert wine. Store in an airtight container for up to 1 week.

SERPETTE *(Lazio)*

Little Snake Cookies

The Castelli Romani are fifteen towns located in the hills southeast of Rome. They were once popular vacation destinations for wealthy families looking to temporarily escape the capital during summer. Among them are Ariccia, famous for its porchetta, whole spit-roasted pig seasoned with herbs and spices; and Castel Gandolfo, overlooking Lake Albano, where Roman Catholic popes have summered since 1623.

Among these hills dotted with vineyards and ancient structures is the town of Monte Porzio Catone, where in the main piazza you'll find Panificio Egidi. The bakery has been turning out these S-shaped butter cookies for five generations. They are a proper dunking cookie, chubby, light and crumbly, made with a classic pasta frolla dough. This is what I like to call an "unplugged" recipe, meaning that the dough is mixed by hand, just as Signora Graziella, the current matriarch, makes her serpette to this day. If you want to speed things up a bit, you can use a hand or stand mixer to mix the wet ingredients but be sure to fold the dry ingredients in by hand so as not to overwork the dough.

MAKES 16 COOKIES

½ cup (100 g) granulated sugar

2 large eggs

3½ ounces (7 tablespoons; 100 g) unsalted butter, melted and cooled

Finely grated zest of ½ lemon

Finely grated zest of ½ orange

2 cups (240 g) unbleached all-purpose flour, plus more for the work surface

1 cup (120 g) pastry flour

1 teaspoon baking powder

¼ teaspoon fine salt

TO FINISH

1 large egg

2 to 3 tablespoons granulated sugar

1. Preheat the oven to 375° F (190° C). Line a rimmed baking sheet with parchment.

2. Combine the sugar and eggs in a large bowl and beat with a hand whisk until lightened and foamy. You can also use a hand mixer for this step. Whisk in the melted and cooled butter, a little at a time, followed by the lemon and orange zests.

3. In a separate bowl, whisk together the flours, baking powder, and salt. Pour this into the wet ingredients and stir with a spatula until well incorporated. Knead briefly with your hands to make a cohesive dough.

4. Divide the dough into 16 equal pieces—they should weigh about 1½ ounces (40 g) each. If the dough is sticky, lightly flour your work surface. Roll each piece into a fat finger about 6 inches (16 cm) long and bend it into an S shape. Arrange the cookies on the baking sheet, in four rows of four.

5. In a small bowl, beat the egg with 1 tablespoon of water. Brush this over the tops of the cookies and sprinkle them with sugar. Bake for 20 to 25 minutes, until they are set and golden in color, with a few light cracks on top. Transfer the baking sheet to a wire rack to cool for 20 minutes; then transfer the cookies from the baking sheet to the rack to cool completely. Store the serpette in an airtight container for up to 2 weeks.

SETTEMBRINI *(Umbria and other regions)*

September Fig Rolls

I can't be the only one who loved Fig Newtons as a child. My mom often packed one or two in my lunch box, and I always looked forward to them. It was only later that I realized she probably bought them because they reminded her of the many varieties of fig-filled cookies in Italy.

Scope out the cookie aisle at any Italian supermarket and you will surely see packages of Mulino Bianco Settembrini cookies on the shelves. The company is one of Italy's largest commercial producers of cookies, if not the largest, and these are among the most popular. They are so named for their filling—figs. September is high fig season, when trees from north to south are laden with fruit and you'll find crates of them stacked at the markets. You'll find even better versions of this cookie at bakeries throughout central Italy—I had especially good ones in Umbria, with tender pastry and sweet centers. They inspired me to make my own.

Even if you've never been big on fig rolls, I encourage you to give these a try. The buttery dough, a variation of classic Pasta Frolla (page 206), is made with a little farro or whole wheat flour. The combination of orange zest and cinnamon in the dough, sweet fig preserves, and finely chopped walnuts really does evoke September. If you have access to fresh figs and are feeling ambitious, you can fill your cookies with homemade Fig and Chocolate Preserves with Cognac (page 212) or Fig Preserves with Citrus Zest (page 211). Store-bought works nicely, too.

MAKES 20 TO 24 COOKIES

DOUGH

- 1½ cups (180 g) unbleached all-purpose flour
- ½ cup (60 g) farro or whole wheat flour (see page 15)
- ⅔ cup (85 g) confectioners' sugar, plus more for dusting
- ¼ teaspoon fine salt
- ½ teaspoon ground cinnamon
- Zest of 1 small orange, such as a clementine
- 4 ounces (1 stick; 113 g) cold, unsalted butter, cut into ½-inch (12-mm) cubes
- 1 large egg, lightly beaten

FILLING

- 1 cup (300 g) Fig and Chocolate Preserves with Cognac (page 212) or Fig Preserves with Citrus Zest (page 211); or store-bought fig jam
- ½ cup (60 g) finely chopped walnuts

1. To make the dough: Combine the flours, confectioners' sugar, salt, cinnamon, and orange zest in the work bowl of a food processor fitted with the metal blade. Pulse to mix thoroughly. Distribute the butter around the inside of the bowl and pulse to break it up into small pieces. Pour in the egg and pulse until the mixture begins to clump together. Turn it out onto a sheet of reusable wrap or plastic wrap and pat it into a disk. Wrap tightly and refrigerate for several hours and up to overnight.

2. Preheat the oven to 350° F (180° C). Line two rimmed baking sheets with parchment. Remove the dough from the refrigerator and let it warm up for 30 minutes while you make the filling.

3. To make the filling: If the preserves are chunky, mash or chop them to break them up. Spoon them into a bowl and stir in the chopped walnuts.

3. Divide the dough in half and rewrap one half. On a floured surface, roll the piece of dough into a 12 x 5-inch (30 x 13-cm) rectangle, ¼ inch (6 mm) thick. Make sure the bottom is not sticking to the work surface. Spoon the jam in a center strip along the length of the dough. Carefully lift the long bottom edge over the jam, using a bench scraper to assist you if you have one. Roll the strip of dough upward until you reach the top edge and have a long log enclosing the filling. Keep rolling a little more to position the seam on the bottom of the log. Roll back and forth lightly to secure the seam, then press down along the top of the log to flatten it slightly.

4. Use the bench scraper or a knife to trim off the ends of the log. Cut the log into 1-inch (2½-cm) pieces. You should end up with 10 to 12 pieces. Arrange them on one baking sheet. Roll, fill, and cut the second piece of dough in the same way and arrange those pieces on the second baking sheet. Bake, one sheet at a time, in the middle of the oven, for 18 to 20 minutes, until the cookies are set and lightly browned on top, with nicely browned bottoms. You may get some cracking on the surface; this is fine. Transfer the baking sheets to wire racks to cool for 20 minutes, then transfer the settembrini to the wire racks to cool completely. Once cooled, you can dust them lightly with confectioners' sugar, but it's not necessary. I prefer their rustic, unadorned look.

Store settembrini in an airtight container for up to 1 week. The cookies will soften over time as the pastry absorbs moisture from the jam, but they will still be delicious.

MERINGHE DI ASSISI *(Umbria)*

Giant Meringues from Assisi

Walk about Assisi's meticulously maintained hilly cobbled streets and you will see meringues displayed in every bakery window, along with nougat and pastries. Some are as big as pie pumpkins, and they are often decorated with drippy drizzles of melted dark chocolate and colorful sprinkles. In recent years more and more bakeries (alas) have taken to selling meringues colored with food dyes, in pale shades of eggshell blue, green, and pink. While these might catch the eyes of tourists, I prefer the creamy hue of the natural ones.

I asked at several bakeries where the tradition of giant meringues came from. No one had a definitive answer, but one speculation that appealed to me was that the lofty cloudlike confections conjure heaven as it has been depicted for centuries in art. A more practical answer is that meringues are a good way to use up all the egg whites left over from making the copious amounts of pastry cream that are used as a gelato base or to fill cream puffs and other pastries.

The prettiest meringues I came across were from Pasticceria Sensi, an artfully decorated café with vaulted brick ceilings, cherubs painted on the walls, and a Venetian chandelier lighting the room. Their window showcased a plate of meringues that were about two sizes smaller than those sold at other shops, elegantly piped swirls lightly garnished with finely chopped nuts. Those became the inspiration for this recipe.

This method of baking the meringues slowly at low temperature and allowing them to cool completely in the oven produces perfectly crisp confections that are pale and creamy in color, with a dry, airy interior. They are crunchy throughout and produce a shower of delicious, messy crumbs when you bite into them. See page 27 for tips on how to successfully make meringues.

MAKES ABOUT 10 SOFTBALL-SIZE MERINGUES

4 large (130 g) egg whites, at room temperature

1 teaspoon lemon juice

1 cup (200 g) superfine sugar

1 teaspoon pure vanilla extract

¼ teaspoon fine salt

¼ cup (35 g) finely chopped toasted and skinned hazelnuts (see page 26)

1. Arrange two racks in the upper-middle and lower parts of the oven. Preheat the oven to 250° F (120° C) and line two rimmed baking sheets with parchment.

2. Make sure that both the stainless-steel bowl and whisk attachment are squeaky clean, with no residual fat from previous baking adventures, or your egg whites will not whip properly. Pour the egg whites into the bowl of the stand mixer fitted with the whisk attachment and whisk on medium until the egg whites are foamy.

3. Add the lemon juice and increase the speed to high. When the whites are creamy, gradually begin adding the sugar, 1 tablespoon at a time, with the mixer running. Once you have added ¾ cup (150 g) of the sugar, add the vanilla and salt. Add the final ¼ cup (50 g) of sugar, 1 tablespoon at a time, until you have added it all. The meringue should be smooth and glossy, with stiff peaks that hold upright or just barely curl at the tip.

Continued >>

4. Scoop the batter into a large piping bag fitted with a large open star tip. You may need to fill the bag in batches to keep the meringue from overflowing. Pipe large swirls of meringue—about the size of a tennis ball or slightly larger (they will expand as they bake) onto the baking sheets, 5 per sheet. Slide the baking sheets into the oven and bake for 45 minutes. Without opening the oven door, lower the heat to 200° F (90° C) and bake for 1 hour more. Turn the oven off and allow the meringues to cool completely before opening the oven door.

5. Once cool, remove the meringues from the oven and carefully lift them off the parchment. Set them on a rack if you're not serving them immediately. Otherwise, carefully pile them onto a decorative platter and serve. Store leftovers in an airtight container for up to 3 weeks.

BAKER'S NOTE: *Meringue batter is fussy. It is best not to make these cookies in humid conditions, as they absorb moisture from the atmosphere and may not dry properly or retain their crunch. I find it's best to make them in winter, when the weather is cold and dry.* *See page 27 for more tips on how to make meringues.*

Meringues are sweet, and one the size of a softball (or larger) might be too much to take in one sitting. You can enjoy these gentle giants in small doses, by crumbling them on top of ice cream or in an Eton Mess–style parfait, layered with whipped cream and strawberries.

You can also make bite-size meringues by using a smaller tip to pipe out smaller swirls of batter. Bake them the same way you would larger meringues, at 250° F (120° C) for 45 minutes, then at 200° F (90° C) for 1 hour. Leave them in the oven to cool completely.

VENTAGLIE *(Lazio . . . and everywhere)*

Puff Pastry Fans

This bakery classic is hardly exclusive to Italy, and it goes by many names: elephant ears, palmiers, and Prussians among them. More pastry than cookie, ventaglie are loved for their flaky texture and the sticky crunch of caramelized sugar that accompanies every bite. You will find ventaglie in bakeries across all over the world, ranging in size from mini to jumbos.

It was at Biscottificio Innocenti (see page 126), an historic cookie bakery in the heart of Rome, where I spied the biggest ventaglie I've ever seen—a row of plate-size elephant ears resting on a tray, each leaning seductively against another, just waiting for someone (me) to come along and grab one. I decided they needed to make an appearance here.

These ventaglie aren't quite as large, maybe more like salad plate size, which is still plenty generous. I use a "rough puff" dough to make them. It's easier than making classic puff pastry and it produces the same flaky results. You'll need to chill the dough several times during the process. Start the dough the day before you plan to serve the ventaglie.

MAKES ABOUT 15 MEDIUM-LARGE COOKIES

3 cups (360 g) unbleached all-purpose flour

¾ teaspoon fine salt

12 ounces (3 sticks; 340 g) cold unsalted butter, cut into ½-inch (12-mm) cubes

10 to 12 tablespoons ice-cold water

About 2 cups (400 g) superfine sugar

1. Whisk the flour and salt together in a large bowl. Scatter the cold butter cubes on top, then use your hands to gently toss them in the flour, coating them well. Begin to incorporate the butter into the flour by pressing the cubes with your fingers to flatten them into large flakes. Don't handle the butter too much, as your warm hands could cause it to soften and you'll end up with pasty dough rather than the layered, rough puff you're aiming for. Feel around in the bowl as you work, flattening any cubes of butter you come across and tossing everything together to keep the butter flakes coated with flour. It is fine if there are still some larger chunks of butter left in the bowl at this point.

2. Begin to sprinkle in the water, 1 to 2 tablespoons at a time, incorporating it by continuing to gently toss the mixture. You could use a large, sturdy spatula, but using your fingers will give you the best sense for when the dough is sufficiently moistened. After you have added 7 or 8 tablespoons of the water, the dough should begin to hold its shape as a raggedy mass, though it will still be too dry to stay together. Tip the mixture onto a clean work surface and pat it together with your hands. Sprinkle a couple more tablespoons of water on top and mix it in until the dough just starts to stick together. Gently pat it into a disk or rectangle–it will still be rough and raggedy–and cover tightly with plastic wrap. Refrigerate the dough for at least 2 hours and up to overnight. It should be completely firm and cold before you begin working with it again.

Continued >>

3. Lightly flour your work surface. Unwrap the chilled dough and set it on top. It will be too cold to roll, so let it sit for a couple of minutes, then pat it into a rough square. Begin rolling and lightly pounding it with your rolling pin to help it along. Lightly flour the dough and the pin as needed as you go to prevent it from sticking. Once the dough is somewhat malleable, roll it out into a 12-inch (30- cm) square that is ½ inch (12 mm) thick–no thinner. Flip the dough over once or twice as you roll to prevent it from sticking to the work surface, but don't overwork it. The flakes of butter in the dough will turn into buttery layers of crisp pastry when baked.

Fold the dough in half, from top to bottom. Then give it a quarter-turn and fold it in half again. Brush off any excess flour with a pastry brush. Wrap the dough tightly and return it to the refrigerator for 30 minutes.

4. Now it's time to begin the series of "business letter" folds that will create the pastry layers. Remove the dough from the fridge, and on a lightly floured work surface, roll it into a 9 x 12-inch (23 x 30-cm) rectangle. Fold it as you would a business letter, bringing the top down past the middle point, then folding the bottom up over it. Rewrap and refrigerate the dough for 30 minutes.

5. Remove the dough from the fridge, and on a lightly floured work surface, roll it into a 9 x 18-inch (23 x 46-cm) rectangle. Once more, fold it, top-down, then bottom-up, as you would a business letter. With a sharp knife, trim off the raggedy edges to neaten the rectangle. Wrap once more and refrigerate for 30 minutes.

6. Sprinkle the work surface liberally with some of the superfine sugar and set the dough on top of it. Sprinkle more sugar on the surface of the dough. Roll the dough into a 9 x 15-inch (23 x 38-cm) rectangle. Flip it over as you roll, sprinkling both sides with sugar. Don't skimp on the sugar! Once again, fold the dough into thirds. Wrap and refrigerate for 20 minutes–no longer, or the sugar will start to dissolve.

7. Sprinkle a light coating of sugar on the work surface if needed, and scatter some over the dough. Roll the dough into a long vertical rectangle, 20 inches (51 cm) in length and ⅜-inch (1 cm) in thickness. Trim off the raggedy ends and sides to make them neat and straight. Sprinkle a coating of sugar on top. Find the middle mark of the rectangle. Fold the top down twice, guiding it to reach the middle on the second fold. Now, fold the bottom up the same way, in two folds, so that the two folded ends of the dough meet in the center. Leave a small amount of space between them. Flip the bottom end over the top so that you have a tidy, six-layered rectangular block of dough. Coat the outside once more with sugar, reserving about ½ cup (100 g) for a final coating. Wrap and refrigerate for 25 minutes. Arrange two racks in the upper and lower thirds of the oven. Preheat the oven to 400° F (200° C) and line two rimmed baking sheets with parchment.

8. Remove the dough from the refrigerator. Trim off one end and slice the dough crosswise into ½-inch- (12-mm-) thick slices. You should end up with 14 to 16 V-shaped slices. Gently dip the slices in the remaining sugar to coat them on all sides. Arrange them on the baking sheets, leaving 2 inches (5 cm) between them and opening up the V shape slightly to help the cookies expand as they bake.

9. Slide the baking sheets into the oven and bake for 10 to 12 minutes, until the edges are tinged a light golden brown. Carefully flip the ventaglie over with a wide angled spatula. Return to the oven, rotating the baking sheets from top to bottom and from back to front for even cooking. Bake for another 5 to 8 minutes, until the ventaglie are a deep golden brown. Watch closely and take care not to overbake or they may burn. Transfer the baking sheets to wire racks and let the cookies cool completely on the sheets. Store the ventaglie in a tightly lidded container for up to 1 week.

COOKIE STORY

THE COOKIE LADY OF TRASTEVERE

There are two protagonists at Biscottificio Artigiano Innocenti, a cookie bakery in Rome. One is owner and principal baker Stefania Innocenti. The other is the enormous, custard-colored conveyor belt oven (see page 222) that takes up a chunk of real estate in the small shop.

It's true the oven is impressive—beautiful even. It is 85 feet (16 meters) long, extending from the kitchen at the back of the shop out to the front. Customers can watch trays of cookies as they slowly emerge from the oven's depths, like luggage passing through a TSA scanner. Stefania refers to the oven as "the heart of Biscottificio Innocenti." But anyone who steps foot in the bakery, located in Rome's ancient, offbeat Trastevere neighborhood, will understand almost immediately that it is Stefania, with her warm demeanor and expressive eyes framed by large glasses, who is the true heart of this place. It is she, along with two assistants, who bakes the many dozens of cookies arranged in baskets and trays in the store's windows, on tables, and on countertops. And it is she who you will likely find behind the counter, helping you select your cookies, weighing them, and placing them into bags or boxes. She starts her day at 7 a.m. and keeps going until the shop closes at 7:30 p.m.

"Yes, this is my work," she says. "But it is also family. My family has lived our life here. My siblings and I grew up here. And here I am."

Stefania's paternal grandfather, Sesto Innocenti, opened the bakery in 1949. Among the small selection of rustic cookies he sold were *gallette*—biscuits that the Italian military supplied to their troops. The hard biscuits were long keeping and stood in for fresh bread when it was not available. As the business grew, Sesto Innocenti hired the daughters of a friend to help out. One of those girls, Anna, fell for the baker's son Enzo. He loved her, too, but he was a seaman, and his work kept him away for long stretches. When Sesto grew ill, it was Anna who took command of the bakery and kept things running. She also took command of her romantic dilemma, telling Enzo that he had to choose between the sea and her. He chose Anna. Stefania is their daughter.

Although her parents are gone, their presence remains, in photographs tacked to the wall, and in that vintage oven. Buying the oven back in 1960 was another brilliant, intuitive move that Anna made, Stefania says. "It cost

5 million lire back then, as much as an apartment. But she had vision, and she was right because the oven still works and by now it is part of our identity." Trays of cookies are fed into the oven back in the kitchen, and depending on the temperature and speed at which the oven is set, they emerge at the other end perfectly baked.

The selection of cookies at Biscottificio Innocenti ranges from whole wheat cutouts and classic ring-shaped wine cookies to airy meringues and oversize *ventaglie*—puff pastry elephant ears (page 123). The bakery also sells seasonal and holiday treats, like panettone—sweet, yeasted Christmas bread. Many of the cookies Stefania bakes are from recipes created by her mother, including an old-fashioned breadstick-shaped cookie called *mielino*, or "little honey," named for the honey in the dough, and made for dunking in coffee. Over the years, she has added her own recipes to the mix. She uses her annual summer break in July to experiment with new ideas and test recipes. When I visited her, she let me taste her most recent addition, a pleasingly crumbly and rustic cookie made with farro flour and raisins.

Until recently, Biscottificio Innocenti has been a *passaparola*, or word-of-mouth, place, frequented by people who live in Trastevere or elsewhere in Rome, and Romans who have left the city but who make it a point to stop by the bakery whenever they return. In recent years, it has gained a loyal international Instagram following, thanks in part to Stefania's daughter, Manuela, who handles the shop's social media, and also to tour operator Rick Steves, whose guides have put the place on travelers' radar. (The first time he came by with a group, Stefania had no idea who he was.)

To Stefania, her bakery remains a neighborhood shop. She is often kept company by friends who live nearby. They perch on a stool near the cash register and chat about goings-on as she serves customers.

"Trastevere is like a big condominium," she says. We care about each other, we help one another." As if to prove her point, two priests walk in, greet her, and begin to talk about their project welcoming new immigrant families. Stefania listens and nods her head, handing each of them a jam-filled cookie without missing a beat.

TOZZETTI ALL' ALCHERMES *(Umbria)*

"Stubby" Cookies with Alchermes Liqueur

Bevagna is a medieval town not far from Assisi. It is small and strikingly beautiful, with a twelfth-century church, good restaurants, and a not-to-miss bakery called La Bottega del Forno, which has been operating since 1967. It was recommended to me by my friend Elizabeth Minchilli, who leads tours in the area and often buys packets of the bakery's cookies for her guests. Owner and baker Dorita Polticchia, daughter of the bakery's founder, turns out more than a dozen kinds of traditional Umbrian cookies, waking every morning at 4:30 a.m. and baking straight through till noon. Her assortment of rustic sweets, some round, some oblong, others sandwiched with jam and nuts, are enticingly displayed in woven reed baskets in the bakery's shop and café.

Among Dorita's creations are these pretty pink *tozzetti*, which roughly translates to "stubby ones." Think of these cookies as the Umbrian version of Tuscany's famous cantucci, the twice-baked crunchy, nut-studded slices that are meant to be dunked in wine or coffee (see page 98). The pink color in this particular version of tozzetti comes from the addition of Alchermes, a scarlet-hued liqueur infused with cinnamon, cloves, and other spices (see page 18). The liqueur's origins are Florentine, and it is popular in both Tuscan and Umbrian baking. After tasting these at Dorita's shop, I came home armed with a bottle of Alchermes, ready to work on my own version. The liqueur is not easy to find, so feel free to substitute a little red wine or another sweet liqueur, such as amaretto, and, if you like, a few drops of red food coloring.

MAKES 48 SMALL COOKIES

½ cup (70 g) golden raisins

½ cup (120 ml) warm water

2 cups (240 g) unbleached all-purpose flour, plus more for the work surface

1 cup (200 g) granulated sugar, plus more for sprinkling

½ teaspoon baking powder

¼ teaspoon fine sea salt

½ cup (75 g) whole raw almonds

1 large egg plus 1 egg white

4 tablespoons Alchermes liqueur, or red wine plus a few drops of red food coloring

1 teaspoon pure vanilla extract

1. Preheat the oven to 350° F (180° C). Line an 11 x 17-inch (28 x 43-cm) rimmed baking sheet with parchment. Place the golden raisins in a small bowl and cover them with the water. Let them steep while you assemble the rest of the ingredients.

2. Place the flour, sugar, baking powder, and salt in the work bowl of a stand mixer fitted with the paddle attachment. Mix on low speed to combine the ingredients. Pour in the almonds and mix briefly to incorporate them.

3. In a separate small bowl, lightly beat the whole egg and add it to the flour mixture, along with the Alchermes and vanilla extract. Mix on low until the dough starts to come together. Drain the raisins and mix on low. If the dough is dry and crumbly, dribble in about 1 tablespoon of the extra egg white, reserving a little for brushing on top after the dough is shaped. The consistency of the dough should be sticky, and it should come together as a soft ball.

4. Transfer the dough to a floured work surface and sprinkle a little flour on top. Flour your hands lightly and pat the dough into an oval or rectangle. Divide it into four equal pieces. Roll and pat each piece out into a long, skinny log about 1¼ to 1½ inches (3 to 4 cm) in diameter and 12 inches (30 cm) long. Position the logs lengthwise on the prepared baking sheet, leaving a couple of inches of space between them. Press down gently on the logs to flatten them out a bit.

5. Beat the remaining egg white lightly and brush it over the tops of the logs. Sprinkle ½ tablespoon of sugar along the tops of each log and slide the baking sheet into the oven. Bake for 20 to 25 minutes, or until barely browned and just set; the logs should be springy to the touch and there should be cracks on the surface. Transfer the baking sheet to a wire rack. Let the logs cool for 10 minutes; then gently pry them off the parchment and set them on the wire rack for 20 minutes.

6. Lower the oven temperature to 300° F (150° C). Place the cooled logs, one at a time, on a cutting board. Using a santoku knife or a serrated bread knife, cut them on the diagonal into 1-inch- (2½-cm-) thick slices. Arrange the slices on the baking sheet and bake for 20 to 25 minutes, until they are no longer moist in the middle. They might feel a bit soft, but they will become hard and crunchy as they cool. Transfer the baking sheet to the wire rack and let the tozzetti cool completely. The tozzetti will keep for up to 2 weeks in an airtight container at room temperature.

BAKER'S NOTE: *If you prefer a more tender cookie, omit the second bake. Let the logs cool, then slice them on the diagonal into 1-inch- (2½-cm-) thick slices. They will keep for about 5 days in an airtight container.*

COOKIES
OF THE SOUTH

Recipes and stories from

ABRUZZO, BASILICATA, CALABRIA, CAMPANIA, MOLISE, PUGLIA

Southern Italy may lack the economic wealth of the north, but it has its riches, including much natural beauty. Dramatic landscapes define these regions, from the Gran Sasso Mountain range in the heart of Abruzzo, where my mom was from, to volcanic Mount Vesuvius, south of Naples, in Campania; and from the green forests of rural Molise, land of my paternal grandmother, to the ancient silver-gray olive trees of Puglia, the heel of Italy's boot. Basilicata, the arch, lies along the Gulf of Taranto and extends north into the craggy peaks of the Dolomite Lucane, the southern Apennines. The long, narrow peninsula of Calabria, the so-called toe that points toward Sicily, is hilly and scrubby, rising up to La Sila, a mountainous plateau populated by dense coniferous forests.

Colorful, chaotic, spectacular Naples is the south's largest city, spilling down into the Mediterranean and fanning out along the coast. In Puglia, along the Adriatic, there is Bari, known for its Old Town, with its maze of streets and nonnas who sit outside hand-shaping and selling the city's famous ear-shaped orecchiette pasta. Farther south is Lecce, a beautiful baroque confection of a city, known as the "Florence of the South." Chieti, the city in Abruzzo where my mother was born and raised, is one of Italy's most ancient, where excavations have found evidence of prehistoric settlements. The city is perched on a hill that looks out toward the Adriatic on one side and toward the Apennines on the other.

In the countryside are olive groves and citrus groves and almond groves. Wild cherry trees. Fig trees that push up through cracks in the rocks. Grapevines. The fruits of all of these agricultural places are central to the rustic baking that continues to thrive here. Olive oil and lard take the place of butter and eggs in the dough. Cookies are often spiked with wine or perfumed with lemon zest or orange zest. Nuts, especially almonds—whole, chopped, ground—are ubiquitous. Rustic jams become filling in tender cookie rolls. In the most traditional recipes, honey or grape must syrup (page 215) is used instead of sugar to sweeten these sweets.

You'll find several recipes for wine cookies in this chapter, including Intorchiate (page 158), almond and white wine twists from Puglia. One of my favorite holiday cookies is also in this chapter. They are Mostaccioli (page 160)—almond cookies spiced with cinnamon and cloves and glazed with dark chocolate. Simpler, but no less seductive, are the Moretti Abruzzesi (page 135), chocolate amaretti—tender, chewy, a sort of Almond Joy in cookie form. On page 136 you'll meet Ilario, the baker who inspired them.

AMARETTI ABRUZZESI *(Abruzzo)*

Rustic Almond and Chocolate-Almond Cookies from Abruzzo

Abruzzo's version of amaretti, almond cookies, is decidedly rustic. The nuts are more coarsely ground than you'll find in other amaretti, and the cookies themselves are generous, oversize balls, plain in appearance but robust in flavor. Among the best I've had are those baked by Ilario Notarmuzzi at his *biscotteria* in Scanno, in the heart of Abruzzo's Apennine mountains. The village is designated one of Italy's most beautiful towns, and deservedly so. It is located deep within a gorge, built from stone and iron and ringed with mountains. It is famous for its filigree gold and silver jewelry and for its fine bobbin lace, known as *tombolo*.

Ilario uses fresh almonds, both sweet and bitter, from Puglia, to make his amaretti, along with egg whites, sugar, and lemon. His chocolate version, *moretti*, contain just almonds, egg whites, sugar, and cocoa powder (see Baker's Note). Ilario sells cookies by weight, packing them to order in plastic bags. One of my first errands, whenever I return to Abruzzo, is to make the considerable detour to visit Ilario and buy a bag of these satisfyingly chewy almond cookies. This recipe is my take, as Ilario has a strict policy against sharing his recipes. Read more about Ilario, one of my favorite Italian cookie bakers, on page 136.

MAKES 20 TO 24 COOKIES

2 cups (280 g) blanched skinned almonds

1 cup (200 g) sugar

1/8 teaspoon fine salt, optional

2 large (60 g) egg whites

1/4 teaspoon freshly squeezed lemon juice

1/4 teaspoon pure almond extract, optional

1. Place the almonds, sugar, and salt (if using), in the work bowl of a food processor fitted with the metal blade. Pulse until the almonds are reduced to tiny bits but not completely pulverized.

2. In a small bowl, whisk together the egg whites and lemon juice until light and foamy. Pour this through the feed tube, along with the almond extract (if using), and pulse until a sticky dough comes together. It should have some roughness from the tiny almond bits. Cover the bowl and let the dough rest for 1 hour at room temperature.

3. Preheat the oven to 325° F (165° C). Line two rimmed baking sheets with parchment. With a small cookie scoop or a tablespoon, scoop out generous walnut-size pieces of dough and roll them into a ball. If you're using a scale, each ball of dough should weigh less than 1 ounce (20 to 22 g). The dough will be sticky. You can moisten your hands, but don't over-moisten, or the cookies will end up with a smooth, rather than characteristically rough, finish. Place the balls of dough on the baking sheets, 10 to 12 per sheet, and press down very lightly on the tops to help them adhere while still maintaining their rounded tops.

4. Bake, one sheet at a time, in the center of the oven for 15 to 18 minutes, until the cookies are barely set, lightly browned on the bottom and pale gold on the surface. Transfer the baking sheets to wire racks to cool for 10 minutes; then transfer the cookies from the baking sheets to the racks to cool completely. Store the amaretti in an airtight container for up to 1 week.

BAKER'S NOTE: *To make Moretti (chocolate-almond cookies), grind the nuts and sugar together as directed in the recipe; then pulse in 3 tablespoons of unsweetened cocoa powder before adding the remaining ingredients. Proceed with the recipe.*

COOKIE STORY

THE BIKER BAKER OF SCANNO

There are two rules that baker Ilario Notarmuzzi never breaks: He does not share his cookie recipes. And, if you want to enjoy his toasty amaretti, oversize mostaccioli, and tender, brownie-like biscotti, and—trust me—you do, you have to go to his bakery in Scanno to buy them. He doesn't ship, distribute, or sell online.

Scanno, population circa 1,700, is not the easiest place in the world to get to. To arrive there, you have to exit the highway and drive into the Marsicani Mountains, then deep into the Sagittarius Gorges. It's a spectacular drive that winds along the shores of two lakes, through narrow stone underpasses, and past a tiny hermitage tucked away on a hillside. I know it well because I've been making the drive at least once a year since I visited Biscotteria Artigianale di Liliana Rosati for the first time back in 2014.

The bakery, which opened in 1990, is named for Ilario's mother, but his family's baking legacy extends back to the nineteenth century. "My father, who opened this shop, was the son of a *fornaio* [a bread baker]. My mother's father—my grandfather—opened a bread bakery in 1956. But his grandfather was also a baker. We've been covered in flour since the 1800s."

Ilario has been running the *biscotteria* for the last decade-plus, with the intention of passing it on to his three sons. You'll find it down a set of stone steps in the small, well-maintained historic center of this medieval village. The shop is tiny; there's barely room for three customers at a time to squeeze in. And yet, there is a feeling of expansiveness about the place. The glass-fronted countertop, which doubles as a display case, is brimming with stacks of fat cookies. Ilario welcomes customers with a booming voice. He is by turns jovial and serious, eager to talk about anything from almonds to world politics.

During one of my earliest visits, maybe even the first, Ilario and I had a long conversation in which he laid out his philosophy. Back then, he sported a leather vest and a bandana around his head and looked more like a biker than a baker. And while he does indeed own a Harley-Davidson, he is a baker at heart. "If I give away my recipes, I am giving away my livelihood," he told me. "And not just mine, but also my sons'." If he started selling his cookies online, he added, then he would be preventing people from coming to Scanno. "A city needs people, or it dies," he said.

To be fair, Scanno is far from dead, and Ilario would be the first to say so. It is one of the *Borghi Più Belli d'Italia*—"most beautiful villages in Italy"—an official designation bestowed upon small towns and villages that are centers of art, culture, and natural beauty. Among Scanno's attractions are its jewelers who produce exquisite gold and silver filigree necklaces, earrings, and brooches and the tombolo artisans who make fine silver-threaded bobbin lace, Ilario's wife, Luna Piccinini among them. The town is surrounded by the green national park, by mountains and meadows, places where you can ski in winter and hike and swim in summer. There is almost always a sprinkling of tourists about. But Scanno is still very much a place where people live their lives.

When I stop in one day, the biscotteria is filled with the scent of sugar and wine and olive oil. Ilario's son Silvio is pulling a fresh batch of wine *tarallucci* (rings) from the ovens tucked in the back corner of the shop. "This is a cookie beloved by everyone," Ilario says. "There are four thousand versions, but each one is different, and they are all good."

While he does not give away his recipes, he does list, in a framed print that hangs in the shop, every ingredient contained in each of his cookies. In fact, he is an absolute stickler when it comes to ingredients: fresh eggs, good olive oil, and—most important—fresh almonds, which he buys whole from Puglia. "The most important part of the almond is the oil," he tells me. "That's where all the nutrients and all the flavor are contained. If you start with nuts that have already been shelled and chopped, you are starting with a lesser product."

He speaks with genuine pride and maybe a little nostalgia, of one of the bakery's most traditional cookies—biscotti al latte, classic dunking cookies made with sugar, milk, eggs, oil, flour, lemon, and a pinch of leavening. Locally, they used to be known as *biscotti della mietatura*, or "harvest cookies," because they were given, along with a glass of wine, to sheepshearers and workers who cut grain. "For many people, that was their day's wages," he says. They were also given to children celebrating their First Communion and brought to the homes of ailing neighbors. "It was a cookie for every purpose."

Ilario's mostaccioli, flat and round, rather than diamond-shaped, and larger than coasters, are typical of Scanno. They are chock-full of almonds and covered in a thin sugar glaze. My Mostaccioli (page 160) are good—really good—but if I'm being honest, Ilario's are better. But my favorite of his offerings are his *Biscotti di Prato Verde*, or "Green Meadow Cookies." These chocolate oblongs are made with cocoa powder, finely chopped almonds, and pieces of dark chocolate. The dough is baked as a loaf and sold whole, ready to be sliced. Since they are not baked twice like typical biscotti, they are not crunchy; instead, they have a crisp-tender outer shell and a soft, fudgy interior, a bit like a brownie but slightly firmer, with a deeper, fruitier, and more complex flavor. I haven't yet come up with my own version, so you'll have to take my word for it. Or, better yet, go to Biscotteria Artigianale di Liliana Rosati and taste for yourself.

ANGINETTI *(Campania)*

Orange and Anise Cookie Knots

These pretty, iced orange knots are a riff on classic lemon cookies from Campania, the region in southern Italy that includes Naples. They are especially popular along the Sorrento peninsula and farther south in the Cilento. The area is famous for its large, sweet lemons, used to make limoncello and a range of lemon-spiked desserts. These cookies are just as beloved, if not more so, among Italian American families, and are a must-have for many at Christmas and Easter.

Traditional versions of anginetti were made with lard, but butter seems to be the fat of choice in more modern recipes, and it's what I use here. The typical shape of the cookie is either a ring or a knot. Between the two, I prefer the knot, which makes a rustic, yet elegant little package. Try my orange version—the zest goes really well with the anise in the dough. For the more traditional take, substitute an equal amount of lemon juice and zest.

MAKES 20 COOKIES

COOKIES

2 cups (240 g) unbleached all-purpose flour

¼ cup (50 g) sugar

2 teaspoons baking powder

¼ teaspoon fine salt

2 teaspoons finely grated orange zest

2 ounces (4 tablespoons; 57 g) cold unsalted butter, cut into ½ inch (12 mm) cubes

1 large egg, lightly beaten

¼ cup (60 ml) sambuca or other anise-flavored liqueur (see page 21)

2 tablespoons milk

ICING

1½ cups (180 g) confectioners' sugar

1 teaspoon finely grated orange zest, plus 1 teaspoon freshly squeezed juice

1 tablespoon sambuca or other anise-flavored liqueur

2 tablespoons boiling water (I use the microwave to heat the water)

1. To make the cookies: Combine the flour, sugar, baking powder, salt, and orange zest in the work bowl of a food processor fitted with the metal blade. Pulse a few times to mix thoroughly. Distribute the butter inside the bowl and pulse to break it up into small crumbs. Pour the egg through the feed tube and pulse to work it in. Pour in the sambuca and milk and pulse just until the dough starts to come together. Transfer the dough to a clean work surface and pat it into a disk. Wrap tightly in reusable wrap or plastic wrap and refrigerate until thoroughly chilled, at least 4 hours or up to overnight.

2. Preheat the oven to 350° F (180° C). Line a rimmed baking sheet with parchment.

3. Cut the dough into 20 equal pieces. If weighing, they should each weigh just under 1 ounce (about 25 g). Form each piece into a 6-inch (15-cm) rope, about the width of your pinkie. Tie each rope into a knot and set them on the baking sheet, leaving about 1 inch (2½ cm) between them. Bake in the middle of the oven for about 20 minutes, until they are set and lightly browned. Transfer the baking sheet to a wire rack to cool completely.

4. To make the icing: Place the confectioners' sugar in a bowl and whisk in the orange zest, orange juice, sambuca, and enough of the boiling water to achieve a smooth medium-thick icing. Use a pastry brush to brush the icing all over the surface of the cookies. Let them sit until the icing has set, at least 2 hours. Store the cookies in layers, separated by parchment or waxed paper, in an airtight container for up to 1 week.

BACI DI DAMA CALABRESI *(Calabria)*

Apricot Jam and Bittersweet Chocolate Kisses

Well . . . more like big fat jam-laced smooches. Two vanilla and almond butter cookies, fused together with sweet-tart apricot jam and dipped in bittersweet chocolate make for one generous treat. To me, they are the Mae West of Italian "kiss" cookies, a delightful contrast to the more reserved Lauren Bacall–like (but equally delicious) Baci di Dama cookies from Piedmont (page 42).

The origins of this cookie are murky, and there is some indication they may have, at some point, made their way down to the toe of Italy's boot from Piedmont. Whatever their provenance, you will love these edible baubles, with their jewel-toned apricot centers, rounded, slightly cracked domes, and cloak of dark chocolate.

MAKES 18 COOKIE SANDWICHES

COOKIES

5 ounces (11 tablespoons; 150 g) unsalted butter, cut into ½ inch (1 cm) cubes, at cool room temperature

1 cup (120 g) confectioners' sugar

1 large egg plus 2 yolks

1 teaspoon honey

1 teaspoon pure vanilla extract

2 cups (240 g) unbleached all-purpose flour

½ cup (50 g) superfine blanched almond flour

1 teaspoon baking powder

¼ teaspoon fine salt

¾ to 1 cup (225 to 300 g) Vanilla Apricot Jam (page 209) or best-quality store-bought apricot jam

DIPPING

6 ounces (170 g) bittersweet chocolate

1. To make the cookies: In the bowl of a stand mixer fitted with the paddle attachment, beat the butter and sugar until lightened and fluffy, 3 to 4 minutes. Beat in the egg and yolks, one at a time, scraping down the sides of the bowl after each addition. Beat in the honey and vanilla extract.

2. Sift the flour, almond flour, baking powder, and salt into a bowl. Pour this into the butter-egg mixture and mix on low speed. Increase the speed to medium and beat for 30 seconds to fully incorporate. Scoop the dough onto a sheet of reusable wrap or plastic wrap and wrap tightly. Refrigerate for at least 4 hours, and up to overnight.

3. Preheat the oven to 350° F (180° C). Line two or three rimmed baking sheets with parchment. If you don't have a third sheet, you can reuse one after the first batch is baked.

4. Divide the dough into 36 equal pieces. If weighing, each piece should weigh about ⅔ ounce (18 g). Roll the pieces into balls and set them on the prepared baking sheets. Press down on them lightly to flatten slightly. Chill the sheets in the refrigerator for 30 minutes, then bake for 13 to 15 minutes, until the cookies are set and lightly golden in color. There may be some cracking on top, which is fine. Transfer the baking sheets to wire racks to cool completely.

5. To finish, turn half of the cookies upside down so their flat bottoms are facing up. Dollop a generous drop of jam onto the upturned cookie halves, then sandwich them together with the remaining cookies.

6. To dip the cookies: Melt and temper the chocolate according to the instructions on page 27. Dip the cookies, one at a time, into the melted chocolate just enough to cover them a little less than halfway. Set the cookies back on the parchment-lined sheets and allow them to set for at least 2 hours. Store the cookies in an airtight container for up to 1 week. To prevent them from sticking or scuffing, store in layers, separated by waxed paper or parchment.

BISCOTTI DA INZUPPO *(Basilicata)*

Cookies for Dunking

There are more than a few recipes in this book for cookies that are good dunkers. But these crispy, fat, chocolate-flecked fingers are the ultimate. I tasted a similar cookie at Panificio Cifarelli, in Matera. The city is home to an astonishing UNESCO heritage site; a collection of ancient white stone cave-like structures carved into the mountainside. People lived in the *sassi*, as the area is known, until the 1950s, when conditions were declared uninhabitable and the last residents relocated. Now the village is a collection of museums, architectural attractions, inns, and restaurants. Although it can be crowded and has a tourist vibe, it is well worth the visit. The entire village is a treasure.

Panificio Cifarelli's founder, Antonio Cifarelli, started working in a bread bakery in the sassi as a young boy. In 1947, he opened his own forno in the modern part of the city, baking Matera's distinctive bread—crescent-shaped loaves with a golden-brown crust and tight, white crumb. Now run by his grandchildren, the bakery still makes bread in the same oven, but it also makes and sells a variety of sweet and savory baked goods, including these cookies. Try the recipe for Strazzate Materane (page 172), inspired by another of Panificio Cifarelli's rustic cookies.

MAKES 30 TO 32 COOKIES

1 cup (200 g) sugar, plus ⅓ cup (70 g) for coating the cookies

2 large eggs

½ cup (120 ml) extra-virgin olive oil

2 teaspoons lemon zest (from 1 small lemon)

1 teaspoon pure vanilla extract

¼ teaspoon fine salt

½ teaspoon baking soda

¼ cup (60 ml) hot milk (about 110° F; 43° C)

3¾ cups (450 g) unbleached all-purpose flour

2 teaspoons baking powder

2 ounces (57 g) finely chopped or shaved bittersweet chocolate

1. Preheat the oven to 350° F (180° C). Line two rimmed baking sheets with parchment.

2. Pour 1 cup sugar into a large bowl and drop in the eggs. Beat with a hand whisk until lightened and foamy. Drizzle in the oil, whisking to emulsify it, then beat in the lemon zest, vanilla, and salt.

3. In a small bowl, stir together the baking soda and hot milk. Slowly whisk this into the egg mixture. Add the flour, baking powder, and chopped chocolate, and fold them in with a sturdy spatula until thoroughly combined. Pat the dough into a ball, then divide it into 30 or 32 equal pieces, depending on how big you want the cookies. If weighing, each piece should weigh just over 1 ounce (30 g). Roll each piece into a fat finger about 3½ inches (9 cm) long and ½ to ¾ inch (12 mm to 2 cm) wide.

4. Place the remaining ⅓ cup (70 g) sugar in a bowl. Roll each dough finger in the sugar and place them on the baking sheets, 15 to 16 per sheet. Bake the cookies, one sheet at a time, in the middle of the oven, for 18 minutes, until they are puffed and set, with cracks on the surface. Transfer the baking sheets to wire racks to cool for 20 minutes; then transfer the cookies from the baking sheets to the racks to cool completely. Store the cookies in an airtight container for up to 2 weeks.

BAKER'S NOTE: *To make chocolate biscotti da inzuppo, substitute ¼ cup of the flour (30 g) with 3 tablespoons (20 g) cocoa powder.*

BISCOTTI DI CEGLIE *(Puglia)*

Cherry-Filled Almond Cookies

Ceglie Messapica is a postcard-pretty town in the Apulian countryside halfway between the Gulf of Taranto and the Adriatic Sea. Its architecture is a mix of ancient churches, baroque palazzi, and squat, whitewashed buildings with painted wrought iron balconies. In the city's historic center, a maze of cobblestone streets open onto sun-blanched piazzas, where you'll find shops, restaurants, and coffee bars and bakeries. Among them is Caffè Centrale, open since 1861—the year Italy became a unified country. The shop specializes in *pasticceria di mandorle*, or sweets made with almonds and almond paste. Their most popular almond treats are these rustic almond cookies, filled with cherry preserves and spiked with house-made citrus liqueur, then baked until they are honey-brown.

Biscotti di Ceglie date back hundreds of years and are recognized by the Slow Food Foundation as an important artisanal product.

Be sure to use a thick-set preserve for the filling to prevent it from escaping during baking—the Confettura di Amarena on page 210 works well.

MAKES 18 COOKIES

2 cups (280 g) blanched and toasted almonds, cooled (see page 26)

½ cup (100 g) sugar

1 large egg

2 teaspoons honey

2 teaspoons limoncello

¼ teaspoon fine salt

2 to 4 tablespoons superfine blanched almond flour

½ cup (50 g) Confettura di Amarena (page 210), or store-bought cherry jam

1. Place the almonds in the work bowl of a food processor fitted with the metal blade and pulse to break them up. Add the sugar and pulse until the nuts are coarsely chopped. In a small bowl, whisk the egg with the honey, limoncello, and salt. Pour this through the feed tube and pulse until well combined and the nuts are ground to a medium-fine texture. They should not be completely ground.

2. Scrape the mixture into a bowl. It should be dense and pliable. If it seems too loose to shape, stir in 2 to 4 tablespoons almond flour. Cover and let the dough rest for 15 to 30 minutes.

3. Preheat the oven to 350° F (180° C). Line two rimmed baking sheets with parchment. Moisten a work surface and your hands with cold water. Divide the dough into 3 equal pieces. Keeping your hands and the work surface lightly moistened, pat one piece into a rectangle 4 to 5 inches (10 to 13 cm) wide and about 6 inches (16 cm) long. Spoon one-third of the preserves along the length of the rectangle, centering it just below the middle. Starting from the bottom, use a bench scraper to lift the long end of the dough over the filling, as though you were making a mini jelly roll. Continue to roll upward until the preserves are completely enclosed in a log of dough and the seam is on the bottom. Moistening your hands once more, roll the log back and forth a few times to lengthen it to about 9 inches (23 cm). Lightly press down along the top to flatten it.

4. With the bench scraper, cut the log crosswise into 6 equal nuggets, about 1½ inches (4 cm) in length. Transfer them to one of the prepared baking sheets. Shape, fill, and cut the other two pieces of dough the same way. You should end up with about 18 nuggets. Bake the cookies, one sheet at a time, in the middle of the oven for 15 to 20 minutes, until they are set and honey-toned in color. Transfer the sheets to wire racks to cool for 20 minutes, then transfer the cookies from the baking sheets to the racks to cool completely. Store the biscotti di Ceglie in an airtight container for 1 week.

CIAMBELLINE AL VINO *(Abruzzo)*

Sugar-Dipped Wine Rings

The crumbly, slightly rough texture of these cookies makes them among my favorites, in spite of their decidedly rustic look. They are not too sweet, and they provide a satisfying, sturdy crunch when you bite into them since there is no leavening in the dough.

Ciambelline, which means "little rings," are typical of several south and central-south regions of Italy, including Puglia and Abruzzo, and also Lazio, the region that includes Rome and borders Abruzzo. The humble ingredients evoke the harvest season: wine and olive oil are the primary components, along with flour, sugar, and fennel or aniseeds. The cookies can be made with white or red wine, but in Abruzzo it is customary to use Montepulciano d'Abruzzo, a hearty red.

The traditional method for making these cookies is *all'occhio*, (by eye), which is to say without really measuring. You just combine a "glass" of wine, a "glass" of olive oil, and a "glass" of sugar; and then work in enough flour to achieve a supple dough that can be rolled into ropes and shaped. I've added more precise measurements to help you out, though in truth you'll be doing yourself a favor if you try it the old way and use your instincts and your *occhio*.

MAKES 40 COOKIES

2 teaspoons whole aniseeds

1 "glass" (generous 3/4 cup; 170 g) granulated sugar, plus 1/2 cup (100 g) for dipping

1 "glass" (generous 3/4 cup; 180 ml) extra-virgin olive oil

1 "glass" (3/4 cup; 180 ml) Montepulciano d'Abruzzo wine or other robust red wine

1/4 teaspoon fine salt

4 1/2 cups (540g) unbleached all-purpose flour

1. Spread the aniseeds out in a small dry skillet and set over medium heat. Toast, stirring the seeds now and again, for 2 to 3 minutes, until they turn a shade or two darker and you can smell their warm chamomile-like scent. Transfer them to a small bowl or plate to cool completely.

2. Combine the 3/4 cup (170 g) sugar and olive oil in a large bowl and whisk well. Pour in the wine and whisk for a minute or two longer to help the sugar dissolve. Stir in the aniseeds and salt. Pour in the flour and stir with a sturdy spatula until all the flour is incorporated. Pat the dough into a ball and knead it briefly. It will be shiny and rough-textured. Pat it once more into a ball, cover the bowl, and let the dough rest for 30 minutes at room temperature.

3. Preheat the oven to 375°F (190°C). Line two rimmed baking sheets with parchment.

4. Fill a small bowl with the remaining 1/2 cup (100 g) sugar. Cut off a walnut-size piece of dough. If weighing, each piece should weigh just under 1 ounce (about 25 g). Roll 1 piece of dough into a thin rope, about 4 inches (10 cm) in length and slightly thinner than your pinkie. Note that this oil-rich dough tends to break apart as you roll. Not to worry; simply squeeze it together and reroll. Bring the ends of the rope together and pinch to form a ring; or, if you like, cross one end over the other to make a *torcetto* (twist). Dip the top of the cookie into the bowl of sugar to coat the surface (leave the underside uncoated) and place it on one of the prepared baking sheets. Continue shaping and dipping cookies. You will fill at least two trays.

5. Bake the cookies, one sheet at a time, for 20 to 22 minutes, until they are golden and browned along the edges. Let them cool for a few minutes on the baking sheet and then transfer them to a rack to cool completely. Store the cookies in an airtight container for up to 2 weeks.

BISCOTTI SPEZIATI AL VINO ROSSO *(general)*

Spiced Red Wine Cookies

Cookies spiked with wine are ubiquitous throughout southern Italy. They can be made with red or white wine, and they can be plain, rustic dunking biscuits, or slightly more sophisticated, like these. Lightly coated in sesame seeds, with a crispy, airy texture, these cookies get an extra boost of flavor from spices and from the red wine in the dough. Use a decent dry, robust red. I like Montepulciano d'Abruzzo. Nero d'Avola, a bold red from Sicily, is another good choice.

This recipe is lightly adapted from one by Adri Barr Crocetti, a wonderful Italian American cook and friend whose erstwhile blog was among my favorites.

MAKES 18 TO 20 COOKIES

½ cup (70 g) sesame seeds

6 tablespoons extra-virgin olive oil, preferably Sicilian

6 tablespoons sugar

¼ teaspoon pure vanilla extract

1½ cups (180 g) unbleached all-purpose flour

1½ teaspoons baking powder

¼ teaspoon baking soda

2½ teaspoons ground cinnamon

½ teaspoon Pisto Napoletano (page 217) or store-bought Quatre Épices

¼ teaspoon fine salt

¼ cup (60 ml) Montepulciano d'Abruzzo or Nero d'Avola wine, or another robust, fruity red wine

1. Preheat the oven to 350° F (180° C). Line a rimmed baking sheet with parchment.

2. Spread the sesame seeds out on a rimmed baking sheet and bake for 8 to 10 minutes, until lightly browned and fragrant. Stir once or twice during baking so they brown evenly. Set aside to cool.

3. Fit a stand mixer with the whisk attachment and beat the olive oil, sugar, and vanilla extract together until the sugar has mostly dissolved and the mixture thickens, 3 to 5 minutes on medium-high speed.

4. In a medium bowl whisk together the flour, baking powder, baking soda, cinnamon, Pisto Napoletano, and salt. Switch to the paddle attachment and mix in half the dry ingredients on low speed. Beat in the wine, followed by the rest of the dry ingredients. Increase to medium speed and mix just until a soft, shiny and slightly ragged dough comes together.

5. Use a tablespoon measure or scoop to form the dough into small (1½ inch; 4 cm) logs with slightly tapered ends, like little footballs. Roll each cookie in toasted sesame seeds to coat. Place the cookies about 1 inch apart on the baking sheet. Bake for about 22 minutes, until set and lightly browned with some cracking on top. Transfer the baking sheet to a wire rack to cool for 10 minutes, then transfer the cookies to the rack to cool completely. Store the cookies in an airtight container for up to 2 weeks.

CALCIONELLI DI GABRIELLA *(Abruzzo)*

Gabriella's Pastry Pockets

On Christmas morning, my mother, Gabriella, would fry up a fresh batch of these sweet pastry pockets filled with almonds and honey, for us to enjoy while we opened presents. Hers is one of many versions found throughout Abruzzo, the region in Italy where she grew up. They go by several similar names, including *calcionetti* and *caggiunitt*—all dialect words that translate to "little socks," referring to the pocket shape of the cookies. Some variations call for filling the pockets with rustic grape jam, cocoa powder, and chopped nuts, others with a sweet chickpea purée. Some are baked, some are fried. They are all delicious. The best thing about calcionelli is that, as good as they are hot out of the fryer, they are just as good at room temperature. See the Baker's Note for an alternative filling with walnuts.

MAKES 55 TO 60 COOKIES

DOUGH

3 cups (360 g) unbleached all-purpose flour, plus more for the work surface

½ cup (100 g) sugar

¼ teaspoon fine sea salt

1 teaspoon finely grated lemon zest

1 teaspoon finely grated orange zest

4 ounces (1 stick; 113 g) cold unsalted butter, cut into cubes

3 large eggs, lightly beaten

1 tablespoon Punch Abruzzo (see page 18) or dark rum, or ½ teaspoon pure vanilla extract

FILLING

2 cups (300 g) blanched almonds

1 teaspoon finely grated lemon zest

1 teaspoon finely grated orange zest

½ cup (170 g) honey

Vegetable oil for deep frying

Confectioners' sugar for dusting

1. To make the dough: Combine the flour, sugar, salt, and lemon and orange zests in the work bowl of a food processor fitted with the metal blade and pulse briefly. Distribute the butter in the work bowl and pulse until it is incorporated and the mixture is crumbly. Add the eggs through the feed tube and pulse until just incorporated. With the motor running add the liqueur to the feed tube and process just until the mixture begins to clump together. Turn the dough out onto a lightly floured work surface and knead it briefly into a ball. The dough should be soft but not sticky. Wrap tightly in reusable wrap or plastic wrap and refrigerate for 1 hour and up to overnight.

2. To make the filling: Pulse the almonds in a food processor fitted with the metal blade until coarsely chopped. Add the lemon and orange zests and process until the mixture is very finely chopped but not completely ground.

3. Pour the honey into a nonstick frying pan and warm it over medium heat. As soon as the honey is loose, stir in the finely chopped almond mixture and stir to combine thoroughly. Remove from the heat and scrape the mixture into a bowl. Let cool.

4. To make the calcionelli: Dust a rimmed baking sheet or a clean tablecloth with flour. Have on hand a 2¾-inch (7-cm) round cookie cutter, a small bowl of water, and a fork, for cutting, shaping, and sealing. Remove the dough from the refrigerator and cut it in half. Rewrap and refrigerate one half. On a lightly floured work surface, roll out the other half into a large thin circle about ⅛ inch (3 mm) thick. Cut out as many circles as possible with the cookie cutter. Mound 1 teaspoon of the filling in the center of each circle. Dip a finger in the water and moisten the edges of the circle. Fold each circle into a half-moon. Press the tines of the fork along the edges to seal. Transfer the calcionelli to the flour-dusted baking sheet or tablecloth. Reroll the scraps to cut out more circles. Fill, shape, and seal. Repeat the process with the remaining half of the dough. You should end up with 55 to 60 calcionelli.

5. Pour oil to a depth of 1 inch (2½ cm) in a high-sided saucepan. Heat over medium-high heat to about 375° F (190° C) on a deep-frying thermometer. Or test by dropping a scrap of dough into the hot oil; if it sizzles and floats to the surface the oil is ready.

6. Place a wire rack lined with paper towels near the stove. Carefully add 6 to 8 calcionelli to the hot oil. They will sizzle and begin to brown almost immediately so keep an eye on them. Fry for about 30 seconds, using a skimmer to turn them over and

move them about. Transfer them to the paper towel–lined rack to cool. Continue to fry the calcionelli a few at a time until you have fried them all. To serve, dust generously with confectioners' sugar. Store the calcionelli in an airtight container for up to 5 days.

BAKER'S NOTE: *These fried cookies are just as delicious made with a walnut filling. To make it, substitute 3 cups (300 g) walnuts for the almonds. Proceed as directed with the recipe.*

CELLI RIPIENI *(Abruzzo)*

Stuffed Little Bird Cookies

These whimsical cookies, shaped like tiny birds, are popular throughout Abruzzo. To me, they reflect the rustic artistry and ingenuity of Abruzzese baking and beautifully showcase the region's edible treasures. The dough is made with olive oil—an important staple in Abruzzese cooking—and the filling contains a thick grape jam called *scrucchjata*, made from the region's Montepulciano d'Abruzzo wine grapes. You'll find a recipe for Scrucchjata on page 214, but you may need to befriend a winemaker to obtain the right grapes. Otherwise, use a good-quality, artisan grape jam, good blackberry jam, or the Fig and Chocolate Preserves with Cognac (page 212).

Neither the dough nor the filling contains sugar or salt. This cookie really is a relic from the days before those ingredients were common in southern Italian baking. Keep in mind that the oil-rich dough can be a little fussy to work with. I hope this won't deter you because, as with any recipe with a degree of difficulty, the more you do it the better you get. Feel free to add a little flour to your work surface to help you along, but try not to overdo it, or you risk toughening the dough and your cookies won't be tender.

Shaping the cookies is easier than you might think. It's really just a matter of rolling the ovals of dough around the filling to enclose it, then shaping the ends to look like beaks and tails. I use a pair of small (clean) nail scissors to make the characteristic snips that give the birds their plumage.

MAKES ABOUT 20 COOKIES

FILLING

- 1/4 cup (80 g) finely chopped toasted almonds (see page 26)
- 1 scant cup (250 g) Scrucchjata (page 214), or artisan grape jam or blackberry jam
- 1 tablespoon grated bittersweet chocolate
- 1 tablespoon unsweetened cocoa powder
- 1/2 teaspoon instant espresso powder

DOUGH

- 1/2 cup (120 ml) extra-virgin olive oil
- 1/2 cup (120 ml) dry white wine
- 2 1/4 cups (270 g) unbleached all-purpose flour, plus more as needed
- Peppercorns or hulled sunflower seeds, for eyes, optional
- Confectioners' sugar, for dusting, optional

Continued >>

1. Preheat the oven to 350° F (180° C). Line two rimmed baking sheets with parchment.

2. To make the filling: In a small bowl, combine the almonds, jam, grated chocolate, cocoa powder, and espresso powder. Fold everything together gently but thoroughly. Set aside.

3. To make the dough: In a large bowl, stir together the olive oil and wine. Sprinkle in the flour, stirring constantly with a fork or a whisk to incorporate the ingredients. Continue to add flour and stir until you have a dough that is shiny, soft and tacky, and just firm enough to handle. Turn the dough out onto a lightly dusted work surface and knead until smooth and shiny, about 3 minutes.

4. Pinch off a small piece of dough–about the size of a walnut–and pat it into a small disk. If weighing, it should weigh just shy of 1 ounce (24 g). Using a rolling pin, gently roll out the disk into a 5 x 3- inch (13 x 8-cm) oval. The dough will be tacky but should roll out easily without sticking to the work surface. Avoid adding too much additional flour, as it will toughen the dough. The best technique is to be confident and use a light touch.

5. Spread 1 teaspoon of filling along the center of the piece of dough, leaving a border all around. Fold the bottom edge over the filling and then roll up to enclose the filling completely. Roll the dough back and forth to seal in the filling and make sure that the seam is on the underside. You will have what looks like a little snake that just ate a big lunch–two thin ends with a fat middle. Now roll the ends to thin them out. Curve the ends upward, giving one end a pointed tip to look like a beak. Press a peppercorn or sunflower seed near the beak to create an eye (this is optional). Fan out the other end to look like a tail. Use the scissors to snip little cuts in the tail and along the body of the "bird" to make the plumage. Carefully lift the bird onto one of the parchment-lined baking sheets. Use an angled spatula to assist you, if you like. Keep in mind that the dough tends to snap back, so you may have to touch up the beak or tail of the bird once you set it on the baking sheet. These little birds are rustic and are not meant to look precise or perfect. Continue to roll, fill, and shape the cookies and arrange them on the baking sheets, 10 per sheet. You should end up with 20 cookies. (You may not use all the filling; store any that is leftover in the refrigerator for up to 1 month–it's delicious spread on toast.)

6. Bake, one sheet at a time, in the middle of the oven, for 20 minutes, or until the cookies are just set and pale golden. Transfer the baking sheets to racks to cool for 5 minutes. Use an angled metal spatula to transfer the cookies from the baking sheets to the racks to cool completely. To serve, arrange the cookies on a decorative platter. Sprinkle with confectioners' sugar (if using). Serve the cookies slightly warm or at room temperature. Store celli ripieni in an airtight container for up to 2 weeks.

ROCCOCÒ *(Campania)*

Almond Ring Cookies

A visit to Naples during the Christmas season never disappoints. The city's churches and other venues display incredibly detailed Nativity scenes, consisting not just of a manger setup but of entire villages, with mountains and lakes, shops, and neighborhoods.

Bakers start making these spiced ringed cookies around December 8, the Feast of the Immaculate Conception. A most traditional Neapolitan cookie, roccocò (sometimes also spelled rococò) are replete with chopped almonds, and except for an egg wash to give the cookies a little gloss, they contain no fat. The rough, "rocky" appearance of the cookies evokes the eighteenth-century rococo style of art and architecture, which featured the ornamental use of rock and shell forms, though the cookies' origins have been traced to the fourteenth century, when they were made by the nuns of the Real Convento della Maddalena. They are meant to be sturdy cookies, good for dunking in wine. These cookies encompass the quintessential flavors of a Neapolitan Christmas—candied orange peel, the buttery taste of almonds, and the medieval mix of Neapolitan pisto spices.

MAKES 20 COOKIES

2 cups (240 g) unbleached all-purpose flour

1 cup (100 g) blanched almond flour

⅔ cup (95 g) toasted almonds (see page 26), chopped medium-fine

¾ cup (150 g) superfine sugar

¾ cup (100 g) finely chopped Candied Orange Peel (page 220)

1 teaspoon finely grated orange zest (from 1 small orange)

2 teaspoons Pisto Napoletano (page 217)

¼ teaspoon fine salt

½ teaspoon baker's ammonia (see page 17) or baking soda

⅓ cup (75 ml) dry white wine, plus 1 tablespoon for brushing

1 medium egg

20 whole almonds, for decorating

1. Preheat the oven to 350° F (180° C). Line two rimmed baking sheets with parchment.

2. Combine the flour, almond flour, almonds, sugar, candied orange peel, orange zest, pisto napoletano, and salt in a large, wide bowl. Make a well in the center and add the baker's ammonia to it. Pour in ⅓ cup (80 ml) wine and mix everything together with a wooden spoon or sturdy spatula. Knead the mixture into a ball.

3. Divide the dough into 20 equal pieces. If weighing, each piece should weigh slightly less than 1½ ounces (40 g). Roll the pieces into 8-inch (20-cm) ropes, about the width of your pinkie. Pinch the ends together to form a ring. Set the rings on the baking sheets, leaving 1½ inches (4 cm) of space between them. Press them down very lightly to flatten the tops slightly. This is the traditional way to shape rococo, but I admit I don't usually do it, as I like the rings more rounded.

4. In a small bowl, beat together the egg and remaining 1 tablespoon of wine. Brush the tops of the rings and stud each one with 1 whole almond.

5. Bake the cookies, one sheet at a time, in the middle of the oven for about 20 to 25 minutes, until they are set and browned. Transfer the baking sheets to wire racks to cool for 10 minutes, then transfer the cookies to the racks to cool completely. The rococo will continue to harden as they cool. Store the cookies in an airtight container for up to 2 weeks.

www.corriere.it
LA SERA
EURO 2,20 | ANNO 149 | N. 105

CEPPELLIATE DI TRIVENTO *(Molise)*

Cherry Jam Pockets

Molise is one of those under-the-radar regions of Italy that even Italians don't seem to know much about. My paternal grandmother was from Isernia, a comparatively large city in the small, mostly rural and mountainous region, and every summer my father would take our family to visit Nonna's elderly brother and sister, who lived in town. That was pretty much my own Molise experience until I began exploring other parts of the region and realized how spectacular it is—lush with forests and dotted with medieval villages, hilltop towns, and sparsely traveled roads that eventually wind down from the mountains out to the Adriatic Coast.

I had a cousin by marriage who was from Trivento, a stone town perched on a mountain ridge, not far from the Abruzzo border. You would not want to leave town without trying Trivento's signature cookie: Ceppelliate. The name, oddly, means "stumpy" and while these cookies certainly are rustic in appearance, I wouldn't go that far. They are delicious jam pockets made with a crumbly, lard-based pasta frolla, and filled with jam made from local sweet cherries. They can be shaped into half-moons or folded more like a cone or an envelope.

I use my homemade jam, which combines fresh and dried sour cherries, but you can use store-bought cherry jam. Ceppelliate are meant to be showered liberally with confectioners' sugar, but I tend to leave them unadorned so that their rustic charm is in plain view.

MAKES 24 POCKETS

2 cups (240 g) unbleached all-purpose flour, plus more for the work surface

½ cup (100 g) sugar

¼ teaspoon baking powder

¼ teaspoon fine salt

1 teaspoon finely grated lemon zest (from about ½ lemon)

3½ ounces (½ cup; 100 g) cold leaf lard, in pieces; or 4 ounces (1 stick; 113 g) unsalted butter

3 large egg yolks

1 teaspoon pure vanilla extract

1½ to 2 cups (450 to 600 g) Confettura di Amarena (page 210) or store-bought thick sour cherry preserves

Confectioners' sugar, for serving, optional

1. Place the flour, sugar, baking powder, salt, and lemon zest in the work bowl of a food processor fitted with the metal blade and pulse to combine. Pulse in the cold lard just until incorporated. In a small bowl, beat the egg yolks with the vanilla. Pour this through the feed tube and pulse until the mixture begins to clump together. Turn it out onto a sheet of reusable wrap or plastic wrap and pat it into a disk. Wrap tightly and refrigerate for at least 2 hours and up to overnight.

2. Preheat the oven to 350° F (180° C). Line two rimmed baking sheets with parchment. Remove the dough from the refrigerator and let it sit at room temperature for about 30 minutes. Lightly flour a clean work surface. Roll the dough into a large circle about ⅛ inch (3 mm) thick. Use a 3-inch (8-cm) round cookie cutter (I use one with scalloped edges) to cut out circles. Spoon a heaping teaspoon of cherry preserves onto each circle. Fold in half to make a half-moon shape, pressing the edges to seal. For an envelope, fold two edges toward the center, letting them overlap slightly, to make a packet with two open ends. To make a cone, fold two sides over toward the center, letting them overlap and meet at the bottom. Set the cookies on the baking sheets, 12 per sheet.

3. Bake, one sheet at a time, in the middle of the oven for 20 minutes, or until the cookies are set and nicely browned around the edges. Transfer the baking sheets to wire racks to cool for 20 minutes, then transfer the cookies to the racks to cool completely. Dust liberally with confectioners' sugar before serving—or not! Store the ceppelliate in an airtight container for up to 1 week.

CHIACCHIERE *(Abruzzo and many other regions)*

Fried Pastry Ribbons

They go by many names. In Abruzzo they are called either *chiacchiere*, which translates loosely to "chatter" or "gossip," or "cioffe," which means . . . I'm not exactly sure what it means. Maybe it refers to the sound of the strips of dough as they puff up exuberantly in the hot oil, or the crunch when you bite into them. Elsewhere in Italy they are known as *bugie* (lies); *cenci* (rags); *crostoli* (a reference to the crunchy texture); *frappe*, or *sfrappole* (no idea). In the U.S. they're sometimes called "bow ties" or "angel's wings" for their shape.

No matter what you call them, they are a must-have during Carnival, the festive period leading up to Lent. The basic recipe is the same: flour + egg + some type of alcohol, whether it's wine, marsala, brandy, or grappa. Most recipes also include a small amount of fat, either lard or butter. You can make the dough the traditional way, by mounding the flour on your countertop and mixing in the other ingredients. But as with pasta dough, a food processor makes quick work of it.

This is not to say that no effort is involved. In order to obtain crisp, light chiacchiere you must roll the dough into very thin strips—as though you were going to make ravioli. I use my pasta machine. Then I use a fluted pastry wheel to cut the strips into small rectangles before shaping them into ribbons or twists or bow ties.

Keep in mind that these pastries fry quickly, within a matter of seconds. I fry them two or three at a time; otherwise, it's a race to corral them with my skimmer and remove them from the hot oil before they get too dark. You will end up with many, many chiacchiere—somewhere around 150. However, they keep well, and they go fast.

MAKES ABOUT 150 FRIED RIBBONS

2⅓ cups (280 g) unbleached all-purpose flour, plus more as needed

¼ cup (50 g) superfine sugar

¼ teaspoon fine salt

1 tablespoon fresh orange zest

2 ounces (4 tablespoons; 57 g) butter, cut into ½-inch (12-mm) cubes, at room temperature

2 large eggs, at room temperature

3 tablespoons grappa or dry white wine (I use 2 tablespoons grappa and 1 tablespoon wine)

About 2 tablespoons milk

Sunflower or neutral vegetable oil for frying

Confectioners' sugar, for dusting

1. Place the flour, sugar, salt, and orange zest in the work bowl of a food processor and pulse to combine. Distribute the butter around the bowl and pulse to work it in. Add the eggs and grappa and pulse again. Dribble in a little milk–just enough for the dough to come together.

2. Turn the dough out onto a lightly floured surface and knead for about 5 minutes, until smooth and elastic. It should be slightly softer than pasta dough but not sticky. Wrap the dough in reusable wrap or plastic wrap and let it rest at room temperature for 30 minutes. Divide it into quarters and rewrap three of them. Run the remaining piece through a pasta machine and stretch it to a thickness of about 1⁄16 inch (2 mm)–very thin.

3. With a fluted pastry wheel, cut the strip into 3 x ¾-inch (8 x 2-cm) rectangles. Make a vertical slice in the center of each rectangle with the pastry wheel or a sharp paring knife and thread one end through it to form the classic twist. Roll out and cut the remaining pieces of dough. Make sure you have enough room for all the little rectangles. If not, roll out, shape, and fry one portion at a time. In addition to the classic twists, you can simply knot strips of dough to make classic bow ties or fry the rectangles without threading the ends through. Be sure to make the center cut, though, or the strips will puff up in the center as they fry.

4. To fry, pour oil to a depth of 2 inches (5 cm) into a deep-sided skillet or Dutch oven. Heat on medium-high until the oil shimmers (375° F; 190° C). Gently drop two or three ribbons into the hot oil, and fry for about 10 seconds, turning them once so they color on both sides–they should be light golden in color. Turn the heat down if they start to darken too quickly.

5. With a spider or slotted spoon, transfer the chiacchiere to a paper towel-lined baking sheet to drain and cool. Pile them onto a plate, dust generously with confectioners' sugar, and serve. Store the chiacchiere in an airtight container, where they will keep for at least 1 week.

INTORCHIATE *(Puglia)*

Almond and Wine Twists

Many Italian cookies are tied to symbolism. In the case of these almond-studded twists, the cookies' shape is meant to evoke an embrace. It is traditional to serve these at baptisms as a symbol of an infant's new bond with God, and also at weddings in celebration of the spouses. Of course, this does not mean you can't make these for whatever reason suits you, or for no reason at all. They are irresistibly crunchy and not too rich, and they last a good long while—up to 2 weeks. Enjoy them dipped in coffee or a glass of wine—two good reasons right there.

MAKES ABOUT 40 COOKIES

3/4 cup (150 g) sugar, plus 1/2 cup (100 g) for rolling

3/4 cup (180 ml) extra-virgin olive oil

3/4 cup (180 ml) dry white wine–Falanghina and Trebbiano are both good southern Italian choices

1/4 teaspoon fine salt

3 1/2 cups (420 g) unbleached all-purpose flour

1 cup (120 g) pastry flour or unbleached all-purpose flour

2 teaspoons baking powder

84 whole raw almonds, or a mix of raw and blanched

1. In a large bowl, whisk together the 3/4 cup (150 g) sugar and olive oil. Pour in the wine and add the salt and continue to whisk for a minute or two to help dissolve the sugar and meld the ingredients. Stir in the flours and baking powder with a sturdy spatula until well incorporated. Knead the mass into a rough ball of dough, wrap tightly in reusable wrap or plastic wrap, and refrigerate for at least 1 hour.

2. Preheat the oven to 350° F (180° C). Line two or three baking sheets with parchment. If you don't have three sheets, you can reuse one after baking the first batch of cookies. Place the remaining 1/2 cup (100 g) sugar in a shallow bowl.

3. Divide the dough into 40 equal pieces. Or, if you don't mind being a little more casual, pinch off pieces of dough about the size of a walnut. If weighing, each piece should weigh just under 1 ounce (about 25 g). Roll each piece into a rope about 8 inches (20 cm) long and about the width of your pinkie. Since this is an oil-rich dough, you should not need to flour the work surface. Fold the rope in half and pinch the ends together to form a ring. Twist the ring to create a figure eight. Dip the twists into the sugar, coating them entirely, and set them on the baking sheets. You should be able to fit 16 on each sheet. Press 2 almonds into each end of the twists, filling the space there.

4. Bake the intorchiate, one sheet at a time, in the middle of the oven for about 25 minutes, until they are set and golden in color. Transfer the baking sheets to wire racks to cool for 10 minutes, then transfer the cookies to the racks to cool completely. Store the intorchiate in an airtight container for up to 2 weeks.

BAKER'S NOTE: *To make a simpler version of this cookie, form them into rings* (ciambelle) *or elongated loops rather than twists and omit the almonds.*

MOSTACCIOLI *(Abruzzo, Campania)*

Almond and Grape Must Cookies

A handful of Italian regions—Abruzzo, Basilicata, Campania, and Puglia among them—lay claim to a spiced Christmas cookie that goes by the name mostaccioli. Versions of the cookie can be traced to ancient Rome, and it remains one of the most popular holiday cookies in Italy.

While recipes vary in ingredients, as well as shaping and baking methods, one thing almost all of them have in common is that they are usually diamond- or rhombus-shaped, though, of course there are exceptions. My favorite bakery mostaccioli come from Biscotteria Artigianale di Lidia Rosati, in Scanno (see page 136). The cookies are as big as coasters, soft and chewy, and covered with a thin sugar glaze.

Another common characteristic is that mostaccioli dough typically contains a mix of spices, especially cinnamon and clove In the days before sugar was a common ingredient, the dough was sweetened with mosto cotto, grape must syrup, which is where the cookie is believed to have gotten its name (see page 215 for more information and a recipe). Many modern recipes replace the grape must syrup with honey. The online purveyor Gustiamo (see Sources, page 225) sells saba, the Emilia-Romagna equivalent of mosto cotto. You can also substitute date syrup or fig syrup.

My recipe here tends toward classic mostaccioli, diamond-shaped and covered in chocolate. I like to add a garnish of candied orange peel.

MAKES ABOUT 36 COOKIES

½ cup (75 g) whole raw almonds

3 cups (360 g) unbleached all-purpose flour, plus more for dusting the work surface

1 cup (200 g) sugar

2 tablespoons unsweetened cocoa powder

1 teaspoon baking powder

1 teaspoon ground cinnamon

¼ teaspoon ground cloves

¾ cup (300 g) mosto cotto, saba, or runny honey

2 large eggs, lightly beaten

1 pound (454 g) bittersweet chocolate, for glazing

2 tablespoons sunflower oil or other neutral oil

36 pieces of Candied Orange Peel (page 220), each about ¾ inch (2 cm) long

1. Preheat the oven to 350° F (180° C) and line two rimmed baking sheets with parchment.

2. Spread the almonds on a small, rimmed pan (I use a small pizza pan) and bake until they are fragrant and start to crackle, 7 to 8 minutes. Remove them from the oven and let cool completely. You can leave the oven on or turn it off and then reheat it while the dough rests.

3. Grind the cooled almonds in a food processor until finely chopped. Add the flour, sugar, cocoa powder, baking powder, cinnamon, and cloves to the work bowl of the processor and pulse until everything is well combined. Using the feed tube, pour in the mosto cotto and eggs and pulse until a soft ball of dough forms. Gather the dough onto a lightly floured surface, knead it briefly, and pat it into a disk. It may not be completely smooth; this is fine. Cover tightly with reusable wrap or plastic wrap and let it rest at room temperature for 30 to 60 minutes. If you turned off the oven, turn it back on to 350° F (180° C).

4. Turn the dough out onto a lightly floured surface and roll it into a rough rectangle a little less than ½ inch (12 mm) thick. With a diamond-shaped cookie cutter, a sharp knife, or a pastry cutter, cut the dough into diamond shapes about 2 x 3 inches (5 by 8 cm). Gather up any scraps and reroll them to make more mostaccioli. You should end up with about 36.

5. Place the mostaccioli ½ inch (12 mm) apart on the parchment-lined baking sheets. Bake, one sheet at a time, in the middle of the oven, until the cookies are set and lightly crackled on the surface, about 15 minutes. Transfer the baking sheets to wire racks to cool for 10 minutes, then transfer the cookies to the racks to cool completely.

6. Melt and temper the chocolate according to the instructions on page 27. Once the chocolate is ready, whisk in the oil until well combined. Use an instant-read

thermometer to check the temperature of the chocolate. It will stay glossy without any white streaking or "blooming" if the temperature remains between 86° and 90° F (30 and 32° C) when the cookies are dipped. If necessary, reheat the chocolate gently to maintain the proper temperature.

7. Line two baking sheets with parchment. (I use the same parchment on which the cookies were baked.) Dip the tops of the mostaccioli into the bowl of melted chocolate, allowing the excess to drip back into the bowl. Set the cookies on the baking sheets and press a piece of candied orange peel into the center of each one. Let the chocolate set completely, at least 2 hours, before serving. Store the mostaccioli in an airtight container for up to 1 week. To prevent scuffing, arrange the cookies in layers, with sheets of waxed paper or parchment between them.

OCCHI DI SANTA LUCIA *(Puglia)*

Eyes of Saint Lucy Anise Cookies

La Festa di Santa Lucia, or Saint Lucy's Feast Day, is celebrated on December 13 in many countries, including Italy. Sweets often accompany the celebration, as does a rather gruesome story that involves poor Saint Lucy having her eyes gouged out. In one version of the story, the assault is meted out as punishment for not renouncing her Christian faith during the Diocletianic Persecutions. In another, it is Lucy who gouges out her own eyes to prevent herself from being distracted from her devotion to her faith by any would-be suitors.

There is a brighter side to this story. The Feast of Saint Lucy is also known as the Festival of Light. According to legend, as part of her devotion to Christianity and to the poor, Lucy would bring food to those hiding in the Roman catacombs, wearing a candlelit wreath on her head to light her way. In Puglia, families mark the feast with these mini *taralli*—ring-shaped wine cookies that bear a passing resemblance to eyes and are thickly coated in a white sugar glaze. Whatever the story, there's something really pleasing about this recipe. No mixer or food processor is required, just a bowl to mix the ingredients and your hands to roll out the cookies.

MAKES ABOUT 24 COOKIES

COOKIES

1 teaspoon whole aniseeds

2 cups (240 g) unbleached all-purpose flour

¼ teaspoon ground cinnamon

¼ teaspoon fine salt

6 tablespoons (90 ml) extra-virgin olive oil

6 tablespoons (90 ml) white wine, such as Fiano or Falanghina, both Pugliese whites with pleasant minerality

ICING

2¼ cups (300 g) confectioners' sugar, plus more if needed

About 3 tablespoons boiling water (I use a microwave)

¼ to ½ teaspoon pure anise extract

1. To make the cookies: Spread the aniseeds out in a small dry skillet and set over medium heat. Toast, stirring the seeds now and again, for 2 to 3 minutes, until they turn a shade or two darker and you can smell their warm chamomile-like scent. Transfer them to a small bowl or plate to cool completely. Crush them with a mortar and pestle to release more of their flavor. A meat pounder or a small, heavy skillet also does the job. You can also blitz them briefly in a spice grinder.

2. Pour the flour into a medium bowl and whisk in the aniseeds, cinnamon, and salt. Make a well in the bowl and pour in the olive oil and wine. Stir everything together with a sturdy spatula, then use your hands to knead the dough into a ball. Cover with reusable wrap or plastic wrap and let the dough rest for 60 minutes.

3. Preheat the oven to 350° F (180° C). Line a rimmed baking sheet with parchment. Divide the dough into 24 equal pieces–they should each weigh about ½ ounce (15 grams). Roll out each ball into a thin rope, 5 to 6 inches (13 to 16 cm) in length. Bring the ends together, crossing them slightly, to form little circles. Arrange the circles on the baking sheet in six rows of four. Bake in the middle of the oven for 25 minutes, or until set on the top and lightly browned on the bottom. Transfer the baking sheet to a wire rack to cool completely.

4. To make the icing: Whisk together the confectioners' sugar, boiling water, and anise extract in a bowl. The icing should be dense and opaque and fall in a thick ribbon from the whisk when you lift it. If it's too loose, you'll end up with a thin coating of icing. For thicker icing add more confectioners' sugar, 1 tablespoon at a time until you reach your desired thickness. Using two forks, dip the cooled taralli, one by one, into the icing, covering them completely. Return them to the parchment-covered baking sheet (no need to waste a fresh sheet of parchment) and let them sit until the icing has set, at least 2 hours. Store the cookies in layers, separated by parchment or waxed paper, in an airtight container for up to 1 week.

PIZZELLE | FERRATELLE *(Abruzzo)*

Classic Waffle Cookies from Abruzzo

The softest spot in my heart is reserved for these delicately crispy waffle cookies from Abruzzo. My mother, who was from Chieti, a city near Abruzzo's Adriatic coast, made them often when I was growing up, and I would enjoy them plain, or spread with a little butter and jam or, more indulgently, a slather of peanut butter and honey—though I didn't truly come to appreciate them until much later (see page 10).

Pizzelle go by several names in Abruzzo: *ferratelle* (based on *ferro*, the Italian word for iron), *neole*, *nevole*, and *cancelle*, or "gates," a reference to the diamond pattern on a traditional rectangular iron. The cookies can be thin and crispy or thick and tender, depending on the iron you use and the type of batter. The recipe I'm sharing here is a classic one that yields pizzelle that are light, crispy, and delicate without being fragile.

I've written this recipe for use with a standard electric aluminum—*not* nonstick—pizzelle iron. But the batter also works with a nonstick iron, as well as with an old-fashioned manual stovetop iron, for those of you who happen to have one. If your iron's plates are a different size or depth than the standard 4 to 5 inches (10 to 13 cm), you'll need to adjust the amount of batter you use to make each pizzella. (Read more about pizzelle irons on page 25.)

Pizzelle cook quickly—usually within 30 seconds (about the amount of time it takes to *quickly* recite the Hail Mary and the Lord's Prayer, tradition holds). If you are new to pizzelle making, read the troubleshooting tips on page 168 before you start. And if you are a pizzelle lover, be sure to try one or more of the variations listed in the Baker's Note at the end of this recipe.

MAKES 20 TO 24 PIZZELLE

- **1/2 cup (120 ml) sunflower or vegetable oil, plus 1/4 cup (60 ml) for oiling the pizzelle iron (use cooking spray instead of oil for the iron if you prefer)**
- **3 large eggs, at room temperature**
- **3/4 cup (150 g) granulated sugar**
- **1 teaspoon pure vanilla extract**
- **1 2/3 to 1 3/4 cups (200 to 210 g) unbleached all-purpose flour**
- **1 1/2 teaspoons baking powder**
- **1/4 teaspoon fine salt**
- **1 teaspoon aniseeds, pounded in a mortar or in a ziplock bag with a mallet until coarsely crushed**

1. Set up your pizzelle-making station. Place the pizzelle iron on a rimmed baking sheet and plug it in, leaving the lid closed. Let it heat for 15 minutes, or according to the manufacturer's instructions. Pour 1/4 cup (60 ml) sunflower oil into a bowl or glass measuring cup and have a silicone pastry brush nearby, along with a small, angled spatula, and a wire rack. Or, instead of oil, have a can of cooking spray nearby.

2. While the iron is heating, make the batter. Crack the eggs into a large bowl and beat them with the remaining 1/2 cup (120 ml) sunflower oil, sugar, and vanilla extract until everything is well combined. I use a handheld electric mixer, but a vigorous beating with a whisk also works.

3. Whisk or beat in 1 2/3 cups flour, baking powder, salt, and crushed aniseeds until well combined, but take care not to overbeat. The batter will be thick and sticky, the consistency of drop cookie dough, and you should be able to scoop it with a spoon or a small scoop. If it is not scoopable, stir in the remaining flour.

4. Season the plates. When the iron is hot, brush the top and bottom plates thoroughly with oil using the silicone brush. Otherwise, coat the plates well with cooking spray. Dollop a generous tablespoonful of batter onto each bottom plate, positioning the batter slightly toward the back of the grid. Close the lid, securing it with the latch, and

Continued >>

bake for 30 to 40 seconds. Don't worry if some oil or a little batter escapes. Lift the lid and use the angled spatula (or a fork) to help you lift the pizzelle out of the iron. These are your trial pizzelle, meant to help season the iron. You can toss them, as they will be oily. (See Pizzelle Troubleshooting Tips on page 168 if the pizzelle have stuck to the grates.)

5. Make the pizzelle. Lightly oil or spray the plates again, using less oil than the first time. Dollop the batter on as before, close the lid, and bake the pizzelle for about 30 seconds, or until lightly golden. Gently transfer them to the rack to cool and crisp. Once they are cool, you can stack them to make room on the rack for more pizzelle. Continue until you have used all the batter, oiling the plates only as needed. You should end up with 20 to 24 pizzelle.

6. Store the pizzelle in an airtight metal container, where they will stay fresh and crispy for at least 1 week. To serve, arrange them on a plate and dust lightly with confectioners' sugar. They are lovely on their own, but also delicious with jam, peanut butter, or broken up into a bowl of ice cream.

FLAVOR AND SHAPE VARIATIONS:

* *Substitute ½ to 1 teaspoon pure anise extract for the aniseeds.*
* *Replace the anise with 1 to 2 teaspoons finely grated lemon zest.*
* *Replace a couple tablespoons of the flour with finely ground almonds or walnuts.*
* *For chocolate pizzelle, replace 2 tablespoons of the flour with cocoa powder.*
* *Shape pizzelle into cups for ice cream by draping them, right after they are cooked, over the bottom of an overturned glass, while they are still warm and pliable.*
* *Shape pizzelle into cones for ice cream by rolling them around a pizzelle or Krumkake mold while still warm and pliable.*
* *Shape pizzelle into cannoli shells by rolling them around cannoli tubes while still warm and pliable. Pipe them with classic ricotta cannoli filling and stud the ends with candied orange peel or glacéed cherries.*

PIZZELLE ALLA GIANDUIA *(Abruzzo)*

Chocolate-Hazelnut Pizzelle

Pizzelle, or ferratelle, as they are more commonly known in Abruzzo, take well to adaptation. My mom often added a few spoonfuls of finely ground almonds or walnuts to her pizzelle batter, which gave the crisp waffle cookies a richer flavor. I borrowed her idea and ran with it, and the result was this chocolate-hazelnut mash-up. They are not too sweet, but the flavor is earthy, buttery, and deep. These are a nice departure from the classic Pizzelle (page 164).

If you are new to making pizzelle, read the Pizzelle Troubleshooting Tips on page 168 before you start.

MAKES ABOUT 20 PIZZELLE

¼ cup (60 ml) sunflower oil, plus ¼ cup (60 ml) more for coating the pizzelle iron (use cooking spray instead of oil for the iron, if you prefer)

3 large eggs

¾ cup (150 g) sugar

1 teaspoon pure vanilla extract

1¼ cups (150 g) unbleached all-purpose flour, plus more as needed

⅓ cup (50 g) finely ground hazelnuts

5 tablespoons (30 g) unsweetened cocoa powder

1 teaspoon baking powder

¼ teaspoon fine salt

1. Set up your pizzelle-making station. Place the pizzelle iron on a rimmed baking sheet and plug it in, leaving the lid closed. Let it heat for 15 minutes, or according to the manufacturer's instructions. Pour ¼ cup (60 ml) sunflower oil into a bowl or glass measuring cup and have a silicone pastry brush nearby, along with a small, angled spatula, and a wire rack. Or, instead of oil, have a can of cooking spray nearby.

2. While the iron is heating, make the batter. Crack the eggs into a large bowl and beat them with the remaining ¼ cup (60 ml) sunflower oil, sugar, and vanilla extract until everything is well combined. I use a handheld electric mixer, but a vigorous beating with a whisk also works.

3. Whisk or beat in the flour, ground hazelnuts, cocoa powder, baking powder, and salt until well combined. The batter will be thick and sticky, like a fudgy frosting, and you should just be able to scoop it with a spoon or a small cookie scoop. If it is not scoopable, stir in another tablespoon of flour.

4. Season the plates. When the iron is hot, brush the top and bottom plates with oil using the silicone brush or coat the plates well with cooking spray. Dollop a generous tablespoonful of batter onto each bottom plate, positioning the batter slightly toward the back of the grid. Close the lid, securing it with the latch, and bake for 30 to 40 seconds. Don't worry if some oil or a little batter escapes. Lift the lid and use the angled spatula (or a fork) to help you lift the pizzelle out of the iron. These are your trial pizzelle, meant to help season the iron. You can toss them, as they will be oily. (See Pizzelle Troubleshooting Tips on page 168 if the pizzelle have stuck to the grates.)

5. Make the pizzelle. Lightly oil or spray the plates again, using less oil than the first time. Dollop the batter on as before, close the lid, and cook the pizzelle for about 30 seconds, or until lightly golden. Gently transfer them to the wire rack to cool and crisp. Once they are cool, you can stack them to make room on the rack for more pizzelle. Continue until you have used all the batter, oiling the plates only as needed. You should end up with 20 pizzelle, depending on the size of your iron.

Store the pizzelle in an airtight metal tin, where they will stay fresh and crispy for at least 1 week. To serve, arrange them on a plate and dust lightly with confectioners' sugar.

PIZZELLE TROUBLESHOOTING TIPS

Pizzelle are easy to make once you get the hang of it, but they can be tricky. Here are some tips to help you.

1. Read the manufacturer's instructions. Your pizzelle iron may be different from mine, so be sure to follow the instructions for heating and seasoning the iron and for properly baking the pizzelle.

2. Helpful tools. These tools help simplify the process of making pizzelle:

Rimmed baking sheet: I place the iron on a rimmed baking sheet to catch any drips of oil and batter, as well as any crumbs that accumulate. It makes for easier cleanup.

Silicone pastry brush: To prevent batter from sticking to the grid, the pizzelle iron must be well oiled. A silicone brush dipped in sunflower or vegetable oil works well; it stands up to high heat and gets into all the crevices of an intricate pizzelle pattern. If you prefer, you can spray the grid with cooking spray.

Small angled spatula: Use this handy tool to help lift the cooked pizzelle off the grid. A fork also does the job well.

Small (1 tablespoon) scoop: A small ice cream or cookie scoop makes dropping the batter onto the hot iron easier. Mine is 1½ inches (4 cm) in diameter.

Wire rack: This allows the pizzelle to cool and dry quickly, which helps them retain their crispy texture.

3. Heat and season the iron. Follow the manual's instructions. For a Palmer pizzelle iron, the brand I use, let the iron heat up for a full 15 minutes before generously oiling it or coating it with cooking spray and making your trial (sacrificial) pizzelle. This will help prevent them from sticking to the grid. Darcy Palmer recommends reseasoning the iron with every use.

4. Sticking batter. If the batter sticks to the plates, don't panic. It's a pain to remove sticky crumbs from the iron and it takes a little time, but it can be done. It helps to have a stiff wire brush and/or a wooden skewer—like a kebab skewer—on hand. (If you have a nonstick iron, you shouldn't have a problem with batter sticking, but it goes without saying that you should never use a stiff metal brush on a nonstick surface.)

Use the wire brush and wooden skewer to get into the crevices to remove the bits of batter and half-cooked pizzelle that are clinging to the grid. If you're worried about getting burned, unplug the iron first and let it cool slightly. Take the time to clean out all the little corners and angles. When you've gotten out as much as you can, brush the grid with the wire brush or even with a pastry brush to brush away the finest crumbs. Reheat the iron and season it again before resuming making pizzelle.

5. Oil or spray the grid as needed. After the first generous oiling, I lightly oil both the top and bottom plates each time I add batter, to make doubly sure I won't have any more issues with batter sticking.

6. Drop the batter onto the grates. Dollop or scoop the batter onto the hot plates, dropping it slightly above the center of the grid, toward the back. This will allow the batter to spread evenly, as it pushes forward when you shut the lid.

7. Oozing batter. If you drop too much batter onto the grates, it will ooze out the sides of the iron when you clamp down the lid. On the other hand, not enough batter and your pizzelle won't have the full imprint of the design. It may take a few tries to get the amount just right. Another helpful trick: Close the lid after dropping the batter onto the plates, but don't squeeze down on the handles immediately. Give it a few seconds, then latch the handles shut. I find this slight delay helps keep batter from escaping. Let the batter cook for at least 30 seconds before opening the lid.

8. Clinging pizzelle. If your cooked pizzelle are clinging to the top plates when you open the lid, you may need more flour in your batter. Stir in another tablespoon or two and try again (the batter should have the consistency of drop cookie dough).

9. Proper cooling. Set the cooked pizzelle on the wire rack immediately to allow them to dry and crisp up. Once they have cooled—this happens quickly—you can stack them to make more room for more pizzelle on the rack.

10. Soft or soggy pizzelle. The crispiness of pizzelle depends on a variety of factors—the consistency of and ingredients in the batter, the depth of the pattern on the iron (thicker pizzelle, like those produced by my manual heart iron, tend to be crispy outside and tender inside), even the amount of humidity in the air. It sometimes happens that pizzelle lose their crisp texture only moments after being baked, which is a bummer if you are counting on crispy pizzelle. Loose batter, or batter that contains milk or extra eggs generally yields softer pizzelle. Humidity can also affect the texture of pizzelle, especially those made with milk. If you are making pizzelle on a humid day, make sure you use a recipe that doesn't have a lot of liquid. Place the pizzelle on a wire rack as soon as they come off the iron to help them cool and dry quickly.

11. Shaping pizzelle. If you want to shape the pizzelle into cups, cones, or tubes, do it while they are still warm and pliable.

12. Cleaning the iron. Clean it as soon as you are done making pizzelle, taking care not to burn yourself. Never immerse your pizzelle iron in water. Unplug the iron and use a wire brush or pastry brush to remove any crumbs from the grid. Wipe the plates clean with a paper towel or clean cloth. Use a clean cloth to wipe the outside of the iron. Store the iron in its box.

13. Storing pizzelle. I've found that the best place to store pizzelle is in an airtight metal cookie tin, where they keep for at least 1 week without losing their fresh taste or crispy texture. A lidded plastic container can be used in a pinch, but it won't keep the pizzelle fresh and crispy for as long.

QUARESIMALI *(Campania)*

Neapolitan Lenten Biscotti

These crunchy twice-baked cookies are Naples's answer to Tuscany's more-famous Cantucci (page 98). And boy, do they deliver, with big pieces of almonds in every bite and rich flavor that is suffused with warm spices.

Quaresima is the Italian word for Lent, the period leading up to Easter, and that is when these cookies make their appearance. In keeping with the Lenten spirit of restraint and penitence, these cookies contain very little fat—just two egg yolks and the fat contained in the nuts. Even without butter, lard, or olive oil, these are immensely satisfying cookies, especially when dipped in your morning cappuccino.

MAKES ABOUT 32 COOKIES

2 cups (280 g) whole blanched and toasted almonds (see page 26)

1½ cups (180 g) unbleached all-purpose flour

½ teaspoon baking powder

¼ teaspoon fine salt

2 teaspoons Pisto Napoletano (page 217)

2 tablespoons minced Candied Orange Peel (page 220) or candied lemon peel, or a mix of both

2 large eggs, separated

¼ teaspoon lemon juice

¾ cup (150 g) sugar, plus 2 tablespoons for sprinkling

1 tablespoon honey

1. Preheat the oven to 350° F (180° C). Line a rimmed baking sheet with parchment. Measure out 1 cup (150 g) of the almonds and chop them very finely with a sharp knife or blitz them in the food processor with the metal blade until finely chopped-nearly ground. Leave the remaining almonds whole.

2. In a large bowl, stir together the flour, baking powder, salt, Pisto Napoletano, and minced candied peel. Stir in both the finely chopped almonds and whole almonds.

3. In a separate, clean stainless-steel bowl, beat the egg whites with the lemon juice until foamy. Add the sugar 1 to 2 tablespoons at a time, until soft peaks form. In a separate, small bowl, whisk together one yolk with the 1 tablespoon honey. Fold this into the egg white mixture, then fold the eggs into the bowl with the flour and nuts and continue to fold gently until a sticky dough comes together. Pat it into a ball and turn it out onto a lightly floured work surface.

4. Divide the dough in two and shape each piece into loaves about 1½ x 9 inches (4 by 23 cm). If the dough is too sticky to shape, moisten your hands very lightly with water. Place the loaves on the baking sheet, leaving at least 2 inches (5 cm) between them. In a small bowl, whisk the remaining yolk with 1 tablespoon water. Brush this over the tops of the loaves and sprinkle with the remaining 2 tablespoons of sugar.

5. Bake the quaresimali in the middle of the oven for 18 to 20 minutes, until browned and shiny on top, with cracks on the surface. Transfer the baking sheet to a wire rack to cool for 30 minutes. Lower the oven temperature to 300° F (150° C).

6. Cut each loaf crosswise into ¾-inch- (2-cm-) thick slices. Place them upright on the baking sheet and return them to the oven for 20 to 25 minutes to dry out. They will crisp further as they cool. Store the quaresimali in an airtight container for 2 weeks.

STRAZZATE MATERANE *(Basilicata)*

"Raggedy" Spiced Cookies from Matera

Many are the cookies in this book that I have described as rustic. These little misshapen clods are perhaps the most rustic of all. And yet, out of all the cookies in this book, they were among my daughter's favorites; for in spite of their coarse aspect, they are quite wonderful. Every bite gives you a satisfying mouthful of nuts, chocolate, orange, and spice.

Strazzate means "torn" or "raggedy" in the dialect of Matera, in Basilicata—Italy's instep—which is where these cookies are from, and it refers to the way they are shaped. You mix the crumbly dough by hand, then pinch off pieces and pack them into rough rounds. The perennially popular cookie is made both by home bakers and commercial bakeries.

One afternoon, I looked on as bakers at Forno Cifarelli, one of the city's historic bakeries (see page 142), stood around a worktable with an enormous mound of strazzate dough in the center and quickly and deftly picked off pieces, filling up baking sheet after baking sheet of these cookies.

Strazzate are a traditional holiday cookie in Matera, as the combination of spices and zest would suggest. These days, thanks to their ever-growing popularity, they are available year-round.

MAKES ABOUT 32 COOKIES

1⅔ cups (230 g) toasted almonds (see page 26), cooled

2 cups (240 g) unbleached all-purpose flour

1¼ cups (250 g) granulated sugar

1 teaspoon baking powder

¼ teaspoon fine salt

½ teaspoon ground cinnamon

¼ teaspoon ground cloves

2 ounces (57 g) bittersweet chocolate, finely chopped

1 teaspoon lemon or orange zest (1 small lemon or orange)

1 large egg

1 tablespoon sunflower or other neutral vegetable oil

4 to 5 tablespoons brewed espresso or coffee, cooled (see page 14)

1. Preheat the oven to 375° F (190° C). Line two rimmed baking sheets with parchment.

2. Chop the almonds coarsely, by hand or in a food processor, and place them in a large bowl. Stir in the flour, sugar, baking powder, salt, cinnamon, cloves, chocolate, and zest.

3. In a small bowl, whisk together the egg and sunflower oil. Make a well in the center of the dry ingredients and pour in the egg mixture, along with 4 tablespoons of the coffee. Mix everything together with a sturdy spatula or your hands. The dough should clump together but still be somewhat loose. Add the remaining 1 tablespoon of coffee, if needed. You're not looking for a cohesive dough, but a texture more like crumb topping, with large, dry-sticky clumps.

4. Pick up a small palmful (about 1 ounce; 30 g, but the idea is to eyeball it as you go). Squeeze the dough just until it sticks together and set it on one of the prepared baking sheets. The pieces you make should be roughly round, but a little misshapen. Rustic is the look you're aiming for. Press the tops of the cookies to flatten them slightly. You should end up with about 30 in all, 15 per sheet.

5. Bake the strazzate, one sheet at a time, in the middle of the oven for 18 to 20 minutes, until they are set, with lightly cracked tops, and lightly browned on the bottom and around the edges. Don't overbake or they may turn hard as they cool—though some bakers make them this way on purpose. Transfer the baking sheets to wire racks to cool for 10 minutes, then transfer the cookies from the sheets to the racks to cool completely. Store the strazzate in an airtight container. They will keep for about 1 week.

TARALLI DOLCI AL LIMONE *(Calabria)*

Iced Lemon Rings

There are *so* many versions of ring-shaped cookies in Italy, particularly in the south, from Campania and Puglia to Calabria and the islands. Some are more like biscuits than cookies—they are boiled first before being partially sliced, baked, and glazed, giving them a dry, airy texture. This version, which is firmly in the "cookie" realm, is made with olive oil in place of butter and finished with a lemon glaze and a shower of colorful sprinkles. The texture is crumbly but not too soft; the cookies are sturdy enough to dunk but also tender enough to enjoy on their own. It's traditional to set out a plate of these at Easter, but like so many Italian cookies, they have become popular year-round. Their bright lemon flavor makes them a good companion for a cup of tea.

MAKES ABOUT 36 COOKIES

COOKIES

3/4 cup (150 g) granulated sugar

2 large eggs plus 1 yolk

1/3 cup (75 ml) extra-virgin olive oil

1/2 cup (120 ml) whole milk, at room temperature

Finely grated zest of 1 lemon

1 teaspoon pure vanilla extract

4 cups plus 2 tablespoons (500 g) unbleached all-purpose flour

2 teaspoons baking powder

1/2 teaspoon fine salt

ICING

4 cups (480 g) confectioners' sugar

7 tablespoons freshly squeezed lemon juice, diluted with 2 tablespoons water

Pastel sprinkles, for decorating

1. To make the cookies: Place the sugar, eggs, and egg yolk in a large bowl and beat with a hand whisk until well combined and lightened in color. Whisk in the olive oil, milk, lemon zest, and vanilla extract.

2. Whisk together the flour, baking powder, and salt in a separate bowl. Pour this into the bowl of wet ingredients and stir with a spatula to create a soft dough. Scrape the dough onto a piece of reusable wrap or plastic wrap, wrap tightly, and refrigerate for at least 4 hours and up to overnight.

3. Preheat the oven to 350° F (180° C). Line two or three rimmed baking sheets with parchment. If you don't have three sheets, you can reuse one after baking the first batch of cookies.

4. Divide the dough into 36 equal pieces. If weighing, each piece should weigh just under 1 ounce (25 g). If the dough is sticky, sprinkle a little flour on the work surface, though this may not be necessary. Roll each piece of dough into a long, thin rope about 12 inches (30 cm) long. Bring the ends together and pinch them to make a loop. Twist the loop to create a double rope. Bring the ends together once more to create twisted rings. Set them on the baking sheets, leaving 1½ inches (4 cm) between them. You should be able to fit 12 cookies onto each sheet.

5. Bake, one sheet at a time, in the middle of the oven, for 23 to 25 minutes, until the cookies are puffed, set, and golden. Transfer the baking sheets to wire racks to cool completely.

6. To make the icing: Pour the confectioners' sugar into a medium to large bowl. Drizzle in enough of the lemon juice-water mixture to make a medium-thick but still pourable icing. Dip the taralli in the icing and set them back on the parchment-lined baking sheets. Before the icing starts to dry-this happens quickly-decorate the cookies with sprinkles. Let the icing dry completely, at least 2 hours, before serving. Store the taralli in an airtight container for up to 2 weeks, or even a little longer. To prevent sticking or scuffing, separate each layer with a piece of waxed paper or parchment.

COOKIES
OF THE ISLANDS

Recipes and stories from

SARDINIA AND SICILY

I received my first marriage proposal in Sicily. My family was staying with friends in Mazara del Vallo, an historic port town on the west coast of the island. I was just nineteen, but my suitor was even younger—four years old to be exact. He was our friends' nephew, a wiry little hellion with nut-brown skin and gold streaks in his hair who took to me probably because I enjoyed entertaining him without giving in to his antics. It's a long-ago memory, just one sweet detail of a carefree week spent tooling around the island, driving past almond and citrus groves, through brown hills dotted with spindly agave trees, squat prickly pears, and splashy bougainvillea. We took in Palermo, the Greek ruins at Agrigento, the salt flats of Trapani, and the ancient city of Erice, perched atop a hill overlooking the sea.

Erice is home to several confectionaries that specialize in almond-based cookies and pastries. Most famous among them is Pasticceria Maria Grammatico. Its proprietor, for whom the bakery is named, was born into poverty and raised in a convent, where she lived in seclusion, worked hard hand-peeling and grinding almonds, and eventually mastered the art of almond pastry. She left the convent as a young woman, opening her bakery in 1964 with nothing but three kilos of almonds. She still runs that wood-paneled bakery—now expanded to accommodate the (seemingly endless) stream of tourists who stop in to buy cookies, cannoli, and marzipan fruits. Here's a tip: Just up the street is a sister confectionary called Antica Pasticceria del Convento, once run by Maria's sister Angela and now managed by her children. It is often less crowded, and the pastries are just as good!

Convents are where many of Sicily's decadent sweets originated centuries ago. In Palermo, the cloistered Dominican nuns of the Monastery of Santa Caterina d'Alessandria once made and sold almond confections according to antique recipes, passing their creations to customers through a wall by way of a rotating metal wheel. The monastery is now a designated museum, and the once-shuttered bakery, called I Segreti del Chiostro (Secrets of the Cloisters) has been revived. On the opposite side of the island, in Noto, pastry chef Corrado Assenza brings a modern, minimalist sensibility to the almond creations at his celebrated bakery Caffè Sicilia (see Almond Joy, page 186).

Almonds are also central to the baking and confections of Sardinia, and artistry is a big part of the tradition. One of the most intriguing pastries I came across was Tiliccas (page 193), traditional wedding and baptism sweets—not quite cookie, but close enough. A pale dough of flour and lard is wrapped around a soft filling of nuts and honey. The pastry is cut and crimped using special brass pastry wheels with teeth that cut intricate patterns. Lengths of filled dough are formed into whimsical shapes like snails and snakes before being baked.

Not all island cookies require complicated techniques or fancy tools. Ciambelline Sarde (page 188) are among my favorites of all the cookies in this book, the recipe given to me by my Sardinian friend Andrea. They are, essentially, a *pasta frolla* (shortcrust pastry) cookie, but the dough is made with lard rather than butter, which makes them extra tender and crumbly. And no serious book about Italian cookies would leave out a recipe for Buccellati (page 183), also known as *cuccidati*, Sicily's signature spiced and iced fig roll cookies. It is a must-have on Italian American Christmas cookie plates, including mine.

AMARETTUS *(Sardinia)*

Sardinian Amaretti

Bakeries in Cagliari, the capital of Sardinia, all sell these classic almond cookies, each garnished with a single almond in the center.

I questioned whether I should include yet another recipe for amaretti—they are sprinkled throughout this book, and the ingredients for most of them are more or less identical. And yet, the results are all quite distinct, thanks to differences in the handling of those ingredients. In fact, it was eye-opening, as I researched this book, to see how many different and unique iterations the same set of ingredients could create.

In the end, I am glad I included these. They are easy to make and they have a particular appeal, puffing up beautifully in the oven and forming small telltale cracks on their sugared surfaces. They are crunchy on the outside and tender and chewy within. Use the freshest almonds you can find to give these cookies their due. Sardinians use a special nut grinder to achieve the correct texture, but a food processor works well. Note that the dough benefits from an overnight rest in the refrigerator, so start them a day before you plan to serve them.

MAKES 48 COOKIES

4 cups (600 g) blanched almonds

2 cups (400 g) granulated sugar, plus ½ cup (100 g) for rolling

¼ teaspoon pure almond extract, optional

2 tablespoons lemon zest (from 2 large lemons), plus ½ teaspoon freshly squeezed juice

¼ teaspoon fine salt

4 large (120 g) egg whites, at room temperature

48 whole almonds, skin-on or blanched

1. Place the nuts in the work bowl of a food processor fitted with the metal blade. Pulse until the nuts are coarsely chopped. Add the 2 cups (400 g) sugar and almond extract (if using), and pulse until the nuts are finely ground and the sugar is well incorporated. Pulsing rather than processing will prevent the machine from heating up too much and releasing the oils in the nuts. Transfer the mixture to a large bowl and sprinkle in the lemon zest and salt, working the zest in with your fingertips.

2. Pour the egg whites into the stainless-steel bowl of a stand mixer fitted with the whisk attachment. Beat on medium until the whites are frothy. Add the lemon juice and whisk on high until the whites are whipped to stiff peaks. Fold ⅔ of the whites into the nut mixture until no whites are visible. If the mixture is dry, add more whites until you have a dense, malleable dough that can be rolled into balls that hold their shape. Cover the bowl and refrigerate the dough overnight.

3. Preheat the oven to 325° F (165° C). Line two baking sheets with parchment (you will reuse both sheets to bake all the cookies).

4. Set the remaining ½ cup (100 g) sugar nearby in a bowl. Using a small cookie scoop or a tablespoon, scoop out generous walnut-size pieces of dough and roll them into a ball. If weighing, each ball should weigh less than 1 ounce (20 to 25 g). The dough will be sticky. If necessary, very lightly moisten your hands to prevent the dough from sticking to them. Roll the balls in the bowl of sugar and place them on the baking sheets, 16 per sheet. Press a single almond into the center of each cookie-you can poke it in vertically or press it in horizontally. The former creates more distinct cracks on the cookies' surface.

5. Bake, one sheet at a time, in the center of the oven for 15 to 18 minutes, until the cookies are barely set, lightly browned on the bottom, and pale gold and cracked on the surface. Transfer the baking sheets to wire racks to cool for 10 minutes; then transfer the cookies from the baking sheets to the racks to cool completely. Store the amaretti in an airtight container for up to 1 week.

ANICINUS | ANICINI *(Sardinia and Sicily)*

Anise Breakfast Cookies

The plain-Jane appearance of these oversize morning biscuits belies just how special they are: ethereally airy, perfectly crispy throughout, and with an unapologetically anise flavor. Like Cantucci di Prato (page 98), these breakfast cookies are sliced and twice-baked, but otherwise they bear little resemblance to their Tuscan cousins. They are typically two to three times longer, and their texture is more akin to rusks, or Melba toasts, due to the amount of air whipped into the batter. They proffer a satisfying crunch from first bite to last and are delicious either plain or spread with good jam—especially the Fig and Chocolate Preserves with Cognac (page 212).

MAKES 18 LARGE COOKIES

Cooking spray or a small amount of vegetable oil, for coating the baking pan

2 tablespoons whole aniseeds

2 cups (240 g) unbleached all-purpose flour

2 teaspoons baking powder

4 large eggs, separated, at room temperature

2 teaspoons lemon zest (from 1 lemon; plus ½ teaspoon freshly squeezed juice

1 cup (200 g) sugar, divided

¼ teaspoon fine salt

2 ounces (4 tablespoons; 57 g) unsalted butter, cut into ½ inch (12 mm) cubes, softened

4 tablespoons sambuca or other anise-flavored liqueur

2 teaspoons pure vanilla extract

1. Preheat the oven to 325° F (165° C). Line a 9 x 13-inch (23 x 33-cm) rimmed baking sheet (quarter-sheet pan) with parchment and coat it with cooking spray or brush with sunflower or vegetable oil.

2. Spread the aniseeds out in a small dry skillet and set over medium heat. Toast, stirring the seeds now and again, for 2 to 3 minutes, until they turn a shade or two darker and you can smell their warm chamomile-like scent. Transfer them to a small bowl or plate to cool completely.

3. Sift the flour and baking powder into a bowl and set aside.

4. In the bowl of a stand mixer fitted with the whisk attachment, beat the egg whites on medium until foamy. Add the lemon juice and beat on high until the whites are creamy. Add ½ cup (100 g) sugar, 1 tablespoon at a time, beating on high until shiny, with peaks that just curl at the tips.

5. In a separate bowl of the stand mixer, once again using the whisk attachment, whip the egg yolks with the remaining ½ cup (100 g) sugar for several minutes until the mixture is noticeably lightened in color and airy in texture. Beat in the lemon zest and salt. Add the butter cubes, 1 or 2 pieces at a time, beating well after each addition. Once the butter is incorporated, drizzle in the sambuca and vanilla extract.

6. Add one-third of the flour mixture, followed by one-third of the egg whites, to the egg yolk mixture. Fold these in with a sturdy spatula, taking care to use a light hand so as not to deflate the eggs. Fold in another third of the flour and another third of the egg whites, folding them in gently. Add the rest of the flour and egg whites and fold until no traces of flour or white egg white streaks remain. Scrape the batter into the prepared rimmed baking sheet and smooth out the top.

7. Bake in the middle of the oven for 20 to 25 minutes, until puffed and light golden on top. Transfer the baking sheet to a wire rack to cool for 30 minutes. Lower the oven temperature to 300° F (150° C). Line another large, rimmed baking sheet with parchment.

8. Remove the loaf from the baking pan and set it on a cutting board. Cut the loaf crosswise into 16 slices, each about ½ inch (12 mm) thick. Lay the slices on the large baking sheet, cut-side up, and bake for 15 minutes; turn the slices over and bake for another 10 to 15 minutes, until they are golden-brown and no longer moist. They will continue to crisp up as they cool. To serve, arrange the anicini on a platter, or stand them upright in a large decorative cup. Store them in an airtight container, where they will keep for up to 2 months, though they will surely not last that long.

BUCCELLATI | CUCCIDATI *(Sicily)*

Spiced Fig and Nut Rolls

If ever there was a cookie made for Christmas, it is these spiced and iced fig rolls from Sicily. Known both as buccellati and cuccidati in Sicilian dialect, they are made from a soft dough enriched with lots of butter (or lard). Enclosed within is a dense filling of dried fruit, nuts, citrus, chocolate and spice. It is heady!

Buccellati are popular throughout Sicily, and they seem to be just as beloved a holiday tradition among Italian Americans. Not surprisingly, recipes abound, each one slightly—or dramatically—different than the next. Every home baker has her blend of filling ingredients, some simple, others elaborate, with several kinds of nuts or dried fruit, and extra touches like honey or fruit jam.

The cookies can be shaped into simple bite-size rolls, or into larger, fanned-out lengths. A thin layer of icing and a scattering of colorful sprinkles give them a proper festive air.

I have my friend Marie Renello, who writes a wonderful blog called Proud Italian Cook, to thank for these classic, beloved cookies. It is her recipe I used as my road map, changing only a few things along the way. Both the dough and the filling for these cookies need to be refrigerated overnight, so start them a day before you plan to serve them.

MAKES ABOUT 40 SMALL ROLLS AND 20 LARGER FANS

FILLING

15 (340 g) dried Turkish or Calimyrna figs

½ cup (70 g) blanched and toasted almonds (see page 26)

½ cup (50 g) toasted walnut pieces (see page 26)

8 dates, pitted and cut into large pieces

¼ cup (35 g) coarsely chopped Candied Orange Peel (page 220)

2 tablespoons honey

2 tablespoons Jamaican rum

½ cup (70 g) golden raisins

2 ounces (57 g) grated bittersweet chocolate

¼ cup (85 g) Vanilla Apricot Jam (page 209) or store-bought apricot jam

COOKIE DOUGH

4 cups (480 g) unbleached all-purpose flour

¾ cup (150 g) sugar

1 teaspoon baking powder

½ teaspoon fine salt

1 teaspoon finely grated orange zest (from 1 small orange, such as a clementine)

8 ounces (2 sticks; 227 g) cold unsalted butter, cut into ½-inch (12-mm) cubes

4 large eggs, lightly beaten

ICING

2 cups (200 g) confectioners' sugar

4 tablespoons boiling water

1 teaspoon pure vanilla extract

¼ teaspoon pure almond extract

Colored nonpareils, for decorating

Continued >>

1. To make the filling: Start the day before you want to serve these, as both the filling and dough benefit from an overnight rest in the refrigerator to allow the flavors to meld. If the figs are on the firm/tough side, put them in a bowl and pour just enough boiling water over them to cover. Let them soften for 15 minutes, then drain.

2. Remove the stems from the figs, cut them into large pieces, and put them in the work bowl of a food processor fitted with the metal blade. Pulse briefly to chop them up. Add the toasted almonds and walnuts and pulse to combine. Add the dates and candied orange peel and pulse a few more times. Drizzle in the honey and rum and add the grated bittersweet chocolate and apricot jam. Pulse until the mixture comes together to form a thick paste. If it is too dense or dry, add a couple tablespoons of water. The paste should be dense enough to scoop but soft enough to pipe with a pastry bag.

3. Scoop the filling into a container with a tight-fitting lid and refrigerate overnight. The filling will keep for at least 2 weeks in the refrigerator, so you can make it days or weeks before you make the cookies.

4. To make the dough: Place the flour, sugar, baking powder, salt, and orange zest in the bowl of a food processor fitted with the metal blade. Pulse to combine the ingredients. Distribute the cubes of butter into the bowl and pulse until well incorporated and the mixture is crumbly. Pour the eggs through the feed tube and pulse until the mixture begins to clump together.

5. Turn the mixture out onto a large sheet of reusable wrap or plastic wrap and pat it into a disk. Wrap tightly and refrigerate overnight.

6. Remove the dough and filling from the refrigerator and let them soften for about 30 minutes. Preheat the oven to 350° F (180° C). Line two or three rimmed baking sheets with parchment. (You will need to reuse them.) Scoop the filling into a large, sturdy pastry bag fitted with a plain wide ($\frac{1}{2}$ inch; 12 mm) tip.

7. Divide the dough into 8 equal pieces. On a lightly floured work surface, roll each piece of the dough into a 4 x 12-inch (10 x 30-cm) rectangle, about $\frac{3}{8}$ inch (1 cm) thick. Make sure the bottom of the dough is not sticking to the work surface. Add a little more flour if needed. Pipe a line of filling along the length of the rectangle. Fold the long edges over the filling to enclose it, then roll the log over so that the seam is on the bottom. Roll the log back and forth a few times to lengthen the log to about 14 inches (35$\frac{1}{2}$ cm). Flatten the top slightly to create a squared-off log. Trim off the ends.

8. There are two traditional ways to cut these cookies. I use half the dough to make small buccellati, and the other half to make larger, more fanciful cookies.

To cut small buccellati, cut the log with a knife or a bench scraper at 1$\frac{1}{2}$-inch (4-cm) intervals into 8 nuggets. Set the cookies on one of the prepared sheets, leaving about 1 inch of space between them. Roll, fill, and cut out more cookies.

To cut the larger fan-shaped cookies, cut the log at 2$\frac{1}{2}$-inch (6-cm) intervals into 5 smaller logs. Now use a paring knife to make a series of crosswise slices in the logs every $\frac{1}{4}$ inch (6 mm) or so. Slice all the way down to the bottom through to your cutting board, but don't slice all the way to the spine (back edge) of the logs; you want the pieces to remain attached. Set the cookies on a prepared baking sheet and bend their spines slightly to form a curve or crescent, then fan out the slices where you made the cuts (see photo, page 182). Roll, fill, and cut out more cookies.

Whichever shape you choose, bake, one sheet at a time, in the middle of the oven, for 18 to 20 minutes, until golden. Transfer the baking sheets to wire racks to cool for 10 minutes, then transfer the cookies to wire racks to cool completely.

9. To make the icing: Whisk together the confectioners' sugar, boiling water, and vanilla and almond extracts in a bowl. The icing should be opaque, but just runny enough to brush onto the cookies. Place the cookies on parchment-lined baking sheets (I reuse the sheets I baked the cookies on). Brush a light coating of icing on the surface of the cookies, and sprinkle with nonpareils. Let the cookies sit for 2 hours until the icing is set. Store them in airtight containers, separating the layers with waxed paper or parchment to prevent the cookies from sticking. They will keep for up to 2 weeks.

BISCOTTI RICCI DEL GATTOPARDO *(Sicily)*

The Leopard's Rippled Almond Cookies

The 1958 novel *Il Gattopardo* (The Leopard) chronicles the decline of Sicilian aristocracy during the 1860s, after Giuseppe Garibaldi's successful takeover of the island as Italy transitions to a newly unified country. The Leopard in the title is Don Fabrizio, prince of Salina, who witnesses the changes wistfully, with a growing sense of inevitability.

These delicately airy almond cookies make a cameo in the book when the prince visits the Monastery of Santo Spirito, where cloistered Benedictine nuns produce them. The convent is not fictitious; it is located in Palma di Montechiaro, south of Agrigento, in western Sicily, and the nuns there have indeed been turning out biscotti ricci for centuries and continue to do so.

Like so many Sicilian sweets, biscotti ricci are made with almond flour or ground almonds. But they contain whole eggs rather than just egg whites, and the effect is noticeably different. They are surprisingly light and crispy, with a coating of sugar and deeply brown ridged edges.

The traditional method for making biscotti ricci is to extrude the stiff dough through a cookie press fit with a star-shaped disk, to create 3-inch- (8-cm-) long logs with ridges that give the cookies their name. I have come up with an easier alternative that, in my opinion, remains true to the original shape and spirit of the cookie. Rather than piping out logs, I simply use the cookie press to stamp out star or flower shapes. It's much quicker, doesn't require you to pop a vein from exertion, and the resulting cookies are every bit as pretty as the logs, with beautifully browned embossed tops and edges.

MAKES 60 COOKIES

2 to 2½ cups (200 to 250 g) superfine blanched almond flour

1 cup (200 g) granulated sugar, plus more for sprinkling

¼ teaspoon fine salt

¼ teaspoon ground cinnamon

1 teaspoon finely grated lemon zest (from ½ lemon)

1 teaspoon finely grated orange zest (from 1 small mandarin orange)

2 large eggs

¼ teaspoon pure almond extract

1. Preheat the oven to 350° F (180° C). Line two or three rimmed baking sheets with parchment. If you don't have three sheets, you can reuse one after baking the first batch of cookies.

2. Sift 2 cups (200 g) almond flour into a large bowl. Add the sugar, salt, cinnamon, and lemon and orange zests and whisk to combine the ingredients.

3. In a small bowl, whisk together the eggs and almond extract. Make a well in the bowl with the flour mixture and pour in the eggs. Stir with a sturdy spatula to make a stiff, cohesive, and sticky dough. If the dough seems too loose or malleable, sift in a little more flour. You are aiming for dough that will hold its shape well during baking.

4. Fit a cookie press with a flower disk and fill the chamber with the almond dough. Press five rows with four cookies per row onto one of the prepared baking sheets. Sprinkle the cookies liberally with sugar. Bake for 10 minutes, or until the cookies are golden-brown around the edges. While they are baking, press out more onto a second baking sheet, but don't sprinkle with sugar until right before you slide them into the oven. Once baked, transfer the baking sheets to wire racks to cool for 10 minutes, then transfer the cookies to the racks to cool completely. Store them in an airtight container for up to 2 weeks.

COOKIE STORY

ALMOND JOY

"Siamo mandorla dipendente." *We are beholden to almonds*, says pastry chef Corrado Assenza. We are sitting in his office, on the second floor of his renowned bakery, Caffè Sicilia, in Noto, Sicily. Downstairs, the pasticceria is humming with activity: regulars stopping in for an afternoon coffee at the bar; waitstaff nimbly carrying trays to and fro; and tourists clustered at outdoor tables, reveling in a taste of the classic and modern sweets for which the bakery has become famous: fresh ricotta-filled cannoli; mini cassata cakes cloaked in marzipan; fluffy white almond granita, served in a bowl, stuffed inside a brioche, or dolloped into a freshly brewed espresso—affogato-style; or the bakery's rich almond cookies.

With few exceptions—cannoli being one—almonds are the star ingredient at Caffè Sicilia. Almonds are kneaded into nougat, churned into gelato and granita, or made into the sweet paste that forms the foundation for the bakery's rustic cookies, painted marzipan confections, and cakes bejeweled with sparkling candied fruit.

The almond Corrado uses in his cookies and pastries is not just any almond; it is a variety called Mandorla Romana, which grows in the countryside between Noto and Avola in southeastern Sicily. It is one of three Sicilian cultivars grown in the region, along with Pizzuta and Fascionello. The Romana stands out, Corrado says, for its delicate, yet intense flavor, which is pure sweet almond with a slight bitter tinge; and for its creamy texture, due to its high fat content—nearly 60%.

"If you take one of our almonds and chew it, holding it in your mouth until it is finely ground, what you end up with is a sort of cream, he says. "If you do the same thing with an almond from California, or from Spain, or even Puglia, in the end what you have in your mouth is saliva and sand. That's the difference."

Almonds have a long history in Sicily. They were introduced by Arab rulers during the ninth century AD, along with citrus, sugar cane, pistachios, and various spices—ingredients that are still essential to Sicilian cooking and baking. The Romana is thought to be a cross between an ancient Arab variety of almond and an almond indigenous to Sicily. Corrado credits the cultivar, the soil, the area's microclimate (which includes moderate rain), and Sicilian farmers for the nut's superior quality.

"There is no industrial cultivation of the Romana," he says. The tree is a low-yield variety. In the 1970s, it was in danger of being wiped out as farmers began yanking it out of orchards and replacing it with varieties that produced more nuts. But the quality was not the same, Corrado says. His insistence on using Romana almonds has helped bring the almond back from the brink of extinction, and he currently relies on thirty small-production farms to supply his pasticceria.

Caffè Sicilia (see page 229) opened in 1892 on Corso Vittorio Emanuele, Noto's picturesque main street. By the time Corrado was born, in 1960, his aunt was running the bakery. She had no children, and from age thirteen, Corrado spent most of his summer vacations and holidays working in the kitchen. But by 1985, he had moved on. He was studying agriculture at the University of Bologna and dating a girl from Riccione, on the coast of Emilia-Romagna. Caffè Sicilia seemed far away.

Then, he got a call from his aunt. Her health was failing, and she wanted him to take over running the bakery. The other option would be to sell it. Saying yes meant giving up his studies and committing to life as a baker in Noto.

"I convinced my girlfriend—now my wife and mother of my children—to come with me," he says. "It was crazy at the beginning. I was twenty-five years old. It took a bit of adjustment and a little—a lot—of recklessness. But we moved ahead, step by step."

In Corrado's hands, Caffè Sicilia has earned recognition as one of Italy's best pasticcerie. In 2018, he and the bakery were featured in an episode of the Netflix series *The Chef's Table*. His philosophy is simple, he says, and can be found in his last name, Assenza. It translates to "absence." He has taken a less-is-more approach to his craft, paring down recipes, removing extraneous ingredients, and finding ways to coax forth the essence of seasonal fruits, fresh ricotta, and those almonds in his pastries and sweets. "We make food with what we have," he says.

While tourists gravitate toward the cannoli, almond granita, and cassata cakes, Corrado waxes poetic about the small round almond cookies called Normanni and Moreschi that occupy the top shelf of one of the bakery's display cases. The cookies are the same, except Normanni are made with blanched almonds and Moreschi with skin-on almonds. The plain brown cookies, favored by locals, are based on a centuries-old convent recipe, and their appearance is deceptive. "It's a half-sphere, a little dome with a crumbly almond paste shell and inside a tender heart of marmalade," Corrado describes. "The moisture from the marmalade eventually transforms the cookie shell, turning it from crumbly to soft and tender." And, in fact, when you bite into one it's hard to believe that something so plain looking can hold so much flavor—the sweet depth of the almonds and the tart sweetness of the citrus marmalade.

"The great classics," Corrado says, "will always be loved and appreciated."

CIAMBELLINE SARDE *(Sardinia)*

Sardinian Cookie Rings

My friend Andrea Locci works as a chef at a gastro pub in London. But he is originally from Cagliari, the capital of Sardinia. And while he is a terrific chef, Andrea really, *really* excels at baking. His repertoire includes an enticing mix of rustic pies and cakes, creamy spoon desserts, and, of course, cookies. When I asked him about his favorite Sardinian cookies, Andrea mentioned these delicate, crumbly rings, traditionally made with lard, and kindly shared his recipe.

These cookies are similar to other pasta frolla (shortcrust pastry) cookies, but using pastry flour, as well as lard in place of butter, gives them a delicate texture and a warm rich flavor. The traditional shape for these cookies is a ring or a flower with a hole in the center, similar to the Canestrelletti di Torriglia (page 50). I've gone a bit rogue, using a variety of cookie cutters to stamp out rings, hearts, and flowers. Andrea brushes the tops of his cookies with a simple egg-white wash, while I've opted for a crackled sugar coating. It makes the cookies even more tempting.

MAKES 4 TO 5 DOZEN COOKIES, DEPENDING ON SIZE AND SHAPES

4 cups (480 g) pastry flour, plus more for the work surface

1 cup (200 g) granulated sugar, plus more for sprinkling

2 teaspoons baking powder

½ teaspoon fine salt

2 teaspoons finely grated lemon zest (from 1 lemon)

7 ounces (1 cup; 200 g) leaf lard, at cool room temperature (65° F; 18° C) (see page 15)

2 large eggs, lightly beaten

1. Place the flour, sugar, baking powder, salt, and lemon zest in the bowl of a stand mixer fitted with the paddle attachment. Mix on low to incorporate the ingredients. With the mixer on medium-low, gradually drop in clumps of the softened lard, allowing the pieces to work themselves into the flour mixture. Once the lard has been incorporated, pour in the eggs and mix on medium until a dough comes together. Wrap the dough tightly in reusable wrap or plastic wrap and refrigerate for several hours, or up to overnight.

2. Preheat the oven to 325° F (165° C). Line two to three rimmed baking sheets with parchment.

3. Lightly flour a work surface. Divide the dough in half and rewrap one half. Roll the other half out into a large circle about ¼ inch (6 mm) thick. Use a 2½-inch (6-cm) ring or flower-shaped cookie cutter—whichever shape you like—to cut out as many cookies as you can. Arrange them on the baking sheets, leaving about 1 inch (2½ cm) of space between them. (You will need to reuse at least one of the baking sheets to bake all the cookies.)

4. Right before baking, brush the tops of the cookies ever so lightly with water, and sprinkle with sugar. (If you have more than one sheet of cookies ready to go, only brush and sugar the cookies that are going into the oven first.) Bake the cookies, one sheet at a time, in the middle of the oven, for 10 to 15 minutes, until they are just set and pale gold, and their sugared tops are crackled. Transfer the baking sheets to wire racks to cool for 10 minutes, then transfer the cookies from the baking sheets to the racks to cool completely. Store the cookies in airtight containers for up to 2 weeks.

PABASSINAS *(Sardinia)*

Iced Raisin Cookies

The bakeries of Sardinia are filled with a splendid array of sweets ranging from fancy, intricately decorated iced confections to homey biscuits and cookies. These raisin-studded spice cookies lean more toward homey, but a finish of creamy white icing and a demure shower of sprinkles brings to them a touch of elegance. The spice in the cookies comes from a traditional Sardinian blend called La Saporita, "the tasty one," which mixes anise, cloves, coriander, nutmeg, and—notably—caraway seed.

The name *pabassinas* (or *papassinas*, as it is also spelled) refers to the raisins in the dough. The Italian term for raisins is *uva passa*, which in Sardinian dialect becomes *pabassa* or *papassa*.

Pabassinas belong to a long list of Italian cookies that are traditionally baked on November 1st and 2nd to celebrate All Saint's Day and Day of the Dead. Their soft, crumbly texture and delicate spice make them a lovely addition to a holiday cookie plate.

MAKES ABOUT 42 COOKIES

COOKIE

½ cup (70 g) golden raisins

2 cups (240 g) unbleached all-purpose flour

½ cup (100 g) sugar

1 teaspoon La Saporita (page 217)

¼ teaspoon fine salt

3½ ounces (7 tablespoons; 100 g) leaf lard or 4 ounces (113 g) cold, unsalted butter, cut into ½-inch (12-mm) cubes

Scant 3 tablespoons whole milk

1 teaspoon baker's ammonia (see page 17) or 1 teaspoon baking powder

1 large egg, lightly beaten

⅓ cup (50 g) blanched almonds, coarsely chopped

½ cup (50 g) walnut halves, coarsely chopped

ICING

1¼ cups (150 g) confectioners' sugar, plus more as needed

1 large (30 g) egg white

Colored nonpareils, for decorating

Continued >>

1. To make the cookies: Place the raisins in a small bowl and pour enough hot water over them to cover. Let them steep for 1 to 2 hours before proceeding with the recipe.

2. Place the flour, sugar, La Saporita, and salt in the work bowl of a food processor fitted with the metal blade. Pulse to combine. Add the lard in pieces and pulse to break up and distribute the fat.

3. Place the milk in a small bowl and heat it in a microwave until it is steaming but not boiling or heat it in a small pan on the stovetop until steaming. Whisk the baker's ammonia into the hot milk. Pour this through the feed tube into the flour mixture and pulse to combine. Pulse in the lightly beaten egg, followed by the chopped almonds and walnuts.

4. Drain the golden raisins, add them to the processor and pulse briefly just to combine. Turn out the dough onto a sheet of reusable wrap or plastic wrap, pat it into a disk, wrap tightly, and refrigerate for several hours or up to overnight.

5. Remove the dough from the fridge and allow it to soften for about 30 minutes. Preheat the oven to 350° F (180° C). Line two or three rimmed baking sheets with parchment–if you don't have three, reuse one after baking the first batch of cookies.

6. Cut the dough into 3 or 4 pieces. Roll each piece out on a lightly floured work surface into a 1-inch- (2½-cm-) thick log–about the thickness of an Italian sausage. If the dough starts to break apart as you are rolling, just press it back together and reroll. With the palm of your hand, flatten the log until it is a little less than ½ inch (12 mm) in height. Cut the flattened log on the diagonal into rhombuses that are 1½ x 2 inches (4 by 5 cm).

7. Arrange the cookies on the baking sheets, 12 to 16 per sheet. Bake, one sheet at a time, in the middle of the oven, for 12 to 15 minutes, until they are set and lightly browned. Transfer the baking sheets to wire racks to cool for 20 minutes, then transfer the cookies to the racks to cool completely.

8. To make the icing: Arrange the cookies on parchment-lined baking sheets (I reuse the parchment on which I baked the cookies). Whisk the confectioners' sugar and egg white in a bowl. The icing should be thick enough to fall in a dense ribbon from the whisk. If it's too thin, add a little more confectioners' sugar. Use a small knife to spread the icing on the cookies, leaving a little space at the edges. Garnish with a light sprinkling of nonpareils. Let the cookies sit for 2 hours, until the icing is set. Store the pabassinas in layers, separated by waxed paper or parchment, in an airtight container, for up to 2 weeks.

TILICCAS *(Sardinia)*

Sardinian Almond and Honey Snails

Sprinkled throughout this book are a just a few recipes for sweets that don't really qualify as cookies. Calcionelli, the fried mini pastries on page 148, and the colorful Favette Triestine, on page 60, are two examples. These Sardinian sweets—more confection than cookie—showcase the ingenuity of Sardinian bakers who turn humble ingredients into extraordinary edible art.

Tiliccas, also called *tiriccas* and *tilicas*, are a traditional wedding and baptism celebration sweet in Sardinia. The pale dough made from semolina flour, water, and lard, is rolled out into a thin strip and cut using a Sardinian pastry cutter with intricately patterned teeth. The strips are filled with a sticky paste typically containing ground almonds cooked with grape must syrup or honey and semolina flour. The dough is wrapped around ropes of this sticky filling and then formed into snakes, snails, and other whimsical shapes. The sweets are baked at a low temperature just until the dough is set but not browned.

I use a pasta machine to roll out the dough to the appropriate thinness (about ⅛ inch; 3 mm) and then cut strips of manageable lengths to create the shapes. These sweets are not for everyone; the casing of dough, which turns slightly crunchy during baking, does not add much flavor; more than anything it is a vessel for the soft, candy-like filling. It's the filling and the whimsical designs that make them worth the effort.

I have deviated from the traditional version of these sweets by using a mix of all-purpose flour and finely ground semolina, known as *semola rimacinata* in Italian.

MAKES ABOUT 16 SWEETS

DOUGH

1½ cups (180 g) unbleached all-purpose flour, plus more for the work surface

½ cup (60 g) semola rimacinata (finely ground semolina flour)

¼ cup (50 g) cold leaf lard

Scant ½ cup (125 ml) tepid water

FILLING

1⅔ cups (230 g) toasted blanched almonds (see page 26)

1 teaspoon finely grated orange zest (from 1 small orange)

1 teaspoon finely grated lemon zest (from ½ lemon)

½ teaspoon ground cinnamon

¾ cup (250 g) honey

2 tablespoons semola rimacinata (finely ground semolina flour)

Colorful nonpareils, for decorating

Continued >>

1. To make the dough: Place the flours in a food processor fitted with the metal blade and pulse to combine them. Scatter the lard in small clumps into the bowl and pulse to incorporate. Pour the water into the feed tube and pulse until the mixture clumps together into a solid piece of dough. Turn out the dough onto a clean work surface and knead it for several minutes into a smooth ball. If the dough misbehaves and doesn't become smooth, wrap it in reusable wrap or plastic wrap and let it rest for 10 minutes, then knead again. Wrap it again and let it rest at room temperature while you make the filling.

2. To make the filling: Pulse the almonds in the food processor fitted with the metal blade until they are coarsely ground. Add the orange and lemon zests and the cinnamon and process until the nuts are finely ground but still have a little texture. Transfer the mixture to a bowl.

3. Place the honey and ¼ cup (60 ml) water in a nonstick skillet or saucepan and set it over medium heat. Stir to combine. When the honey is loose, stir in the nut mixture, stirring until the nuts are well moistened. Stir in the semolina, reduce the heat to medium-low, and cook until the mixture is as thick as polenta and beginning to pull away from the sides and bottom of the pan. Scrape the paste into a bowl and let it cool to room temperature; it will stiffen as it cools.

4. Preheat the oven to 325° F (165° C). Line two rimmed baking sheets with parchment. Set up a pasta machine or fit a stand mixer with the pasta rolling attachment. Cut the pasta dough into quarters and rewrap three. Feed the fourth quarter through the pasta rollers, beginning at the widest setting and moving on to narrower settings until you have a strip of dough that is about ⅛ inch (3 mm) thick or slightly thinner. If the strip of dough is tacky, lightly flour the work surface. Lay the strip out before you and use a fluted pastry wheel to cut it into 6- to- 8-inch (16- to- 20-cm) lengths that are 1½ to 2 inches (4 to 5 cm) wide.

5. Moisten your hands with water. Pinch off some of the cooled filling and roll it into a rope about 6 to 8 inches (16 to 20 cm) in length and ½ inch (12 mm) thick. Lay the rope onto one of the lengths of dough. Lift up the long sides of the dough to fit around the filling, leaving the top open so that a little of the filling is visible. Now bend or roll up the lengths to form S shapes, snails, or open circles. Set the shapes on one of the prepared baking sheets, leaving only a little space between them (they won't expand). You should be able to fit 6 to 8 on each sheet.

6. Bake, one sheet at a time, in the middle of the oven, for about 10 minutes, until they are set but not browned. The dough should remain pale in color. Transfer the baking sheets to wire racks to cool completely. Store the tiliccas in an airtight container for up to 1 week.

FROLLINI AL PISTACCHIO *(Sicily)*

Pistachio Butter Cookies

I cannot claim that these are traditional Sicilian cookies. They are simply butter cookies that contain ground pistachios or pistachio flour. But I've included them here because they feel Sicilian in spirit. Pistachios are the star ingredient, and some of the world's best pistachios come from Sicily, specifically Bronte, situated on the slopes of Mount Etna. The nuts that grow here are sweet, buttery, and fruity, and when peeled they practically glow a pale lime green, a color Sicilians refer to as *oro verde*, or "green gold."

Pistachio flour is not as widely available as almond flour, but you can find it online (see Sources, page 225), and, while expensive, it is worth seeking out for its rich green color and consistent texture. Otherwise, substitute pistachios and grind them yourself in a food processor. Look for raw pistachios that are skinned as well as shelled; they are bright green in color.

You can taste the nuts' buttery flavor in every bite of these cookies. No gilding is necessary. However, if you want to take them over the top, try sandwiching the cookies with a layer of sweet pistachio cream.

MAKES 40 SINGLE COOKIES OR 20 COOKIE SANDWICHES

2 cups (240 g) unbleached all-purpose flour

1 cup (120 g) pistachio flour (see Sources, page 225), or 1 cup (120 g) finely ground pistachios

¾ cup (150 g) sugar

½ teaspoon fine salt

1 teaspoon baking powder

2 teaspoons lemon zest (from 1 lemon)

6 ounces (12 tablespoons; 170 g) unsalted butter, cut into ½-inch (12-mm) cubes, at cool room temperature

1 large egg, plus 2 yolks

1 teaspoon pure vanilla extract

1 (7-ounce/200-g) jar sweet pistachio cream (see Sources, page 225), for sandwiching the cookies, optional

1. Place the flour, pistachio flour (or ground pistachios), sugar, salt, baking powder, and lemon zest in the work bowl of a food processor fitted with the blade attachment. Pulse to combine the ingredients. Distribute the butter around the inside of the work bowl and pulse until the cubes of butter are broken up and the mixture resembles crumbs. In a small bowl, whisk the egg and yolks with the vanilla. Pour this through the feed tube and pulse just until the dough begins to clump but is still crumbly.

2. Scrape the dough out onto a clean work surface, gather it together and pat it firmly into a disk. Wrap tightly in reusable wrap or plastic wrap and refrigerate for at least 2 hours or up to overnight.

3. Remove the dough from the refrigerator and let it sit for 30 minutes to soften slightly. Preheat the oven to 325° F (165° C). Line two rimmed baking sheets with parchment.

4. On a lightly floured work surface, roll the dough out into a large circle about ¼ inch (6 mm) thick. Use a 2-inch (5-cm) fluted round cookie cutter to cut out as many circles as you can, placing them on the prepared sheets as you go. Gather and reroll the scraps and cut out more circles. You should end up with about 40. If you want to make sandwich cookies, use a smaller (¾ inch; 2 cm) cutter to cut out the centers of half the cookies. (I save these centers and bake them separately; they make dainty little cookies.)

5. Bake the cookies, one sheet at a time, in the middle of the oven for 18 to 20 minutes, until they are set on top and lightly browned on the bottom. Transfer the baking sheets to wire racks to cool for 10 minutes, then transfer the cookies to the racks to cool completely.

6. If making sandwiches, spread 1 to 2 teaspoons of pistachio cream on the bottom cookies (those without the centers cut out). Sandwich them with a top cookie, pressing lightly. Store the cookies in an airtight container for up to 1 week. For sandwich cookies, separate each layer with a sheet of waxed paper or parchment.

BAKER'S NOTE: *These frollini are also delicious drizzled with melted bittersweet or white chocolate. See page 27 for instructions on melting and tempering chocolate.*

PASTE DI PISTACCHIO *(Sicily)*

Pistachio S Cookies

This variation on soft amaretti cookies substitutes pistachio flour for half the almond flour. The result is a lovely cookie, delicately chewy in texture, with a toasty note and a subtly green hue. It is traditional to shape these cookies into an S, which makes them perfect for dunking. However, you can also roll them into balls, which is a bit easier to manage and produces pretty domed spheres with a crackled surface.

You can substitute almonds and pistachios for the flours, if you prefer. Use blanched almonds and skinned pistachios and grind them finely in a food processor, taking care not to overprocess, or you will release the oil from the nuts.

It's not traditional, but I add a smattering of minced candied lemon peel to the cookie dough. The combination of the warm almonds and pistachios and sweet citrus is irresistible. The dough for these cookies needs to be refrigerated overnight, so start them a day before you plan to serve them.

MAKES 24 COOKIES

1½ cups (150 g) superfine blanched almond flour, or 1¼ cups (150 g) finely ground blanched almonds

1¼ cups (150 g) pistachio flour, or 1¼ cups (150 g) finely ground pistachios

1 cup (200 g) granulated sugar

1 tablespoon minced Candied Lemon Peel (page 220), or 2 teaspoons finely grated lemon zest (from 1 lemon)

¼ teaspoon fine salt

2 (64 g) large egg whites, at room temperature

¼ teaspoon freshly squeezed lemon juice

1 tablespoon honey

1 cup (120 g) confectioners' sugar plus more to decorate

1. Place the almond flour, pistachio flour, and the sugar in the work bowl of a food processor fitted with the metal blade. Pulse to combine the ingredients thoroughly. Add the candied lemon peel and salt and pulse a few times to incorporate. Transfer the mixture to a large bowl.

2. In a separate bowl, whisk together the egg whites, lemon juice, and honey until the mixture is pale and frothy. Pour this into the flour mixture and fold it in with a sturdy spatula. You will end up with a sticky dough. Wrap it tightly in reusable wrap or plastic wrap and refrigerate overnight.

3. Preheat the oven to 350° F (180° C). Line two rimmed baking sheets with parchment.

4. Spread the confectioners' sugar onto a clean work surface. Divide the dough in half. Roll each piece on the sugar-coated surface into a log about 8 inches (20 cm) long and 2 inches (5 cm) in diameter. With a sharp knife or bench scraper, cut each log into 12 equal slices, to yield 24 slices.

5. With sugar-coated hands, roll out each slice into a 3- to 4-inch (7½- to 10-cm) log and bend the ends to form an S. Arrange the cookies on the baking sheets, lightly pressing down on their tops to flatten them slightly.

6. Bake the cookies, one sheet at a time, in the middle of the oven for 10 to 12 minutes, or until their edges are just beginning to brown and their tops are starting to crack. The cookies should still be quite soft; they will firm up as they cool. Transfer the baking sheets to racks to cool completely.

7. Serve the cookies as they are or shower them with a fresh coating of confectioners' sugar. Store them in an airtight container for up to 1 week.

PASTICCINI DI MANDORLA *(Sicily)*

Little Almond Cookies

How I love these elegant little almond sweets. Their ingredients are similar to other almond-based cookies in this book. But it's the pretty piping and finishing flourishes, plus a splash of amaretto liqueur, that elevate them beyond an everyday cookie. Pasticcini di mandorla are a classic of Sicilian pasticceria and every bakery sells them. They vary in character; some are more like little mouthfuls of marzipan, others are like cookies in texture, with a crispy exterior and tender center. Some are piped, others molded by hand into little rounds or misshapen nuggets. The typical decoration for these cookies is red and green glacé cherries, but you can stud them with almonds, if you prefer. I tend to do some of each. The final touch is a light brushing of honey once the cookies come out of the oven, which gives them an alluring shine.

MAKES ABOUT 32 COOKIES

2 cups (200 g) superfine blanched almond flour, plus more if needed

1 cup (200 g) sugar

¼ teaspoon fine salt

1 teaspoon finely grated lemon zest (about ½ lemon), plus ¼ teaspoon freshly squeezed juice

3 large (90 g) egg whites, at room temperature

1 tablespoon amaretto liqueur

½ teaspoon pure almond extract

DECORATION

Glacé red and green cherries

Whole blanched almonds

½ cup (170 g) honey

1. Measure the almond flour, sugar, salt, and lemon zest in a bowl. Whisk well to combine and to break up any lumps of almond flour.

2. In a separate bowl, whisk together the egg whites and lemon juice until foamy. Pour this into the almond flour mixture, along with the amaretto and almond extract. Stir everything together with a sturdy spatula until you have a soft, sticky dough. It should be firm enough to pipe and hold its shape. Sprinkle in a little more almond flour if it is too wet or soft. Cover the bowl and refrigerate for 1 hour.

3. Preheat the oven to 350° F (180° C). Line two rimmed baking sheets with parchment. Scoop the chilled dough into a large, sturdy pastry bag fitted with a ½-inch (5-mm) closed-star tip. Holding the tip directly over the parchment, pipe out grooved stars about 1½ inches (4 cm) in diameter, leaving about 1½ inches (4 cm) of space between them. You should be able to fit 16 cookies onto each sheet. Garnish each cookie with a glacé cherry or blanched almond.

4. Bake the pasticcini, one sheet at a time, in the middle of the oven, for about 12 minutes, until the edges are golden brown. Take care not to overbake or the cookies may be tough. Transfer the baking sheets to wire racks.

5. Warm the honey in the microwave until it is loose. While the cookies are still warm, brush them with a light coating of honey. Let the pasticcini cool completely. Store them in an airtight container for up to 1 week.

REGINELLE *(Sicily)*

The Queen's Cookies

These squat, sesame-encrusted fingers are a fixture in the bakeries of Palermo, Sicily's capital. But their reach and popularity extend far beyond the confines of the city, and you'll find them not only in bakeries across Sicily but across the Atlantic Ocean in many Italian American bakeries. Their name honors Margherita di Savoia, or Regina Margherita, Italy's first queen after the country's unification in 1861.

Also known as *biscotti della Regina* and *biscotti inciminati* (from *cimino*, the Sicilian word for sesame), reginelle have earned their popularity. They crunch and crumble when you bite into them, and they are infused with the quintessential Sicilian flavors of citrus and vanilla, along with a warm hit of cinnamon. Traditional recipes call for lard, which is what I have used here. You can substitute butter and the cookies will still be delicious, though they won't have that rich undertone that good leaf lard imparts (see page 15).

MAKES 24 COOKIES

2¼ cups (270 g) unbleached all-purpose flour

½ cup (100 g) granulated sugar

½ teaspoon ground cinnamon

¼ teaspoon fine salt

1 teaspoon finely grated lemon zest (from ½ lemon)

1 teaspoon finely grated orange zest (from 1 small orange, such as a clementine)

3 ounces (6 tablespoons; 85 g) cold leaf lard; or 3 ounces (6 tablespoons; 85 g) cold unsalted butter, cut into ½ inch (12 mm) cubes

1 large egg

2 teaspoons pure vanilla extract

¼ cup (60 ml) whole milk

1 teaspoon ammonium bicarbonate or 2 teaspoons baking powder (see Baker's Note)

¾ cup (105 g) sesame seeds

1. Measure the flour, sugar, cinnamon, salt, and lemon and orange zests into a large bowl and stir to combine the ingredients. Add the lard in small clumps and work them in with your fingers, until you have a flaky, crumbly mixture.

2. In a small bowl, whisk together the egg and vanilla. Pour this into the bowl of dry ingredients. In another small bowl, stir together the milk and ammonium bicarbonate. Add this to the dry ingredients and mix everything together with a sturdy spatula or wooden spoon until it comes together. Briefly knead the dough to work in any dry bits and smooth it out. Pat it into a disk, wrap tightly in reusable wrap or plastic wrap, and refrigerate for at least 2 hours or up to overnight.

3. Preheat the oven to 400° F (200° C). Line two rimmed baking sheets with parchment.

4. Toast the sesame seeds. Heat a dry skillet on medium heat. When the skillet is hot, pour in the sesame seeds. Toast, stirring the seeds around often to prevent scorching or uneven darkening, for 3 to 4 minutes, until they are fragrant and have turned a couple of shades darker. Pour them onto a plate or into a shallow bowl to cool.

5. Remove the dough from the refrigerator and divide it into 4 quarters. Roll out each piece into a rope about 16 inches (40 cm) long and 1 inch (2½ cm) thick. Cut the ropes crosswise into 2-inch (5-cm) nuggets. You should end up with 32 total. Roll each piece in the toasted sesame seeds, coating them generously. If the seeds are not sticking well, moisten your hands to help them adhere. Set the cookies on the prepared baking sheets, 15 to 16 cookies per sheet.

6. Bake, one sheet at a time, in the middle of the oven, for 25 minutes, until the cookies are puffed, set, and richly browned, with cracks on the surface. Transfer the baking sheets to wire racks to cool for 10 minutes, then transfer the cookies to the racks to cool completely. Store the reginelle in an airtight container for up to 2 weeks.

BAKER'S NOTE: *If using baking powder, stir it into the dry ingredients at the beginning of the recipe.*

BASICS
AND EMBELLISHMENTS

Recipes for

FOUNDATIONS, FILLINGS, AND FLOURISHES

PASTA FROLLA

Basic Italian Shortcrust Pastry

The words "pasta frolla" appear throughout this book. It is, essentially, the Italian version of shortcrust pastry, an egg and butter-rich (or lard-rich) dough used in countless cookie and tart crust recipes. There are as many versions of pasta frolla as there are bakers in Italy, and they differ in any number of ways. Some employ more butter and fewer eggs; others use only egg yolks rather than whole eggs. Some doughs are worked by hand, others in the mixer. Some include a leavening agent for lightness. The doughs can be flavored with vanilla, rum, citrus zest, or cocoa powder. You'll find quite a few of these variations among the recipes in this book.

Here, I am sharing my simplest, most basic pasta frolla recipe, and a rich chocolate variation. The dough comes together easily in the food processor and rolls out like a bolt of silk. You can use either of these doughs to make any number of cookies—cutouts, roll-and-slice, sandwiches and more. And you can use them both together to make bicolor cookies, such as Biscotti Girandola (page 96), beautiful black and white spirals. By the way, these two doughs also make tender tart crusts that hold their shape and don't get soggy. I use them to make classic jam crostata, as well as ricotta and cream-filled tarts.

MAKES ABOUT 1½ POUNDS, ENOUGH FOR SEVERAL DOZEN COOKIES, DEPENDING ON SIZE

3 cups (360 g) pastry flour

3/4 cup (100 g) confectioners' sugar

1/2 teaspoon finely grated lemon zest

1/2 teaspoon finely grated orange zest

1/4 teaspoon fine salt

8 ounces (2 sticks; 227 g) cold unsalted butter, cut into 1/2-inch (12- mm) cubes

3 large egg yolks

1/2 teaspoon pure vanilla extract

1. Place the flour, confectioners' sugar, lemon and orange zests, and salt in the work bowl of a food processor fitted with the metal blade and pulse to combine the ingredients. Distribute the butter around the inside of the bowl and pulse to break up the pieces.

2. Drop in the egg yolks and add the vanilla extract. Pulse just until the dough starts to clump together. Turn the dough out onto a clean work surface, pat it together into a ball, and knead briefly to make it smooth. Wrap the dough tightly in reusable wrap or plastic wrap and refrigerate until thoroughly chilled–overnight is best.

CHOCOLATE PASTA FROLLA VARIATION: *To make chocolate pasta frolla, replace ½ cup (60 g) of the pastry flour with ½ cup (40 g) unsweetened cocoa powder. Omit the lemon and orange zests–or use just orange zest, if you want a bit of citrus flavor–and increase the amount of vanilla extract to 1 teaspoon. Proceed with the recipe as directed above.*

BISCOTTI DI INZUPPO AL CIOCCOLATO 12-24
CALCIONELLI Dough
PASTA DI PISTACCHI
Celli Ripieni Dough
ISTRIAN WEDDING COOKIE Dough enough for 10
Ricciarelli Dough

CONFETTURA DI ALBICOCCA

Vanilla Apricot Jam

Fresh apricots have a short season and can be hard to come by. Luckily, dried apricots make excellent jam, with a rich, sweet-tart flavor and perfect sticky, spreadable consistency that doesn't require pectin. In addition to filling the Baci di Dama Calabresi (page 141), this glowing orange-hued jam can be spread on cake layers and is delicious on croissants or just plain toast.

Dried apricots are available at most supermarkets, as well as online. Look for apricots that are bright in color and still have some moisture in them. These plump up nicely when reconstituted in water and make the prettiest jam.

MAKES 1½ PINTS (750 G)

8 ounces (227 g) dried apricots, preferably sulfured, about 2 scant cups

2 cups (475 ml) water

2½ cups (500 g) granulated sugar

1 vanilla bean

EQUIPMENT

Food processor

3 sanitized ½-pint (250-ml) jars and their lids

Candy thermometer

Basic water-bath canning equipment (optional)

1. Place the apricots in the work bowl of a food processor fitted with a metal blade. Pulse to chop the apricots coarsely, taking care not to overprocess. Scrape into a bowl and pour in the water. Gently mix, cover, and let the apricots steep for several hours or up to overnight, until the fruit is soft and has absorbed most of the water.

2. Pour the apricots and any remaining liquid into a medium heavy-bottom saucepan. Stir in the sugar. Split the vanilla bean open lengthwise, scrape the seeds into the pan and add the pod. Cook on medium-low heat for about 10 minutes, stirring to dissolve the sugar and break up any clumps of vanilla seeds. Raise the heat to medium-high and bring to a boil. Lower the heat to medium and cook at a lively simmer, stirring, for about 20 minutes, or until the mixture registers 220° F (104° C) on a candy thermometer. You should be able to drag a path along the bottom of the pot with a silicone spatula. If you don't have a thermometer, use the freezer test: Place 2 or 3 small bowls or plates in the freezer to chill while you cook the preserves. When the mixture has thickened, spoon a little onto one of the cold plates and return it to the freezer for about 2 minutes. The spread should be thick enough that it moves sluggishly when you tilt the plate. If it's too runny, let the preserves cook another 3 to 5 minutes and retest.

3. Remove the vanilla bean pod. Ladle the jam into three clean half-pint (250 ml) jars, leaving ¼-inch (6-mm) headspace. Wipe the rims with a clean, damp cloth, and screw on the lids. Process the jars in a boiling water bath for 10 minutes. Remove the jars from the water and set them upright on a clean kitchen towel to cool completely. Within a couple of minutes, you should hear the jar lids "ping" signifying that they have sealed properly. Processed jars will keep in a cool dark spot for up to 1 year. Store any jars that have not sealed in the refrigerator for up to 1 month.

If you don't want to process the jars, simply ladle the jam into sturdy freezer-safe containers. Let it cool to room temperature before storing in the freezer for up to 1 year. You can also refrigerate the jam for up to 3 months, but be sure to check for mold before using, and discard any jam that shows signs of molding or discoloration, bubbles or foam (fermentation), or that smells off or unpleasant.

CONFETTURA DI AMARENA

Sour Cherry Preserves

This sweet-tart preserve is more like a spoon fruit than jam, with generous pieces of cherries suspended in a sticky, soft-set jam. Use it as a filling for Biscotti di Ceglie (page 144), Ceppelliate di Trivento (page 155), and Occhi di Bue (page 72).

It's also delicious spread on morning toast or swirled into yogurt.

MAKES 1½ PINTS (750 G)

1½ pounds (680 g) sour cherries, pitted, with pits reserved (see Baker's Note)

1 cup (140 g) dried sour cherries

2 cups (400 g) granulated sugar

2 tablespoons freshly squeezed lemon juice

1 vanilla bean

EQUIPMENT

3 sanitized ½-pint (250-ml) jars and their lids

Tight-weave cheesecloth

Kitchen twine

Candy thermometer

Basic water-bath canning equipment, optional

1. Combine the fresh and dried cherries, sugar, and lemon juice in a nonreactive heavy-bottomed saucepan. Split the vanilla bean open lengthwise, scrape the seeds into the pot, and add the pod as well. Gently mix everything together and let the cherries macerate for about 1 hour. Place the reserved pits in a piece of cheesecloth, tie it closed with the twine, and add the bundle to the pot.

2. Set the pot over medium-high heat and bring to a boil. Reduce the heat to medium and cook the mixture at a simmer until it has darkened and begun to thicken, 20 to 30 minutes. Continue until the mixture reaches 220° F (104° C). You should be able to drag a path along the bottom of the pot with a silicone spatula. If you don't have a thermometer, use the freezer test: Place 2 or 3 small bowls or plates in the freezer to chill while you cook the preserves. When the mixture has thickened, spoon a little onto one of the cold plates and return it to the freezer for about 2 minutes. The spread should be thick enough that it moves sluggishly when you tilt the plate. If it's too runny, let the preserves cook another 3 to 5 minutes and retest.

3. Remove and discard the vanilla bean pod and the cheesecloth bundle. Ladle the hot fruit into jars, leaving ¼-inch (6-mm) headspace. Wipe the rims clean with a clean damp cloth and screw the lids on the jars.

4. Process the jars in a boiling water bath for 10 minutes. Remove the jars from the water and set them upright on a clean kitchen towel to cool completely. Within a couple of minutes, you should hear the jar lids "ping" signifying that they have sealed properly. Processed jars will keep in a cool dark spot for up to 1 year. Store any jars that have not sealed in the refrigerator for up to 1 month.

If you don't want to process the jars, simply ladle the jam into sturdy freezer-safe containers. Let it cool to room temperature before storing in the freezer for up to 1 year. You can also refrigerate the jam for up to 3 months, but be sure to check for mold before using, and discard any jam that shows signs of molding or discoloration, bubbles or foam (fermentation), or that smells off or unpleasant.

BAKER'S NOTE: *To remove the pits from sour cherries, use the paper clip trick: Unbend a clean paper clip into a long S shape. Gently push the smaller curved end into the cherry through the stem end and scoop out the pit.*

CONFETTURA DI FICHI

Fig Preserves with Citrus Zest

This is a classic fig preserve, with finely chopped orange and lemon zest contributing a bright note to the sweet fruit. The recipe is simple, as it requires no pectin or peeling of fruit. Use these luscious preserves to sandwich Occhi di Bue butter cookies (page 72) or as a filling for Settembrini (page 118). I've minced the orange and lemon zest, rather than finely grating it, to give the citrus more of a presence in the finished preserve.

MAKES 1½ PINTS (ABOUT 750 G)

2 pounds (910 g) ripe figs, gently washed

2 cups (400 g) granulated sugar

Finely minced zest and freshly squeezed juice of 1 small orange

Finely minced zest and freshly squeezed juice of 1 lemon

EQUIPMENT

3 sanitized ½-pint (250-ml) jars and their lids

Candy thermometer

Basic water-bath canning equipment, optional

1. Cut the tops of the stems off the figs then quarter the fruit lengthwise. Place them in a heavy-bottomed nonreactive saucepan. Add the sugar, orange juice and lemon juice. Sprinkle the zest on top. Gently mix everything together with a silicone spatula or wooden spoon and let the figs macerate for 30 to 60 minutes.

2. Have ready 3 half-pint (250 ml) sterilized jars and their rings and lids. Place 2 or 3 small bowls or plates in the freezer (you will use these to test the jelling point of the preserves).

3. Set the pot over medium-high heat and bring to a boil; reduce the heat to medium and cook at a lively simmer for 15 to 20 minutes, or until the mixture has thickened and turned a couple of shades darker. Continue until the mixture reaches 220° F (104° C). You should be able to drag a path along the bottom of the pot with a silicone spatula. If you don't have a thermometer, use the freezer test: Place 2 or 3 small bowls or plates in the freezer to chill while you cook the preserves. When the mixture has thickened, spoon a little onto one of the cold plates and return it to the freezer for about 2 minutes. The spread should be thick enough that it moves sluggishly when you tilt the plate. If it's too runny, let the preserves cook another 3 to 5 minutes and retest.

4. Ladle the hot preserves into the jars, leaving ¼-inch (6-mm) headspace. Wipe the rims clean with a clean, damp cloth, and screw the lids on the jars. Process the jars in a boiling water bath for 10 minutes. Remove the jars and set them upright on a clean kitchen towel. Within a couple of minutes, you should hear the jar lids "ping" signifying that they have sealed properly. Let the jars cool to room temperature before storing in a cool, dark place. Processed jars will keep in a cool dark spot for up to 1 year. Store any jars that have not sealed in the refrigerator for up to 1 month.

If you don't want to process the jars, simply ladle the jam into sturdy freezer-safe containers. Let it cool to room temperature before storing in the freezer for up to 1 year. You can also refrigerate the jam for up to 3 months, but be sure to check for mold before using, and discard any jam that shows signs of molding or discoloration, bubbles or foam (fermentation), or that smells off or unpleasant.

CONFETTURA DI FICHI CON CIOCCOLATO E COGNAC

Fig and Chocolate Preserves with Cognac

I have a Brown Turkey fig tree in my backyard that is extremely generous, in spite of benign neglect (I do not have a green thumb). Every year toward the end of summer, the many little fruits dangling like ornaments from the leafy branches turn ripe, seemingly all at once. The figs aren't very large or juicy, so they're not great for eating out of hand. But they make excellent preserves. Every year, I try a new variation—fig and plum, fig and blueberry, fig and amaretto liqueur. One year, I came up with this version, with bittersweet chocolate and cognac stirred in. It's perfect as a filling for Italian cookies, including Hazelnut and Jam Mattoncini (page 108) and Settembrini (page 118).

MAKES 2½ PINTS (ABOUT 1.25 KG)

3 pounds (1.4 kg) ripe figs, gently washed (I use Brown Turkey)

2½ cups (500 g) granulated sugar

3 strips lemon zest, plus the juice of ½ lemon

1 cinnamon stick

2 whole star anise

About 10 whole cloves

1 vanilla bean

⅔ cup (160 ml) cognac

3 ounces (85 g) bittersweet chocolate, finely chopped

EQUIPMENT

5 sanitized ½-pint (250-ml) jars and their lids

Tight-weave cheesecloth

Candy thermometer

Basic water-bath canning equipment, optional

1. Cut the hard little stems off the figs and quarter the fruit lengthwise. Place them in a heavy-bottomed nonreactive pot or saucepan. Add the sugar, lemon zest, and lemon juice. Tie the cinnamon stick, star anise, and cloves into a cheesecloth bundle and add it to the pot. Split the vanilla bean, scrape the seeds into the pot, and add the pod. Gently mix everything together with a silicone spatula or wooden spoon and let the figs macerate for 30 minutes.

2. Set the pot over medium to medium-high heat and bring to a boil. Lower the heat to medium and cook at a lively simmer for 15 to 20 minutes, or until the mixture has thickened and turned a couple of shades darker. Continue until the mixture reaches 220° F (104° C). You should be able to drag a path along the bottom of the pot with a silicone spatula. If you don't have a thermometer, use the freezer test: Place 2 or 3 small bowls or plates in the freezer to chill while you cook the preserves. When the mixture has thickened, spoon a little onto one of the cold plates and return it to the freezer for about 2 minutes. The spread should be thick enough that it moves sluggishly when you tilt the plate. If it's too runny, let the preserves cook another 3 to 5 minutes and retest.

3. When the preserves are ready, remove and discard the spice bundle and the vanilla bean pod. Stir in the cognac and let it bubble for a minute or so; don't let up on the stirring. Remove the pot from the heat and stir in the chocolate, stirring until it is fully melted and thoroughly mixed into the preserves.

4. Ladle the hot preserves into the jars, leaving ¼-inch (6-mm) headspace. Wipe the rims with a clean, damp cloth, and screw the lids on the jars. Process the jars in a boiling water bath for 10 minutes. Remove the jars from the water and set them upright on a clean kitchen towel to cool completely. Within a couple of minutes, you should hear the jar lids "ping" signifying that they have sealed properly. Processed jars will keep in a cool dark spot for up to 1 year. Store any jars that have not sealed in the refrigerator for up to 1 month.

If you don't want to process the jars, simply ladle the jam into sturdy freezer-safe containers. Let it cool to room temperature before storing in the freezer for up to 1 year. You can also refrigerate the jam for up to 3 months, but be sure to check for mold before using, and discard any jam that shows signs of molding or discoloration, bubbles or foam (fermentation), or that smells off or unpleasant.

Ball
SureTight

SCRUCCHJATA

Rustic Grape Jam

Every fall, winemakers across Abruzzo turn dusky, blue-skinned Montepulciano grapes into the region's best-known wine. Montepulciano d'Abruzzo is bright, tannic, and fruity, with notes of berry, cherry, and pomegranate. A small portion of those dusky grapes get turned into a thick, full-bodied jam known as *scrucchjata* or *scrucchiata* (pronounced skrook-YAH-tah). The word, which is in Abruzzese dialect, roughly translates to "squished." The dense, purple-black jam is used in tarts and as a filling for a variety of cookies, including Celli Ripieni (page 150) and Calcionelli di Gabriella (page 148).

Montepulciano d'Abruzzo grapes aren't cultivated in the U.S., but with the proliferation of wineries and vineyards in more and more states, it has gotten easier to find grapes beyond Concord or supermarket table grapes. It's worth seeking out good red wine grapes for this rustic jam. See page 225 for online sources.

MAKES 1 TO 1½ PINTS (500 TO 750 G), DEPENDING ON THE GRAPE

4 pounds (1.8 kg) wine grapes, such as Montepulciano d'Abruzzo or Syrah, stemmed

Up to ½ cup (100 g) granulated sugar

1 vanilla bean, optional

EQUIPMENT

2 or 3 sanitized ½-pint (250-ml) jars and their lids

Food mill fitted with the disk with the smallest holes

Basic water-bath canning equipment, optional

1. Place the grapes in a large nonreactive heavy-bottom saucepan and mash them up with a potato masher to break their skins and release their juices. Set the pot over medium heat and bring to a boil. The grapes should begin to break down within 15 minutes. Lower the heat to medium-low and cook, stirring, for another 15 to 20 minutes, until the grapes have turned into a pulpy mass.

2. Let the mass cool briefly; then pass it through the food mill into a bowl to get rid of the seeds and skins. You should have about 2½ cups (375 ml) of pulp. Taste and add up to ½ cup (100 g) sugar, taking care not to sweeten the mixture too much. Scrape the seeds of the vanilla bean into the grape mixture, if you like (this is not traditional, but I like the full fruity flavor the vanilla adds).

3. Transfer the sweetened pulp to a clean saucepan and bring to a boil over medium-high heat. Lower the heat if necessary to prevent scorching but continue to cook the fruit at a simmer until it is thick and glossy, and the temperature reaches 220° F (104° C). You should be able to drag a path along the bottom of the pot with a silicone spatula or wooden spoon. If you don't have a thermometer, use the freezer test: Place 2 or 3 small bowls or plates in the freezer to chill while you cook the jam. When the mixture has thickened, spoon a little onto one of the cold plates and return it to the freezer for about 2 minutes. It should be thick enough that it moves sluggishly when you tilt the plate. If it's too runny, let the jam cook another 3 to 5 minutes and retest.

4. Ladle the jam into the jars, leaving ¼-inch (6-mm) headspace. Wipe the rims with a clean, damp cloth, and screw on the lids. Process the jars in a boiling water bath for 10 minutes. Remove the jars from the water and set them upright on a clean kitchen towel to cool completely. Within a couple of minutes, you should hear the jar lids "ping" signifying that they have sealed properly. Processed jars will keep in a cool dark spot for up to 1 year. Store any jars that have not sealed in the refrigerator for up to 1 month.

If you don't want to process the jars, simply ladle the jam into sturdy freezer-safe containers. Let it cool to room temperature before storing in the freezer for up to 1 year. You can also refrigerate the jam for up to 3 months, but be sure to check for mold before using, and discard any jam that shows signs of molding or discoloration, bubbles or foam (fermentation), or that smells off or unpleasant.

MOSTO COTTO

Grape Must Syrup

This dark, fruity syrup, made from the juice of freshly pressed red wine grapes is both a condiment and an ingredient in Italian baking. In Abruzzo and other parts of the south it is called *mosto cotto*, or "cooked must." Farther north, in Emilia-Romagna, it is known as "saba." In Sardinia, where it is also commonly used, it is "sapa." You can find mosto cotto or saba at specialty Italian groceries or online (see page 225), but if you have access to wine grapes, it is fun to make your own.

Once cooked, the syrup is bottled and left to age. It is here that the real transformation takes place. Over weeks and months, the mosto cotto darkens to a deep, rich brown. Its character mellows and it takes on notes of spice and dried fruit—prunes, raisins, figs, cherries.

In Italy, mosto cotto was used as a sweetener for baked goods before sugar was widely available (see the recipe for Mostaccioli on page 160). It imparts a complex, fruity flavor and gives cookies a tender bite. There really is nothing like it. Beyond its uses in baking, the syrup is a delicious with fresh ricotta or aged cheeses, whisked into dressings and sauces, and—naturally—drizzled on top of ice cream.

In Virginia, where I live, I've found winemakers who are intrigued by the idea of grape must syrup and more than willing to sell me a gallon or two of must to make a batch at home. (I've used Cabernet Franc, Syrah, and Petit Verdot, among other grapes, to make mosto cotto in the U.S.) Failing that, look for Concord grapes at fall farmers' markets. They lack the complexity of wine grapes like Montepulciano d'Abruzzo but they will do in a pinch.

MAKES ABOUT 3 CUPS (680 ML)

1 gallon freshly pressed wine grape must

EQUIPMENT

Fine-mesh strainer

Tight-weave cheesecloth

Narrow funnel

1 sterilized 1 quart (1 L) swing-top bottle

1. Pour the must through a fine-mesh strainer lined with damp cheesecloth into a large heavy-bottomed Dutch oven or sauce pot. Bring to a boil over medium-high heat. Reduce the heat to medium or medium-low and let it simmer for 1½ to 2 hours, skimming off any foam that rises to the top. As the must cooks, it will reduce in volume and begin to thicken slightly. It will start to smell "cooked." This is when you need to be alert, as the must can go from perfectly cooked to overdone very quickly. Reduce the heat to low and continue to simmer the liquid very gently until it is reduced to about ¼ its original volume. It will be thickened but not too dense. It should coat the back of a spoon but still pour easily. If you start to smell burnt caramel, pull the pot off the heat immediately.

2. Let the syrup cool to room temperature. Strain it through a fine-mesh sieve lined with damp cheesecloth and funnel it into the prepared bottle. Store the mosto cotto in a cool, dark spot, where it will keep for at least 1 year. Its flavor will continue to improve as the months go by.

MISCELE DI SPEZIE

Spice Blends

Spice blends are used in several recipes in this book. They give cookies medieval and Renaissance allure, and they are a potent reminder of Italy's role in the spice trade. The republic of Venice, in particular, was a key player in the development of trade routes from Asia to Europe, and by the fifteenth century, the city held a monopoly on the spice trade. Spices such as cinnamon, cloves, ginger, nutmeg, and pepper were expensive, a luxury reserved for the wealthy, who used them lavishly in both savory and sweet dishes. Convents and monasteries employed spices for medicinal purposes, and eventually these precious ingredients found their way into confections produced by religious orders.

Each of these three spice blends is associated with a specific cookie. But feel free to try them in other baked goods—spice cake, for example—or even in savory dishes, such as roasted or braised meat. Be sure to use fresh (not expired) whole or ground spices to capture their full potency.

CAVALLUCCI SPICE

This suggestive Tuscan spice blend is the key ingredient in Cavallucci page 107), spiced Christmas cookies from Siena that date to the sixteenth century.

MAKES ½ CUP (60 G)

2 tablespoons whole aniseeds

2 tablespoons whole coriander

2 tablespoons ground cinnamon

2 tablespoons freshly grated or ground nutmeg

1. Place the aniseeds and coriander seeds in a small dry skillet and toast over medium heat for 3 to 4 minutes, until the spices are a shade darker in color and fragrant. Transfer them to a plate or bowl and let them cool completely. Then grind them in a spice grinder until they are reduced to a powder.

2. Mix all of the spices together in a bowl, then transfer to a jar with a tight-fitting lid. The blend will keep for up to 1 year.

LA SAPORITA

Invented in Piedmont in the 1920s, this unusual spice blend with many variations was used in everything from roasts to ravioli filling. Eventually it traveled beyond the confines of Piedmont and became popular in Sardinian cooking and baking. Caraway is not used with much frequency in Italian cuisine, but it is a key component in this blend. It is the "secret" ingredient to the Sardinian Pabassinas (page 191).

MAKES ABOUT ¼ CUP (60 ML)

2 teaspoons whole aniseeds

2 teaspoons caraway seeds

2 teaspoons whole cloves

2 teaspoons whole coriander seeds

2 teaspoons freshly grated nutmeg

1. Place the aniseeds and caraway seeds in a small dry skillet and toast over medium heat for 3 to 4 minutes, until they turn a shade darker and are fragrant. Add the cloves and coriander seeds and toast for 1 minute more, then remove from the heat and let cool completely. Grind the spices in a spice grinder until they are reduced to a powder.

2. Mix all the spices together in a bowl, then transfer to a jar with a tight-fitting lid. The spice blend will keep for up to 1 year.

PISTO NAPOLETANO

For Neapolitans, the perfume of the holidays and the perfume of this redolent spice are one and the same. It is the essential ingredient in both Roccocò (page 153), traditional Neapolitan Christmas cookies; and Quaresimali (page 171), crunchy Lenten almond cookies.

MAKES ABOUT ⅓ CUP (40 G)

1 tablespoon whole cloves

1 tablespoon whole star anise

1 tablespoon whole coriander seed

1 tablespoon whole black peppercorns

3 tablespoons ground cinnamon

1. Place the cloves, star anise, coriander seeds, and peppercorns in a small skillet over medium heat and toast for 3 to 4 minutes, until the spices are fragrant, then remove from the heat and let cool completely. Grind the spices in a spice grinder until they are reduced to a powder.

2. Mix all the spices together in a bowl, then transfer to a jar with a tight-fitting lid. The spice blend will keep for up to 1 year.

PASTA DI MANDORLA

PASTA DI MANDORLA

Almond Paste

Sweet almond paste is a central ingredient in many Italian cookies, and in a huge number of sweets in Sardinia and Sicily. It is different from marzipan, which has more sugar and is smoother in texture. Marzipan is used to make Sicily's famous *frutta Martorana*, mini-size fruits—figs, peaches, oranges, and so on—that are painted with colorful vegetable dyes to look like their real counterparts. Almond paste is used primarily as an ingredient in baking. It's possible to find good-quality almond paste at gourmet shops and some supermarkets, and it is available online. However, homemade almond paste is easy to make in a food processor. Whenever I have a surplus of almonds hanging around the pantry, I make a batch and freeze it for when I need it. It's worth splurging, if you can, on Sicilian almonds to make a paste that is infused with the nut's sweet, slightly bitter and aromatic flavor. Use homemade almond paste to make Baci di Alassio (page 40) and Pinolate Genovesi (page 80).

MAKES ABOUT 1 POUND (454 G)

1½ cups (200 g) blanched almonds

1 cup (200 g) granulated sugar

2 to 3 tablespoons water

½ to 1 teaspoon pure almond extract

1. Place the almonds in the bowl of a food processor fitted with the blade attachment. Sprinkle in 3 tablespoons of the sugar and process until the nuts are powdery–they will first look like coarse sand and then like fine cornmeal. Add the rest of the sugar and pulse until well combined.

2. With the motor running, add 2 tablespoons of water and the almond extract, using more or less of the extract according to your preference. Add more water by the teaspoon if necessary to bring the paste together.

3. Turn the paste out onto a clean work surface and divide it in half. Knead each piece into a rough log about 6 inches (16 cm) long. Place each log onto a separate sheet of plastic wrap and wrap tightly. Roll the logs back and forth, one at a time, to make them smooth and even. Tie the ends with kitchen string and refrigerate. The almond paste will keep in the refrigerator for up to 1 month, and in the freezer for up to 1 year. Let it thaw in the refrigerator before using.

SCORZA DI ARANCIA CANDITA

Candied Orange Peel

Many of the cookie recipes in this book call for candied orange or lemon peel, either finely chopped or in pieces. Candied peel adds color, texture, and bright flavor. It works beautifully with a spectrum of cookies, from vanilla and chocolate to spiced and iced. I consider it essential. I have yet to find a commercial brand of candied peel that tastes like real fruit, so I make my own.

The process calls for simmering the fruit in water, then poaching it in sugar syrup. As the peel absorbs the hot syrup, it is transformed into a chewy-soft confection. Once the peel has been candied, you can, if you like, coat the strips in sugar to make them sparkle. You can use this same process to candy lemon, lime, and other citrus peel.

MAKES ABOUT 2 CUPS (200 G)

3 organic navel oranges, preferably with thick peel, rinsed well

1½ cups (300 g) granulated sugar

2 cups (475 ml) water

About ½ cup (100 g) superfine sugar, for coating, optional

1. Use a sharp paring knife to slice off the top and bottom of each orange. Score the oranges, making vertical slices at 1-inch (2½-cm) intervals and cutting just through the peel and pith but not into the flesh. Pull off the segments of peel and slice them vertically into strips about ¼ inch (6 mm) wide. (Reserve the flesh for another use.)

2. Place the strips of peel in a saucepan with water to cover by at least 1 inch (2½ cm). Bring to a boil over medium-high heat, reduce the heat to low, and cook the peels gently for about 45 minutes, until just tender. Drain in a colander set in the sink.

3. Set a wire rack on a rimmed baking sheet.

4. Combine the granulated sugar and the 2 cups (475 ml) of water in the same saucepan over medium-high heat; bring to a boil, stirring to dissolve the sugar, then reduce the heat to low and add the drained peels. Cook gently, stirring from time to time, for 45 minutes to 1 hour, until the peels are tender and most (but not all) of the syrup has been absorbed. Use a slotted spoon to transfer the peels to the rack and arrange them so that they are not touching. Let dry for at least 2 hours, until they are no longer wet but still slightly tacky.

5. To coat the strips in sugar, spoon the superfine sugar into a 1-quart (1 L) ziplock bag. Add 3 or 4 strips of peel to the bag and shake to coat them evenly. Place coated strips back on the rack, taking care to keep them separate. Continue until you have coated all the strips. Let them dry overnight, turning them once or twice, before serving or storing. Store the peels in a large glass jar in the refrigerator, where they will keep for at least 6 months.

BAKER'S NOTE: *Candied orange peel dipped in chocolate is a delicious after-dinner treat. Melt some chocolate following the instructions for tempering on page 27 and dip one-third of each strip into the chocolate. Set the strips on a parchment-lined baking sheet and allow the chocolate to set completely before serving.*

PEPERONCINO
SESAMO
ROSMARINO
SEMPLICI
INTEGRALI AI SEMI
MIEL
2,20 AL PEZZO

ACKNOWLEDGMENTS

I am grateful to all of the people who breathed life and beauty into this book.

To Leslie Jonath, my agent, this book would not have happened without your support and wholehearted enthusiasm. Thank you.

Thank you to the supremely talented duo of Lauren Volo and Maeve Sheridan, photographer and stylist, who managed to magically conjure sunny Italy in a New York studio in January. And to Debbie Kim, whose keen eye and attention to detail made sure that every single cookie was ready for its glam shot.

To Daniela Bracco, whose sweet, whimsical illustrations grace pages and end papers of this book: *Grazie di cuore!*

My heartfelt thanks to Jenna Heald, who made the hand-drawn stencil so that I could accurately re-create the *Pupazze Frascatane* (page 112).

To everyone at Gibbs Smith: Thank you for giving this book a welcoming home. Special thanks to my editor, Michelle Branson, for your patience and 100% commitment to this project; to Amy Treadwell, for your copyediting precision—what a treat to be working with you again—and to Sarah Gorecki. My thanks also to the design team—Ryan Thomann, Sheryl Dickert, and Renee Bond—for seamlessly joining together the many visual parts of this project into such a beautiful book; and to the publicity and sales team, Michelle Bayuk, Moneka Hewlett, Kellie Robles, Kim Eddy, and Paulina Siparsky, for working so hard on its behalf.

To all the bakers who shared their stories, opened their kitchens, and shared and inspired the recipes in this book, *grazie infinite*. Special thanks to: Paola Rosazza Battore, Stefania Innocenti, Ilario Notarmuzzi, Corrado Assenza, Paolo Lazzaroni, Massimiliano and Ricardo Lunardi, Gianni Cifarelli, Dorita Polticchia, Anna Portinaro, Paola Bacchia, Adri Barr Crocetti, Andrea Locci, and Marie Renello. Many thanks also to Beatrice Ughi for steering me toward the best Italian producers and products.

To my family: Scott, Nick, and Adriana: Thank you for being there every step of the way and for gamely trying *all* the cookies.

Fragole
L'ortofrutticola
HORTOITALIA
€1,60
Marsala
COMAL

SOURCES

BAKE SUPPLY PLUS

bakesupplyplus.com

Baker's ammonia (ammonium carbonate)

C. PALMER MFG. CO., INC.

cpalmermfg.com

Pizzelle irons

CONSUMER FRESH WINEMAKERS

cfpwinemakers.com

Wine grapes and grape must

DELAURENTI

delaurenti.com

Mosto cotto and saba (grape must syrup)

THE FAT LADY

thefatladytallow.com

Leaf lard

FORMAGGIO KITCHEN

formaggiokitchen.com

Mosto cotto and saba (grape must syrup)

GIANNETTI ARTISANS

giannettiartisans.com

Pistachio flour; and skin-on Sicilian almonds

GRAPE MUST

grapemust.com

Wine grapes and grape must

GUSTIAMO

gustiamo.com

Mosto cotto and saba (grape must syrup); Skinned hazelnuts from Piedmont; skin-on or blanched Sicilian almonds; sweet pistachio cream; and Italian pine nuts

KING ARTHUR BAKING

kingarthurbaking.com

Parchment paper sheets and other baking supplies

NUTS.COM

nuts.com

Mediterranean pine nuts (grown in Italy, Portugal, and Spain); shelled pistachios; and a wide variety of dried and candied fruits

PENZEYS SPICES

penzeys.com

Whole and ground spices and Quatre Épices spice blend

USA PAN

usapan.com

Baking sheets and biscotti pans

WINE GRAPES DIRECT

winegrapesdirect.com

Wine grapes and grape must

Liquor

EVANGELISTA

evangelistaliquori.it/en

Punch Abruzzo: The availability of this sweet, potent liqueur from Abruzzo is unreliable. The two primary producers are Evangelista and Jannamico. I recommend asking your local liquor store or wine shop if they stock it or are able to special order it. It's worth the splurge!

HEIRLOOM LIQUEURS (MADE IN THE U.S.)

heirloomliqueurs.com

Alchermes

JANNAMICO

iannamicoliquori.com/en

Punch Abruzzo

LIQUOR EXPRESS

liquorexpress.us

Alchermes

Ratafia (cherry liqueur)

COOKIE BAKERIES IN ITALY

There are several types of bakeries in Italy:

Biscotteria or Biscottificio As its name implies, this type of bakery specializes in cookies, though it may also sell bread and other baked goods. There are far fewer cookie bakeries than bread or pastry shops, so if you come across one, be sure to go inside.

Forno The word *forno* means "oven" in Italian. These days, the forno is similar to the panificio—a place where bread, pizza, and rustic savory and sweet bakes are produced—and the two are sometimes used interchangeably, depending on regional word use. But forno can also have a different connotation. Many towns throughout Italy once had a communal oven, a place where women brought loaves of unbaked bread or other foods that they prepared at home to be baked. This was before many families had ovens in their own homes. These forni were usually wood-fired, and they produced their own breads and baked goods beyond those that were brought to them to be cooked. Some of these forni, like Cifarelli, in Matera (page 142), are still in operation.

Panetteria Like a panificio and a forno, a panetteria sells bread and other baked goods. However, the products sold are not always baked in-house.

Panificio You generally won't find fancy fresh pastries at the panificio, but you will find bread, pizzas and other savory bakes, as well as a range of rustic cookies. In some cases, the baking happens off the premises, in a commercial or industrial kitchen, but in others, the baking takes place in the back, with a shop in front that serves customers.

Pasticceria This is where you go for breakfast pastries, as well as freshly baked cakes, tarts, and other desserts known as *pasticceria fresca* because they include yeasted and cream-based sweets. A pasticceria is often also a bar, where you can get your morning cappuccino, afternoon espresso, and even an evening aperitivo.

Here is a list of bakeries that are mentioned in this book, plus a few more that I visited while doing research. This is by no means a comprehensive list, and there are many famous big-city bakeries and Michelin-starred pasticcerie whose names do not appear here. If you have plans to travel to Italy, my heartfelt advice is that, wherever you go in the country, look for the local bakeries just as you might look for the local farmers' market.

Northern Italy

LIGURIA

ALIMENTARI NOVELLA

Via Giacomo Buranello, 29, Torriglia

127-year-old shop selling produce, pantry staples, and sundries in addition to freshly baked Canestrelletti di Torriglia. Paola Rosazza Battore's are among the best.

CAFFÈ BALZOLA 1902

Piazza Matteotti, 26, Alassio
balzola1902.com

A jewellike belle epoque-era caffè and pastry shop in the colorful seaside town of Alassio, where the original Baci di Alassio were first produced.

PASTICCERIA GUANO

Piazza Cavour, 2r, Torriglia

The charming pink and green interior, and the perfume of anise and butter are two good reasons to stop at this family-run bakery. Their canestrelletti cookies is a third.

LOMBARDY

BERGAMO DOLCE

Via Bartolomeo Colleoni, 22b, Bergamo
bergamodolce.it

Cookie and pastry shop in the beautiful historic center of Bergamo selling a variety of regional cookies and pastries.

PASTICCERIA BIANCHI

Via S. Antonio, 1, Gallarate

Historic bakery since 1934, opened by Oreste Bianchi and his wife, Maria, in 1934 and now run by the couple's descendants. Specializing in hand-pinched amaretti di Gallarate cookies.

PASTICCERIA RISTORANTE ALBERGO BIGIO

Viale Papa Giovanni XXIII, 56, San Pellegrino Terme
bigio.info/it/bar-pasticceria

Historic caffè, bakery and hotel in a stunning spa town. Famous for its crescent-moon-shaped crunchy butter cookies, ideal for dipping in cappuccino or milk. The founder's collection of marionettes adorns the bakery walls.

PIEDMONT

ARTIGIANI NOVARESI CAMPORELLI

Vicolo Monte Ariolo, 3, Novara
camporelli1852.it

Family bakery producing signature crispy oval cookies since 1852.

CAFFÈ DEL MORO

Via Goffredo Mameli, 41, Gavi

Old-fashioned bakery with a wood-paneled tearoom and delicious soft amaretti.

PASTICCERIA BONFANTE

Via Torino, 29, Chivasso
nocciolinidichivasso.com/it

Historic bakery producing button-size Nocciolini di Chivasso.

PASTICCERIA ROSSI

Via G. Lanza, 17, Casale Monferrato
krumirirossi.it

Historic bakery specializing in dense, U-shaped butter cookies.

TRENTINO-ALTO ADIGE

PASTICCERIA BRONZETTI

Via Cembra 1, Lavis (Trento)
pasticceriabronzetti.it

Contemporary bakery with fancy cakes, fresh pastries, and a selection of pretty, piped amaretti, butter cookies, ladyfingers, and more.

VALLE D'AOSTA

PASTICCERIA MAURO MORANDIN

Via Chanoux, 105, Saint-Vincent
mauromorandin.it

Popular bakery in the pretty town of Saint-Vincent, in the Aosta Valley, known for its panettone (sweet Christmas bread) and other pastries, including the region's Torcetti di Saint-Vincent.

Central Italy

LAZIO

ANTICO PANIFICIO EGIDI

Piazza Porzio Catone, Monte Porzio Catone

Bread bakery in the Castelli Romani, the hills outside of Rome, specializing in Serpette—S-shaped butter cookies since 1900.

BISCOTTIFICIO ARTIGIANO INNOCENTI

Via della Luce, 21, Rome

Historic bakery in the heart of Trastevere, where you'll find owner Stefania Innocenti behind the counter selling a range of cookies, all made without animal fat. Be sure to ogle the custard-colored vintage 1960s conveyor-belt oven, which she still uses.

PASTICCERIA P. CIPRIANI

Via Carlo Botta, 21/23, Rome

Wood-paneled bakery in center of Rome dating to 1906 with a wide selection of rustic cookies sold by weight and displayed in the bakery's large vintage bins.

TUSCANY

BISCOTTIFICIO ANTONIO MATTEI

Via Ricasoli, 20, Prato
antoniomattei.it/it/home

The original shop of the original producer of cantucci, Tuscany's famous twice-baked almond cookies.

FRATELLI LUNARDI

Via Lucciano 33/39, Quarrata
fratellilunardi.it

Whimsical modern bakery nevertheless steeped in tradition, located in the suburbs of Pistoia. Known for their cantucci, as well as other cookies and a tempting selection of bread, pizzas, and prepared foods.

PANIFICIO IL MAGNIFICO

Via dei Pellegrini, 27, Siena
ilmagnifico.siena.it

Charming shop in the heart of Siena, with breads and cookies, including cantucci and ricciarelli, the city's famous sugar-coated almond cookies.

PASTICCERIA CARLI

Piazza Francesco Berni, 20, Lamporecchio

Bakery dating to 1870 offering a variety of fresh pastries and tarts, plus their famous anise-scented wafers called Brigidini.

UMBRIA

LA BOTTEGA DEL FORNO

Corso Giacomo Matteotti, 24, Bevagna
labottegadelforno.com

Bread and cookie bakery in a spectacular medieval town, with an enticing display of traditional and creative cookies made by baker Dorita Polticchia.

GRANARIUM

Via Madonna della Pia, Bevagna
granarium.it

Family-owned mill and rustic bakery in the Valley of Assisi, offering excellent pizzas, breads, and cookies made with their own flours.

PASTICCERIA SENSI

Corso Mazzini Giuseppe, 14, Assisi
pasticceriasensi.it

Small family-run pastry shop and coffee bar selling a range of fresh Umbrian pastries and cookies, including pretty piped meringues.

Southern Italy

ABRUZZO

BISCOTTERIA ARTIGIANALE DI ROSATI LILIANA

Strada Silla, 43, Scanno

One of Italy's smallest bakeries, and well worth the drive into the interior of Abruzzo to stroll around this picturesque town and sample the bakery's rustic cookies, including oversize amaretti and chocolate amaretti, and big, tender mostaccioli.

BASILICATA

IL FORNAIO

Piazza S. Oronzo, 23, Lecce
ilfornaiolecce.it

Bakery in the heart of Lecce's historic center offering a mix of breads, pizzas, and rustic cookies for more than seventy years.

FORNO CIFARELLI

Via Istria, 17, Matera
panificiocifarelli.it

Wood-fired bread bakery since 1947, selling the area's famed golden Matera loaves and a range of rustic cookies.

MOLISE

BISCOTTIFICIO CIANCIULLO

Via Generale Carlo d'Amico, Jelsi
cianciullo.com

Family-run bakery since 1967, located in a picturesque village in the Molise countryside, offering a variety of sweet yeasted breads, rustic cakes, and regional cookies made with local grains.

PUGLIA

CAFFÈ CENTRALE

Corso Garibaldi, 22, Ceglie Messapica
caffecentrale1861.com

Known for their selection of cherry jam-filled Biscotti di Ceglie.

SICILY AND SARDINIA

ANTICA PASTICCERIA DEL CONVENTO

Via G.F. Guarnotti, 1, Erice
anticapasticceriadelconvento.it

Historic bakery in a hilltop town west of Palermo specializing in marzipan and other almond sweets, as well as custard-filled pastries called Genovesi. Run by relatives of renowned pastry chef Maria Grammatico.

I SEGRETI DEL CHIOSTRO

Piazza Bellini, 1, Palermo
isegretidelchiostro.shop

Bakery and sweet shop located in the cloisters of a former Dominican convent. All of the cookies and confections are made according to antique convent recipes, many of them with almonds as a base.

L'ANTICO DOLCE SELARGINO DA LOLA

Via Palestro, 35, Selargius
anticodolceselargino.it

A charming bakery painted robin's egg blue and white, in a suburb of Cagliari. The display cases are replete with traditional Sardinian cookies and confections, meticulously decorated with icing and delicate piping and neatly arranged on large platters.

PASTICCERIA MARIA GRAMMATICO

Via Vittorio Emanuele, 14, Erice
mariagrammatico.it

Iconic bakery in a picturesque ancient hilltop town west of Palermo, where the proprietor, who was raised in a convent, has been producing painted marzipan fruits, cannoli, confections, and almond cookies since 1964.

ITALIAN BAKERIES IN THE U.S.

Millions of Italians immigrated to the U.S. in the late nineteenth and early twentieth centuries, bringing their culinary traditions with them. Italian bakeries sprang up in cities from Boston to San Francisco, serving a range of goods from rum-soaked sponge cakes and cream-filled pastries to an array of cookies. Some of the OGs are still in business, run by descendants of their founders. Here is a list of mostly historic bakeries with a few contemporary ones sprinkled in. As with the list of bakeries in Italy, this is by no means comprehensive, but rather a snapshot of the Italian bakery landscape in the U.S.

California

DIANDA'S BAKERY, SAN FRANCISCO

Italian American pastry shop in the heart of the Mission district, with a second location in San Mateo. Dianda's was opened in 1962 by a couple from Lucca, Tuscany, and is now run by three longtime employees who bought the business from the original owners.

VICTORIA PASTRY COMPANY

700 Filbert St., San Francisco
victoriapastrycompany.com

Historic bakery with a range of cakes, tarts, and pastries, plus a mix of biscotti, Italian butter cookies, amaretti, and pine nut cookies

Connecticut

LIBBY'S ITALIAN PASTRY SHOP

130 Wooster St., New Haven
libbyscookies.com

Family-run bakery operating in New Haven's Little Italy since 1921, with a selection of traditional Italian cookies available for sale in-shop and online.

LUCIBELLO'S ITALIAN PASTRY SHOP

935 Grand Ave., New Haven
lucibellospastry.com

Opened in 1929, the bakery has been run by the Faggio family since 1959. Assorted cookies include almond paste, anginetti, anise, butter shortbread, fig, and rainbow slices.

Illinois

D'AMATO'S BAKERY & SUBS

1124 W. Grand Ave., Chicago
damatoschicago.com

A Chicago stalwart since 1970, this shop is known for its submarine sandwiches and panini, made with bread baked in a coal-fired oven Sweets include cannoli and a classic assortment of Italian cookies.

SCAFURI BAKERY

1337 W. Taylor St., Chicago
scafuribakery.com

Anise cookies, lemon knots, hazelnut biscotti, and chocolate-dipped butter cookies are among the assortment sold by this family-run bakery. First opened in 1904, Scafuri closed in 2008 but was reopened by family members in 2010.

SICILIAN BAKERY, CHICAGO

sicilianbakeryinc.com

Family bakery opened in the 1950s by Sicilian immigrant Silvio Gagliardi, the bakery was taken over by nephew Phil Rubino, and is now run by Phil and his son Anthony. The bakery's cookie selection includes piped butter cookies, fig cookies, sesame cookies, and lemon knots.

Louisiana

ANGELO BROCATO

214 N. Carrollton Ave., New Orleans
angelobrocatoicecream.com

Founder Angelo Brocato learned to make gelato and fruit granita in his native Palermo. He and his brother, Giuseppe, opened their ice cream parlor and bakery in New Orleans's French Quarter in 1905. Now located in Mid-City, the bakery still offers gelato, pastries, cannoli, and a classic selection of Sicilian cookies, including anise biscotti, amaretti, anise drops, and biscotti regina (sesame cookies).

Maryland

VACCARO'S ITALIAN PASTRY SHOP

222 Albemarle St., Baltimore
vaccarospastry.com

Classic Italian American bakery in Baltimore's small Little Italy neighborhood, with two additional locations. Offering cakes, cannoli, pastries, and three dozen types of cookies, including a handful made with almond paste.

Massachusetts

MIKE'S PASTRY

300 Hanover St., Boston
mikespastry.com

Founded in 1946 in Boston's North End and known for its cannoli. The bakery also sells a mix of biscotti, amaretti, macaroons, and rainbow cookies.

MODERN PASTRY SHOP

257 & 263 Hanover St., Boston
modernpastry.com

Family-run bakery in Boston's North End, established in 1930 by Giovanni Picariello. The bakery sells a range of elegant cakes, plus classic Italian cookies such as amaretti, pistachio macaroons, butter and jam cookies, biscotti, and pizzelle.

New Jersey

LAROSA'S FAMOUS PASTRY SHOP

79 Newman Springs Rd., Shrewsbury
larosaspastryshop.com

A fifth-generation bakery that began with a pushcart in Manhattan in 1901. They have a wide range of cookies, including apricot Linzer tarts, butter cookies, Florentine lace cookies, lemon cookies, walnut sandwiches, and a mix of biscotti from almond and chocolate hazelnut to cherry vanilla.

PALAZZONE 1960

190 Rt. 23 North, Wayne
palazzone1960.com

Bakery and café with a mix of traditional and contemporary offerings. The shop was opened in 2012 by Giancarlo Palazzone, whose parents owned a bakery in Clifton, New Jersey, in the 1960s and '70s. The bakery's artfully made cookies include chocolate and vanilla-almond biscotti, pignoli, and jam-filled butter cookies.

PRATO BAKERY

371 4th St., Jersey City
pratobakery.com

This shop specializing in Tuscan baking opened in Jersey City in 2015, moving from its original location in Greenwich Village. The bakery, which now has four locations, offers a range of cookies from classic twice-baked almond cantucci to brutti ma buoni ("ugly but good" cookies); plus pastries and schiacciata (Tuscan focaccia).

New York

CIRCO'S PASTRY SHOP

312 Knickerbocker Ave., Brooklyn
circospastryshop.com

Family bakery in Bushwick since 1945 run by Sicilian native Nino Pierdipino and his two sons, Salvatore and Anthony. The bakery still uses its 100-year-old recipe to make Savoiardi (ladyfingers), among other traditional cookies.

COURT PASTRY SHOP

298 Court Street, Brooklyn

This classic Sicilian bakery in the Carroll Gardens neighborhood has been turning out handmade cannoli, biscotti, sprinkle cookies, cuccidati, chocolate meringues, piped butter cookies and other treats since 1948.

DELILLO PASTRY SHOP

610 E. 187 St., Bronx
delillopastryshop.com

Hundred-year-old bakery opened by two brothers from Puglia in 1925 and now run by the family of its onetime head baker, Luigi Florio. Specializing in celebration cakes, wedding cakes, cannoli, and assorted Italian cookies.

EGIDIO PASTRY SHOP, BRONX, NY

egidiopastry.com

Family-owned bakery since 1912, Egidio sells a wide selection of cookies; it is known especially for Quaresimali, almond-studded Neapolitan biscotti. Owner Maria Carmela Lucciola keeps all of the bakery's original recipes, written on onionskin paper, in a Tupperware box in the kitchen.

FERRARA PASTICCERIA

195 Grand St., New York

Historic bakery in New York's Little Italy since 1892. Pine nut cookies, rainbow cookies, biscotti, and jam sandwiches are among the cookie offerings.

FLORENTINE PASTRY SHOP

667 Bleeker St., Utica

A stalwart in the city since 1928 offering cannoli, pasticciotti, sfogliatelle, and napoleons, along with an assortment of classic and not-so-classic cookies including cashew-almond macaroons, sold by the pound.

MADONIA BAKERY

2348 Arthur Ave., Bronx
madoniabakery.com

Family-owned bread bakery and pastry shop since 1918. Known for their selection of crusty and stuffed breads as well as a large selection of biscotti and other Italian cookies.

VENIERO'S PASTICCERIA

342 E. 11th Street., New York
venieros.com

Founder Antonio Veniero hailed from Sorrento, south of Naples. The bakery is still family-run in the same location and offers a selection of classic Italian bakes, including anise toasts, pignoli, coconut macaroons, and S cookies.

VILLA ITALIA

226 Broadway, Schenectady
villaitaliabakery.com

Third-generation family bakery selling cakes, pastries, bread and panettone, and an assortment of cookies, from almond crescents and cantuccini to jam-filled butter cookies and rainbow slices.

Pennsylvania

ENRICO BISCOTTI

2022 Penn Ave., Pittsburgh
enricobiscotti.com

Bakery in the city's Strip District specializing in biscotti. The wide-ranging flavors include everything from anise almond to pumpkin walnut and salted caramel.

ISGRO PASTRIES

1009 Christian St., Philadelphia
isgropastries.com

Established in 1904 by Sicilian immigrant Mario Isgro, who had worked as a baker in Vienna. Still in its original location, Isgro's sells a range of pastries and Italian cookies: fruit-filled butter cookies, amaretti, pignoli, butter cookies, and biscotti. Pillowy ricotta cookies are their most popular cookie.

MOIO'S PASTRY SHOP

4209 William Penn Highway, Monroeville
moios.com

Traditional Italian bakery opened in 1936 in Pittsburgh by Raphael Moio, who was born in Calabria. Now located in Monroeville, the bakery is run by the founder's grandson Tony, who turns out rum cakes, pastries and a wide selection of cookies, including almond and coconut macaroons, butter cookies, and biscotti.

TERMINI BROTHERS BAKERY

1523 South 8th St., Philadelphia
termini.com

Founded in 1921 by brothers Gaetano and Giuseppe Termini, the historic South Philly bakery now has three locations and is run by Giuseppe's grandsons Joseph and Vincent. Signature cookies include hand-piped fingers sandwiched with raspberry jam, lemon taralli, pignoli cookies, and coconut macaroons.

Rhode Island

SCIALO BROS. BAKERY

257 Atwells Ave., Providence, RI
scialobakery1916.com

The bakery, which sells an array of cakes, trifles, tarts, pastries, and cookies, has been a fixture on Federal Hill since it opened in 1916. It closed its doors in 2020 during the COVID-19 pandemic but was reopened a year later by a group of investors. Locals still vouch for its quality.

Virginia

BISNONNA BAKESHOP

10782-D Fairfax Blvd., Fairfax, VA
bisnonnabakeshop.com

Inspired by her great-grandmother, Nicole Liberatore started her made-to-order bakery with husband Dominick in 2019 ("Bisnonna" means "grandmother" in Italian). The shop specializes in seasonal flavors of cannoli, celebration cakes, and Italian cookies, including rainbow slices, lemon-ricotta cookies, pignoli, Italian leaf butter cookies, amaretti, biscotti, cuccidati, and pizzelle.

Wisconsin

PETER SCIORTINO BAKERY

1101 E. Brady St., Milwaukee, WI
petersciortinosbakery.com

Opened in 1947 by Peter Sciortino and his wife, Grace, the bakery was sold in 1997 to three employees: Maria, Joe, and Luigi Vella. The bakery has a large selection of classic Italian cookies: amaretti, apricot-filled tea cookies, chocolate butter cookies, macaroons, lemon cookies, and filbert kisses (baci di Alassio).

BIBLIOGRAPHY

Artusi, Pellegrino: *The Art of Eating Well* (translated by Kyle M. Phillips III). Random House, New York, 1996.

Boni, Ada: *Il Talismano della Felicità*, Serie d'Oro. Editore Colombo, Rome (undated).

Dell'Anno, Giuseppe: *Giuseppe's Easy Bakes: Sweet Italian Treats*. Quadrille, 2023.

Dell'Anno, Giuseppe: *Giuseppe's Italian Bakes: Over 60 Classic Cakes, Desserts & Savoury Bakes*. Quadrille, 2022.

Field, Carol: *The Italian Baker*. HarperCollins, New York, 1985.

Gosetti, Fernanda: *I Dolci della Cucina Regionale Italiana*. Gruppo Editoriale Fabbri S.p.A., Milan, 1993.

Granof, Victoria: *Sicily, My Sweet: Love Notes to an Island, with Recipes for Cakes, Cookies, Puddings, and Preserves*. Hardie Grant North America, 2024.

Marchetti, Domenica: *Ciao Biscotti: Sweet and Savory Recipes Celebrating Italy's Favorite Cookie*. Chronicle Books, San Francisco, 2015.

Marchetti, Domenica: *Preserving Italy: Canning, Curing, Infusing, and Bottling Italian Flavors and Traditions*. Houghton Mifflin Harcourt, Boston, 2016.

Mims, Ben: *Crumbs: Cookies and Sweets from Around the World*. Phaidon Press Limited, New York, 2024.

Schwartz, Arthur: *Naples at Table*. HarperCollins, New York, 1988.

Websites

Gambero Rosso: gamberorosso.it

Giallo Zafferano: giallozafferano.it

La Cucina Italiana: lacucinaitaliana.it

Proud Italian Cook: prouditaliancook.com

Sale e Pepe: salepepe.it

Slow Food Italia: slowfood.it

INDEX

ABOUT THE AUTHOR AND CONTRIBUTORS

Domenica Marchetti is the author of numerous books on Italian home cooking, including *The Glorious Pasta of Italy*; *Preserving Italy: Canning, Curing, Infusing, and Bottling Italian Flavors and Traditions*; and *Williams-Sonoma Everyday Italian*. A former newspaper reporter who earned her master's degree in journalism at Columbia University, Domenica has published articles and recipes in many publications, including *The Washington Post*, *Eating Well*, *Food and Wine*, and, in Italy, *La Cucina Italiana* and *Sale e Pepe*.

Domenica is a professional recipe developer and cooking class instructor who has taught all over the country and online. She also leads occasional small-group culinary tours and food writing workshops in Italy. She splits her time between Abruzzo, Italy, where her family is from, and Virginia. She also writes the popular weekly recipe newsletter *Buona Domenica*. *Italian Cookies* is her ninth cookbook.

Originally from Connecticut, **Lauren Volo** has lived in New York City for over twenty years and now calls Brooklyn home. She earned a BFA in art photography from Syracuse University and is currently pursuing a master's degree in art education at Brooklyn College. She has photographed over fifty cookbooks and worked on numerous advertising campaigns, bringing a thoughtful, detail-oriented approach to each project. Outside of her studies, she's a mom of two boys, volunteers at their school fundraisers, and enjoys contemporary dance. Her favorite food is pizza.

Daniela Bracco is a Sicilian illustrator who lives and works in Rome. She has a master's degree in graphic design from Università IUAV di Venezia. She started her career as part of the editorial staff of *Il Sole 24 Ore* in Milan, with the role of illustrator. She now works as a freelance illustrator and graphic designer collaborating with various agencies, magazines, and individuals such as *Il Gambero Rosso* magazine, *Lonely Planet* magazine, *Monocle* magazine, *La Repubblica*, *Sky*, *Tennis and Padel Federation*, and *Slow Food Editore*.